'*Law and Morality* is a collection of excellent essays on some of the core issues that have animated the debate between legal positivism and natural law theory, that has in turn been the focal point of much of jurisprudential scholarship over the past two hundred years. The contributors are distinguished scholars whose essays, taken together, provide an excellent introduction to the debates for those just getting their 'feet wet', while also pursuing topics that readers deeply engaged already will find fresh and stimulating. A rare achievement, and one fully worthy of the attention it will receive.'

Jules Coleman, *Wesley Newcomb Hohfeld Professor of Jurisprudence and Philosophy (Retired), Yale University*

Law and Morality

Philosophers considering the relationship between law and morality are often divided into two schools: natural law theory and legal positivism. Broadly speaking, natural law theorists assert that law is intrinsically linked to the moral order and that ethical considerations are integral to the identification and interpretation of legal norms. Legal positivists, by contrast, maintain that law is essentially a human construct and that its connection to morality, if any, is contingent rather than necessary. This volume presents a collection of accessible yet intellectually rigorous perspectives on this ongoing debate. The primary objective is to introduce the reader to the traditions of natural law and legal positivism and familiarise them with the important figures and issues. The work discusses the nature of jurisprudence and its role in human communities. The section on natural law essentially takes a historical approach, charting the origins of natural law thought in ancient Greece, then discussing the natural law thought of St. Thomas Aquinas, and concluding with a discussion of contemporary restatement of the natural law thought in the works of John Finnis. The section on legal positivism comprises ruminations on the works of the two most important legal theorists of the last century: H. L. A. Hart and Hans Kelsen. It also includes a chapter on the planning theory of law, a recent development in legal positivism. The inclusion of a chapter on Islamic tradition situates these debates in an Islamic intellectual context and gives a comparative perspective on the debate. Written by scholars who are at the forefront of the debate on the relationship between natural law and legal positivism, the work offers fresh perspectives on the debate concerning the relationship between law and morality. Building upon a long tradition of thought and advancing the debate, their contributions are expected to stimulate and inform further work on these crucial questions. The collection will be of interest to academics and students working in the areas of legal philosophy, jurisprudence, legal and political theory, and law and religion.

Mir Ahmad Murtiza is a Pakistan-based lawyer and the Global Research Fellow (Non-Resident) at the Global Institute of Law, Oxford, UK.

Routledge Research in Legal Philosophy

Metaethical Issues in Contemporary Legal Philosophy
A Constitutivist Approach
Edited by Stefano Bertea and Jorge Silva Sampaio

Purely Formal Legal Theory
Deontic Networks
Ottavio Quirico

Judges, Decision Making and Empathy
Insights from the Bench
Mateusz Stępień and Ewa Wilczek-Rużyczka

The Illegality Defence in Law
A Constitutional and Human Rights Perspective
Edit Deutch

Legal and Ethical Retributivism
A Restorative Analysis
Halil Cesur

Democracy and the Rule of Law in Indonesia
A Legal Philosophical Analysis
Stefanus Hendrianto

Law and Morality
Perspectives on Natural Law Theory and Legal Positivism
Edited by Mir Ahmad Murtiza

For more information about this series, please visit: https://www.routledge.com/Routledge-Research-in-Legal-Philosophy/book-series/RRLP

Law and Morality

Perspectives on Natural Law Theory and Legal Positivism

Edited by Mir Ahmad Murtiza

Assistant Editors

Noor Ul Huda
Haleema Sadia

Routledge
Taylor & Francis Group
LONDON AND NEW YORK

First published 2026
by Routledge
4 Park Square, Milton Park, Abingdon, Oxon OX14 4RN

and by Routledge
605 Third Avenue, New York, NY 10158

Routledge is an imprint of the Taylor & Francis Group, an informa business

British Library Cataloguing-in-Publication Data
A catalogue record for this book is available from the British Library

Library of Congress Cataloging-in-Publication Data
Names: Murtiza, Mir Ahmad editor
Title: Law and morality : perspectives on natural law theory and legal positivism / edited by Mir Ahmad Murtiza ; Assistant Editors, Noor Ul Huda, Haleema Sadia.
Description: Abingdon, Oxon [UK] ; New York, NY : Routledge, 2026. | Series: Routledge research in legal philosophy | Includes bibliographical references and index.
Identifiers: LCCN 2025046148 (print) | LCCN 2025046149 (ebook) | ISBN 9781041217091 hardback | ISBN 9781041217114 paperback | ISBN 9781003728603 ebook
Subjects: LCSH: Law—Moral and ethical aspects | Law and ethics | Natural law—Influence | Legal positivism | Law—Philosophy
Classification: LCC K247.6 .L395 2026 (print) | LCC K247.6 (ebook)
LC record available at https://lccn.loc.gov/2025046148
LC ebook record available at https://lccn.loc.gov/2025046149

ISBN: 978-1-041-21709-1 (hbk)
ISBN: 978-1-041-21711-4 (pbk)
ISBN: 978-1-003-72860-3 (ebk)

DOI: 10.4324/9781003728603

Typeset in Galliard
by Apex CoVantage, LLC

Contents

Contributors

Tony Burns is an emeritus professor in the School of Politics and International Relations at the University of Nottingham, UK. He is also a senior research fellow at the Centre for Aristotelian Studies and Critical Theory at Mykolas Romeris University. Additionally, he is the Co-Director of the Centre for the Study of Social and Global Justice (CSSGJ) in the UK. His research interests include the history of political thought, the Aristotelian natural law tradition, the Hegel-Marx connection, and continental political thought.

Jonathan Crowe is a distinguished legal philosopher. He currently serves as the Dean of the School of Law and Justice at the University of Southern Queensland. Previously, he held academic positions at Bond University and the University of Queensland and has been a visiting scholar at Georgetown University and the University of Texas at Austin. In addition, he is a founding director of Rape and Sexual Assault Research and Advocacy (RASARA) and a co-editor of the *Journal of Legal Philosophy*. He has also served as president of the Australasian Society of Legal Philosophy. His research focuses on legal philosophy, ethics, and public law.

Fr. Kevin Flannery, S.J., is a Catholic scholar and Jesuit priest. He served as professor of the history of ancient philosophy at the Pontifical Gregorian University and is now there professor emeritus (although still teaching seminars); he is also a consultor of the Dicastery for the Doctrine of the Faith. Additionally, he is Ralph McInerny Distinguished Research Fellow at the Jacques Maritain Center at the University of Notre Dame (South Bend, Indiana) and a member of the Pontifical Academy of Saint Thomas Aquinas. Previously, he served as president of the American Catholic Philosophical Association. His research expertise spans moral philosophy, natural law theory, and the ethical and logical works of Aristotle. He has also authored numerous works on Catholic moral theology, the philosophy of action, and the intersection of ethics and law.

Clemens Jabloner is an Austrian jurist and statesman. He currently leads the research unit 'Kelsen and his Circle' at the University of Vienna, focusing on the legal and intellectual legacy of Hans Kelsen. He is also the director of the Hans Kelsen-Institut in Vienna. From 1993 to 2013, he served as president of the Supreme Administrative Court of Austria. In 2019, he held the positions of Vice-Chancellor and Minister of Justice of Austria.

Muhammad Ammar Khan Nasir is a distinguished Islamic scholar and academic. He serves as a faculty member in the Department of Islamic Studies at GIFT University, Gujranwala. He is also the Director of the Ibn Khaldun Institute in Gujranwala and a Fellow at Al-Mawrid Institute of Islamic Sciences, Lahore. He has made significant contributions to Islamic scholarship, particularly in the areas of jurisprudence, theology, and contemporary Islamic thought.

Philip N. Pettit is a renowned philosopher and political theorist. He is L. S. Rockefeller University Professor of Human Values at Princeton University with a joint appointment as a distinguished professor of philosophy at the Australian National University (ANU) in Canberra. He was appointed a Companion of the Order of Australia in 2017. He holds fellowships, or equivalent positions, in the Australian Academies of Humanities and Social Sciences (1986–1987); in the American Academy of Arts and Sciences (2009); the Royal Irish Academy (2010); the British Academy (2013); and l'Académie des Sciences Morales et Politiques, Institut de France (2019). His research interests span a diverse range of topics, including moral and political theory, the philosophy of mind and metaphysics, ethics, social and political philosophy, democratic theory, and the philosophy of law. Among his many books are *Republicanism* (1997), *On the People's Terms* (2012), and *The State* (2023).

Scott J. Shapiro is a distinguished legal philosopher known for his contributions to legal philosophy, international law, and cybersecurity. He is currently the Charles F. Southmayd Professor of Law and Professor of Philosophy at Yale Law School. In addition, he serves as a Special Government Expert at the U.S. Cybersecurity and Infrastructure Agency (CISA) and is the Founding Director of the Yale CyberSecurity Lab. He is also an editor for *Legal Theory* and the *Stanford Encyclopedia of Philosophy*. His research interests include the philosophy of law, international law, criminal law, cybersecurity, and artificial intelligence.

Nigel E. Simmonds is a distinguished English legal philosopher. He is currently Emeritus Professor of Jurisprudence at the University of Cambridge and a Life Fellow of Corpus Christi College, where he previously served as dean. He has authored several books and numerous articles in leading legal and philosophical journals. His research focuses primarily on the nature of law, legal reasoning, and the moral foundations of legal order.

Christopher Tollefsen is a professor of philosophy at the University of South Carolina. His research focuses on natural law theory, ethics, and bioethics. He has authored several works, including *Lying and Christian Ethics* and *The Way of Medicine* (co-authored with Farr Curlin). His scholarship engages with issues of moral realism, personal autonomy, and the intersection of law and ethics.

Envoi

It is a privilege to have the opportunity to wish this volume and its editors every success in arousing intelligent and critical interest in the always-relevant moral reasons for instituting, maintaining, and cooperating with positive law that, to the greatest reasonable extent, is identifiable by reference only to publicly ascertainable historical facts about its enactment or its institution by social custom or judicial decision by courts of record.

As it happened, this opportunity arose, by invitation from the editors, on the very day I completed a biographical memoir of my esteemed former long-time colleague Joseph Raz, in which I have been able to express my admiration and appreciation for his achievements as a critical investigator of law's nature and rational structure, normativity, and institutional characteristics. Famed though he became as a proponent of 'legal positivism' of an 'exclusive' kind, it is less well known than it ought to be—but he himself made unambiguously clear on several occasions—that the progress of scholarly reflection and debate, subsequent to the writings in which he proposed the 'positivism' that others have called 'exclusive', has shown that the philosophy of law need not and should not conceive its sound theses as positivist or non-positivist. In my entry on 'Natural Law Theory [of Law]' in the *Stanford Encyclopedia of Philosophy*, I articulate in sec. 5.2 essentially the same position.

It is encouraging to see the authentic moral and social-factual issues involved in the human project of having positive law (and thus, of promoting the rule of law) being examined as they are in this volume—which I wish Godspeed—examined and debated, that is to say, with less attention to textbook labels and categories than to the human goods which we citizens and lawyers are morally responsible for protecting and advancing by means and methods of cooperation and just dispute resolution which a sound, historically informed legal philosophy shows are actually likely, in fact, to fulfil that responsibility as best it can be fulfilled.

John Finnis
Oxford, 30 March 2025

Preface

Few questions have attracted so much attention in the history of legal and political thought as the question of the relationship between law and morality. Throughout history, this question has been the subject of debate among philosophers, theologians, and statesmen of almost all civilisations and has significantly influenced the ways in which human societies have viewed their legal and political institutions. The debate has encompassed diverse questions, such as (1) are there any objective principles of human morality; (2) if there are any such principles, how are they related to the will of an omnipotent God; (3) what is the relation between objective principles of morality and human nature (4); to what extent should a human-made law embody principles of morality; and (5) how does the justice or injustice of human laws affect our obligation to obey them, to name a few.

This debate has unfolded in diverse contexts across various historical periods and regions, with each context illuminating different dimensions of the relationship between law and morality. In contemporary philosophical discourse, the central divide is broadly between natural law theorists and legal positivists. While the intellectual roots of both traditions extend deep into much earlier sources, the distinctive contours of the modern debate are shaped by particular developments in 20th-century philosophy. Given the richness and internal diversity of each tradition, any attempt to characterise these schools is necessarily open to contestation. Nonetheless, a general characterisation may be offered: natural law theorists assert that law is intrinsically linked to the moral order and that ethical considerations are integral to the identification and interpretation of legal norms. Legal positivists, by contrast, maintain that law is essentially a human construct and that its connection to morality, if any, is contingent rather than necessary. This, of course, is only a simplified sketch. For a richer understanding, the reader is encouraged to explore the chapters that follow.

The debate is far from settled; it continues to shape contemporary legal and political theory. The present book is intended to contribute to understanding this debate. It brings together scholarly contributions that explore various dimensions of these traditions. It is divided into three sections. The first section contains chapters on various aspects of the natural law tradition. The second section is devoted to the school of legal positivism. Both of these sections begin with introductory chapters. The last section contains a chapter on the debates concerning law and morality in Islamic tradition.

This book is intended for a broad and diverse audience. Judges, practising and academic lawyers, law students, scholars and students of philosophy, and any inquisitive reader with an interest in the relationship between law and morality will find value in its pages.

There are many to whom we are indebted for bringing this project to fruition. We are deeply grateful to the contributors for placing their trust in us and sharing their valuable work. It is they who deserve the fullest credit for the substance and success of this volume. We are especially honoured by the kindness of Professor John Finnis, who generously agreed to write the envoi for this book, offering it his blessing and wishing it Godspeed. His words grace this volume, and his lifelong scholarship has been a source of inspiration and wisdom for many of us. We are also sincerely grateful to Professor Jules Coleman for his gracious endorsement of the book. His support is both encouraging and deeply appreciated. Moreover, we are thankful to Alison Kirk, Senior Editor at Routledge, for her guidance and expert editorial support. Finally, we are indebted to many friends and mentors, particularly Afzaal Ahmad Butt and Gul Sher Butt, whose support in various forms has been invaluable throughout the course of this project.

We hope that this book will inspire interest in these debates and both stimulate and inform further work in the field.

Editor
Lahore, 21 May 2025

Acknowledgments

We express our sincere gratitude to the respective journals and authors for granting permission to reprint the following articles. We acknowledge their rights with appreciation.

- N. E. Simmonds, 'On the Centrality of Jurisprudence,' *American Journal of Jurisprudence*, 2019, Volume 64, Issue 1, Pages 1–18. Reprinted with permission of the author and the editor.
- Philip N. Pettit, 'Social Norms and the Internal Point of View: An Elaboration of Hart's Genealogy of Law,' *Oxford Journal of Legal Studies*, 2019, Volume 39, Issue 2, Pages 229–258, by permission of Oxford University Press.

We deeply appreciate their generosity in allowing the inclusion of these works.

1 On the Centrality of Jurisprudence*

N. E. Simmonds

I. Values and Law

Perhaps human groups may sometimes be governed by the simplest facts of force and violence: crude threats are made, and people respond accordingly. In such circumstances, the practical conduct of life does not invite or require philosophical inquiry: one simply needs to understand the risks to which one is exposed and to take appropriate action as best one can. When force rules, philosophy retreats into the private sphere and sustains itself upon the hope of better times. But governance by unadorned force, if it is possible at all, is certainly unusual and probably pathological, a sign of social breakdown rather than the normal state of affairs. More typically, human communities try to organize themselves by invoking values that command our allegiance. Even communities that rely heavily upon the use of force nevertheless seek to legitimate that force by an appeal to values. Sometimes, these appeals may be no more than a misleading patina that conceals the real mechanisms of power. But, more often, the appeals are in good faith and have a real significance in shaping the character of the community. They possess the power to summon the allegiance and compliance of citizens, even if the nature of that power is muddied and obscured by its entanglement with coercion.

Values may be conveyed and renewed by ancestral legends, by myths and stories, including stories of the community's own history. But they can also become the focus of more explicit appeals to abstract ideas such as justice, freedom, civility and equality. Once the governance of a community relies upon an appeal to ideas such as these, it is on a path that makes philosophical thought an integral part of its collective life. The discourse of philosophy then shapes, sustains and renews the ideas by which we govern our lives together.

Many communities in the world today organize themselves around an idea which can appear to be straightforward, but is in fact profoundly elusive and problematic: the idea of "law." At first we may think of "law" as simply a body

* This paper was originally published in the ***American Journal of Jurisprudence***, 2019, Volume 64, Issue 1, Pages 1–18. We bear responsibility for any errors that may have occurred in reprinting or editing.

DOI: 10.4324/9781003728603-1

of decrees issued by the powerful. Considered in that way, law does not look like a value so much as an established social fact. While an understanding of values such as justice or liberty requires philosophical reflection, a grasp of the nature of law might seem to call for careful description: knowledge of law's nature can superficially appear to be a matter for historians or social scientists rather than philosophers. Laws may be just or unjust, and their content therefore cannot be discovered by thinking about justice or other values. One discovers the law's content by investigating the ways in which power has been exercised: What statutes have been enacted? What judicial decisions have been handed down?

But this picture of law as the raw exercise of power is too simple. Consider, for example, the way in which legislators would characterize their own enactments. They would not speak of those enactments as "decrees" or "orders" or "dictats." They see themselves, not as issuing orders, but as creating *laws.* And the observation that such statutes are "laws" is not a matter of neutral classification serving only values of intellectual tidiness. The status of legislative enactments as law is seen as very central to the claim that the statutes have upon the conduct of the citizen. If asked "Why should I comply with your statute?" the legislators would probably say "Because it is the law!" But what is this status which is being ascribed to the statute? Since we know that laws may be unjust, and may fail to serve the common good, why should the status of a rule as law ground some claim to our compliance?

Judges strive to decide cases by reference to the law. They invoke the law's requirements as the justification for their decisions. This is what the litigants expect and insist upon. Our understanding of justice may perhaps inform and shape our view of what precisely the law requires, and some will take the view that the principal requirement of justice is the enforcement of the citizen's legal rights and duties. In these ways and many others, justice is pervasively relevant to the judge's task. But no one imagines that it would be right and legitimate for the judge simply to set on one side all the statutes and precedents and invoke his or her own convictions regarding justice in the abstract and apart from the legal rules. In all but the most extreme situations, the critical question for the judge is always "What does the law require?"

Legislators, judges and citizens, therefore, regard the legal status of a rule as bearing directly upon its capacity to bind us and to justify the actions of public authority. If law is an exercise of power (which, in some sense, it clearly is) it is a particular form in which power is exercised, and a form to which we attach huge significance. But what precisely is that form? And what is the basis of its significance?

We are unclear about how our various values fit together. Indeed, we are unclear about *whether* they fit together, or whether they clash and compete and force upon us hard choices. Are liberty and equality compatible or competing? How does "justice" relate to "civility"? How do "rights" relate to "the common good"? These are obviously central and difficult questions for philosophical inquiry. Similar questions arise in relation to "law." Most obviously we may ask how law relates to justice. But here there is also an additional difficulty, since it is not entirely clear how far the idea of "law" represents an orienting value of some sort, and how far it simply labels an interestingly distinctive way in which power may be exercised, sometimes for good purposes and sometimes for bad. Values seem to be very different from practices: they provide critical standards by reference to which practices must be judged; and, for that very reason, their content cannot be determined by examining the facts of actual practice. Law, on the other hand seems to be primarily a matter of practice and decision. As a fallible product of accepted authority, law may be just or unjust, good or bad. Yet law is also a guiding idea by which we live, being regularly invoked as the *basis* of authority and the *justification* for the state's deployment of force. A product of authority, yet the basis of authority. A practice to be judged by independent critical standards of justice, yet itself a guiding idea. This is the ambiguous ground explored by jurisprudence.

II. Life

If guiding values play a central role within our political communities, thereby giving a philosophical cast to public debate, something similar is true within our individual lives, at least when those lives are led responsibly. For the concerns which shape our lives most fundamentally are not simple biological givens but are the fruit of life in community, possessing a depth that provokes philosophical thought. Our comprehension of them is enriched by reflection, just as with our political values. One should not imagine that a flourishing life consists of a steady flow of discrete pleasurable sensations. Even the most transient pleasures are informed by their deep cultural resonance: we taste not simply the wine but also the culture from which it springs. And no succession of such pleasures, however prolonged, will itself amount to a flourishing life. Beneath the transient pleasures, we want our lives to form some coherent and meaningful narrative, and a narrative within which our agency and our relations to others form a central part. Even shallow acquisitiveness may be less concerned with the assets acquired and more concerned with the manner of their acquisition: for many it may be true that, "Possessing some particular bundle of material goods . . . is not nearly so important as possessing those goods because of one's own actions and choices."[1] We want to be valued colleagues, trusted friends, good parents, responsible citizens, companions, and perhaps sophisticated participants in the fruits of civilization. Each of these aspects of our well-being is an ideal of conduct and personal virtue rather than

1 John Tomasi, *Free Market Fairness* (Princeton University Press 2012) xi.

a pleasurable experience.[2] It is something to which we may approximate but from which we will always fall short; something which may be understood in different ways, and the character of which invites reflective inquiry.

A life that is in this way structured by ideas is, in that respect, an essentially human life. It is a life where individual agents endeavor to shape their conduct by reference to common standards and ideals, and where the relevant ideals are explored and endowed with their richness of meaning through a mixture of concrete example, experience and dialogue. It is a life where I am governed, not simply by a succession of intellectually opaque urges, but by enduring and evolving judgements concerning the authority and soundness (or otherwise) of my feelings and attitudes, and the way in which my action may or may not contribute to a worthwhile life. While those judgements, if they are to guide my decisions, must be my own, they will draw upon standards or ideals that are endorsed by others, informing their lives as they inform mine.

Such a life is one wherein my capacity so to govern my conduct is publicly acknowledged by others and by the practices in which I and they jointly participate. It is a life wherein my understanding is enriched by dialogic encounter with both comrades and strangers, whose perceptions and experiences of this world can help to ensure that the values whereby I live my life reflect profound features of the human condition. I become an agent only within this context of the mutual recognition of persons and the shared acknowledgment of values.

Political philosophy sometimes proceeds as if it is entirely concerned with a problem of cooperation between agents each of whom possesses a set of clearly conceived fundamental interests that exist and are identifiable prior to such cooperation. Politics is then taken to address issues concerning the just distribution of the "benefits and burdens" of social life, where "benefits and burdens" are understood by reference to some pre-political notion of self-interest. Or it is taken to concern the ways in which convergence may be achieved between the common good (perhaps erroneously understood as some sort of aggregate) and the individual goods pursued by each agent. But these pictures neglect the way in which our collective practices give identity to the goods pursued within individual lives. Human communities are the matrix within which meaning is conferred upon our lives.

2 Can one lead a flourishing life while believing one's life to be an utter failure and consequently taking no pleasure in it? The answer, I would suggest, is that one can. The erroneous judgement about the value of one's life, and the consequent despair, would detract from, but not negate, the value of that life. Something similar is true of pleasurable experience. A life with few pleasurable experiences certainly gives us, in that respect, some cause for regret. A lot, however, turns upon the explanation for the shortfall. If I have foolishly neglected opportunities for pleasurable experience, or needlessly indulged my tendency towards gloom and despondency, the quality of my life may have been seriously marred by these missteps. But, where my life has lacked pleasure because of unavoidable circumstances, it may nevertheless constitute a triumph to be celebrated.

To be fully human involves the finitude of one's life, and the nature of one's relationships with others, being issues which compel attention and confer upon all that we do such meaning as it can possess. Similarly, a human form of association is one that is shaped by reflection upon its own character and value. A wolf pack doubtless has its own mode of association, with hierarchies of dominance and submission, group loyalties and group bonding. But the behavior of wolves is not guided by the *idea* of the wolf pack, as a group of humans might be guided by ideas. Such ideas can, with variable success, be consciously adopted and instilled as part of a program to change behavior: consider the governing images and rhetoric (including the idea of wolf-pack solidarity) which might be instilled into the ethos of some military units. More commonly, however, our guiding ideas emerge from reflection upon existing ways of life, even though those ideas will often set critical standards from which existing practice falls short.

III. Practice and Value

The intimate relationship which obtains between our values and our practices is often overlooked or implicitly denied. It can come to seem obvious that practices are simply facts about how we behave, open to neutral description, while values are something quite different. Values appear to endure apart, standing in judgement upon practice and setting standards from which our practices may diverge. Reflecting upon this, we may be tempted to think of values as inhabitants of another realm: visitants that touch us, but that remain for the most part remote (alluring at best, judgmental at worst). Or we may be tempted to think of them as simply expressions of individual subjective attitude (our hopes and yearnings) rather than intersubjective realities about which we may hold fallible beliefs. From either of these points of view (values as remote metaphysical objects, and values as subjective attitudes) the suggestion that practice and value are mutually dependent seems only to result in muddle. It appears to be in danger *either* of obliterating the critical capacity of values, thereby sanctifying the facts of power and conformity, *or* of allowing our subjectivity to color and obstruct attempts at an objective understanding of the social world.

However, while the potential (and, all too frequently, actual) gap between what is done and what ought to be done is undeniable, that gap is not at all incompatible with the close dependencies that may obtain between practice and value. Sometimes a practice may appear to be the central instantiation of a value, without which we could have no firm grasp of the value's contours: consider, for example, the way in which the practice of trial and judgement informs our sense of justice as a distinct moral virtue.[3] In general, the judge

3 It is worth noting that the iconography of justice seems to refer both to the practice (of trial and judgment) and to the ideal (by reference to which the practice may itself be judged).

has a duty to consider only the legal rights and wrongs obtaining between the litigants. Once those rights and wrongs are established, the judge must not override them in the interest of third parties, or even in the interests of the community as a whole: the plaintiff cannot be deprived of his damages simply because the money would be better spent by the defendant. It is worth asking whether we would have a firm grasp of the concept of justice as something distinct from collective well-being if we were not familiar with such a practice of adjudication. Would the notion of justice not be in danger of simply dissolving into the general impartiality that is required by any assessment of collective welfare?

A practice may derive its character (as a practice of doing this or that) from its appearance of pervasive concern with a certain value. The departure of a practice from the values with which it is normally associated can be so great that it forfeits its claim to be a practice of this or that type. Thus it has sometimes been suggested that, although the law may frequently be unjust, the enactments and decisions of those who exercise power may sometimes be so *grossly* unjust that they forfeit their character as law. Values may inform the identity of practices, and practices may give substance to the content of values, without values losing their critical edge. A little reflection is sufficient to reveal that this seemingly puzzling relationship between practice and value is really quite familiar, and by no means limited to the jurisprudential questions that form our subject matter.

Universities, for example, are best understood as institutions oriented towards the discovery of truth. This is, of course, not to deny that many universities may become perverted into something else: into money-making businesses; or institutions that simply provide vocational training; or institutions that unconsciously and uncritically (or even knowingly and cynically) foster a particular ideology and suppress rival viewpoints. But we think of such institutions as falling short of an ideal that is internal to their claim to be universities. If someone suggested that such institutions are "not really universities" we would understand what they meant. And it would be an error to suggest that such claims simply assert that the institutions in question are *bad*. The institutions in question do not simply fall short of values that we hold dear: they fall short of values that they themselves implicitly invoke by their very claim to be universities. Too great a proliferation of such institutions might lead to the suggestion that the very *concept* of a university had changed (indeed, a world where universities are understood to be about training for work, rather than about the disciplined inquiry into truth, may not be at all far away). But, short of such a fundamental shift, we are more likely to conclude that commitment to the value of inquiry into truth is part of what it means to be a university. Yet, in spite of being part of the university's identity as a university, that very value nevertheless provides a centrally relevant basis for the critical scrutiny of the university's practices.

Conversely, would we really have an understanding of the notion of truth as a value, if we did not have some knowledge of institutions such as our great universities, shaped as they are by practices of teaching and learning that have been pursued and reinforced by many generations of devoted scholars? Would we understand the value of truth if we lacked any knowledge of the practices of scientific inquiry and scholarship? In a world without those practices, would the value of truth not come to be thought of as simply the prohibition on lying, or perhaps as the pragmatic value of serviceably accurate cognition to aid our plans and projects?

The same is true of at least some, and perhaps all, other values. Would the value of friendship be grasped by one who had never encountered friends? Could we understand the value of enduring love if we were not familiar with the institution of the family? Could we attain any grasp of the notion of civility (with all of its rich political evocations) if we had not first encountered the formalized practices of courtesy?[4]

We come to understand values by a combination of habituation and reflection. That is to say, we learn to engage in certain practices, such learning frequently involving the acquisition of habits of perception and response that could not be articulated in the form of a set of rules. Beyond the most elementary stage, we learn by observing the experts and trying to copy. Only then do we reflect upon the significance of the practices in question, perhaps framing some general idea of the values served by the practice. And one who is not a practitioner may be singularly ill-equipped to enter into or assess such reflections.

Pursuing the example of the university once again, we may notice that many students may enter the university hoping to increase their employability by gaining qualifications. But, if they are assiduous in their work, and their university is a serious institution, they will learn, from their experience, something concerning the intrinsic value of truth and understanding, together with associated values such as reasoned argument and civility towards those with whom we disagree. This can change the orientation of their lives, and not simply facilitate the attainment of objectives that they held prior to their studies.

IV. Philosophy

The intimate relationship that obtains between some practices and the ideals that orient those practices is revealed by the practice of philosophy itself. For philosophy is a practice that necessitates reflection upon its own character; and it is a practice which, since Socrates, has been viewed by many as an important constituent of a fully flourishing life.

In considering the general nature of philosophical inquiry, we are reflecting upon an actual human activity that encompasses considerable diversity yet also exhibits a surprising degree of unity and of historical continuity. Not

4 N. E. Simmonds, "The Bondwoman's Son and the Beautiful Soul" (2013) 58 *American Journal of Jurisprudence* 117–119.

infrequently, across the long history of the subject, philosophers have claimed to discover the correct path that the inquiry should henceforth follow, and they have sometimes urged a radical break with the approaches of the past. Yet philosophy, unlike the natural sciences, never truly leaves its past behind: we constantly revisit the works of Plato and Aristotle and a host of others, and seem to find in them new insights and a new understanding of the road ahead. Consider, then, the following observation from Collingwood:

> [W]hen we distinguish philosophy from the other activities of our minds, we do not think of it as something that merely happens in us like the circulation of the blood; we think of it as something we try to do, an activity which we are trying to bring into conformity with an idea of what it ought to be.[5]

In being "an activity" that we try to bring "into conformity with an idea of what it ought to be," philosophy resembles many other important human practices. We try to understand such practices as oriented towards an idea. And our grasp of the orienting idea is not prior to our engagement with, and reflection upon, the practice. Thus, although Kant tells us that philosophy is merely the idea of a *possible* science which does not exist *in concreto*, but "to which, by many different paths, we endeavour to approximate," he also points out that an understanding of the relevant "archetype" can only be attained by our critical and reflective engagements with actually existing "attempts" at philosophy.[6]

What then can we learn, concerning the inquiry which is jurisprudence, from reflection upon the origins of philosophical thought concerning law and justice?

The Greek Sophists revealed that values such as justice are not a fundamental part of the ordering of the cosmos, akin to the laws of planetary motion. Some believed that this revelation exposed justice as a fraud or a delusion. Since their day, many have agreed: Thrasymachus always seems to be with us, in one form or another. But many more have disagreed and have looked to Plato and his heirs as offering a basis for a thoroughgoing rejection of the Sophist view. Consequently, Plato is often read as seeking a straightforward reversal of the Sophist revolution, grounding value in a metaphysical status that is entirely prior to human thought and practice.[7] Plato's texts can appear to lend plausibility to this reading by linking the inquiry into value

5 R. G. Collingwood, *An Essay on Philosophical Method* (Clarendon Press 1933) 4. Collingwood emphasizes that "the question what philosophy is, cannot be separated from the question what philosophy ought to be." But he also emphasizes the dangers of what he calls a "philosophical utopianism" which loses sight of the actual practice of philosophers of the past.

6 Kant, *Critique of Pure Reason*, B866.

7 G. A. Cohen, *Lectures on the History of Moral and Political Philosophy* (Princeton University Press 2014) Ch. 1.

with a search for enduring objects of knowledge beneath the Heraclitean flux of observable nature. Some of the most famous features of the *Republic* suggest a similar impetus away from the world of human practice and towards an obscure metaphysics. For the philosopher is portrayed in that work as required to embark upon a wholly individual quest, seeking to discover a reality that lies beyond the cave-like arena of human dialogue and human concerns.

To see the potential error in such an understanding of Plato,[8] we need to remember that the work of the Sophists was but one manifestation of a gradually dawning awareness of the special character of human action as something distinct from unreflective nature. Other manifestations of that same awareness were the emergence of history (as something independent of cosmological and theocratic myth)[9] and the Socratic turn towards the consideration of human affairs. Socrates shifts philosophical inquiry away from an investigation of the cosmos and towards the question of how we should live. If we are careful to read Plato within the context of that Socratic turn, we may come to conclude that his philosophy is not aimed at a simple reversal of the Sophist's view. And, if we judge by Socrates's own example, the question of how we ought to live is to be explored in dialogue with others, within the public space of conversation between equal citizens. The good is to be discovered, not by a transfiguring moment of solitary escape from the cave, or an excursion into metaphysics as something distinct from ethical discourse, but by the consideration of first-order ethical questions. We come to understand the sovereignty of good by careful attention to the human condition, to particular human lives and human practices, guided always by our concern to understand the nature of a life well-lived and of a flourishing community.[10] Even our understanding of the way in which practices fall short of the values that they serve is itself the result of quotidian experience.[11] Perhaps admirers of Plato who take an exotic metaphysics to be central to his thought make precisely the same error that was made by the Sophists, while rejecting the Sophists' genuinely transformative insight: they assume that the truth and objectivity of justice and the good can be preserved only by a denial of the dependence of such values upon practice. This, it seems to me, is a mistake.

Whereas the Sophists had asserted a clear distinction between nature and convention, Plato and Aristotle offered a more nuanced account, wherein

8 We should at least be aware of the possibility of reading Plato differently. While criticizing Plato's "hypostasis" of ideas, Kant observes that "the exalted language, which he employed in this sphere, is quite capable of a milder interpretation." Kant, *Critique of Pure Reason*, A 314/B 371n.

9 R. G. Collingwood, *The Idea of History* (Clarendon Press 1946) Part 1.

10 See Iris Murdoch, *The Sovereignty of Good* (Routledge and Kegan Paul 1970).

11 Plato imagines the prisoner from the cave being "forcibly dragged" up the steep ascent to the light. But what could motivate a voluntary ascent? Only indications to be found within the phenomena of the cave could lead us to suspect the existence of a more unified source of light, and so lead us to embark upon the journey.

the uniqueness of human action and speech was fully acknowledged but the civil and political structures thereby constructed were viewed as containing *in potentia* a full realization of human nature rather than a distortive imposition upon it. Consequently, for this tradition, an understanding of the nature and possibility of a fully human life requires careful thought regarding the significance of actual institutions and modes of association.

There are those who think of morality as something entirely inward and personal, to be identified through personal conscience, or perhaps through intellectual reflection on such abstract principles as the categorical imperative or the principle of utility. The domain of actual practice is thought of as the object to which such elevated ideas are to be applied in criticism: it is not thought of as something which might inform and enrich our understanding even of our most fundamental values. By contrast with this, the tradition of moral thought that runs through Aristotle turns its gaze outward, towards established practice, institutions and ways of life. As Aristotle explains, virtues of character are akin to skills in so far as we acquire them by engaging in the relevant practice. Thus "virtues arise in us neither by nature nor contrary to nature, but nature gives us the capacity to acquire them, and completion comes by habituation."[12] So immersion in the practice must precede full understanding; and ethical inquiry is not exclusively a matter of turning the gaze inwards to our own moral intuitions, but outwards also to the practices of which those intuitions are an aspect.

This should not be taken as suggesting a static picture of morality as simply a body of inherited precepts. Fully to possess a virtue it is not enough to internalize and conform to certain precepts and prohibitions: one must also possess an understanding of the value served by those precepts and prohibitions. The honest person is not simply the one who avoids telling lies, but the person who prizes truth and pursues the value of truth. To understand a value is to see how it forms a constituent of a fully flourishing life, and this requires us to reconstruct in thought and imagination an entire world of practice. As Gadamer points out, moral knowledge always pertains to right living in general and tacitly contemplates an entire way of life. Moral requirements are never fully knowable in advance of the particular problems that they must confront, and moral precepts can never be more than schemata which take on a precise content only in particular contexts.[13] To respect and sustain the practice we must seek to understand the values served by the practice. But to understand those values we must grasp the way in which the practice fits within a broader way of life. This creates the dialogue between practice and value, engagement and

12 Aristotle, *Nicomachean Ethics* (Roger Crisp tr, Cambridge University Press 2000) 2.1.1103a23–26.

13 Hans-Georg Gadamer, *Truth and Method* (Joel Weinsheimer and Donald G. Marshall trs, 2nd rev. edn, Continuum Books 2004) 318.

reflection, of which jurisprudence is one manifestation. Jurisprudence seeks to understand the law in the light of the value that the idea of law represents.

Suppose that we incline towards the view that morality is a body of standards arrived at by individual inquiry quite independently of practice, and with which outward practice should strive to comply. We will then regard any consideration of that practice as either purely descriptive or fundamentally judgmental. That is to say, we will assume that it must be concerned either with accurate description of what occurs in fact, or with the question of how far the practice complies with our favored values and moral prescriptions. Down this route lies the picture of positive law as related to a "higher law," with which it may or may not comply; similarly, we find here the picture of jurisprudence as a purely "analytical" or "clarificatory" inquiry that is quite distinct from any concern with substantive values. The general framework of thought does not invite the possibility that the practice might be, in itself, an articulation of values which cannot properly be understood apart from the practice. But this is the very possibility that underlies philosophical inquiry into the nature of law, when that inquiry is properly understood.

History and political philosophy were born together, in the context of that perhaps hitherto unknown form of association that we call the polity. Historical understanding emerges only when human action begins to be grasped as something distinct from the regular course of nature. A narrative of past events befalling human beings (conquests, enslavements, defeats, migrations) is not a history if the events are viewed as part of a deterministic natural order indistinguishable from the weather or the movements of the heavens. Nor is it a history if the agency behind the events is ascribed to a divinity or an inscrutable fate.[14] Similarly, political community cannot be understood if relations between human beings are equated with collisions or causal influences between physical bodies, or if human agents are regarded as simply responding unreflectively to biological drives, or as the puppets of divine providence. To understand history is to understand agency. Agency is not best understood in terms of mechanical responses to blind passions or urges, but in terms of reasons. Agents act upon reasons, and the capacity to act upon reason involves judgements of value. Actions are bearers of meaning, and are guided by our beliefs concerning value. The forms of human association are the arena within which meanings are conferred, and values collectively articulated and realized. The political community is the association within which this enterprise aspires to full self-awareness.

Like the study of history, political philosophy too engages with a world where the guidance of action by reason is understood to be different from the causal processes that govern the natural world. The perspective of reason, rather than causality, is one that we adopt when we consider our own actions. For, even though we may be well aware of the large role played by accident

14 Collingwood (n 9) Part 1.

and contingency in our lives, we do not regard those lives as a succession of things that simply happen to us: in the midst of all the happenstance there is a core narrative of choices and actions for which we are responsible. To understand the actions and practices of others we must view those others as similarly responsible, and similarly guided by what the actors take to be reasons. Such reasons are always framed in terms of our ideas about what matters: our ideas about value. And such values are never wholly individual, but always and necessarily involve our relationship with others.

From time to time philosophers have attempted a rational reconstruction of the nature of the political community, by imagining the contractual emergence of political communities from a pre-political "state of nature." If one were to pursue this path, and one tried to be true to the moral phenomena, the simple contractual view (portraying the polity as a cooperative arrangement to satisfy pre-political desires[15]) would need to be significantly modified even if it was not abandoned altogether. At a minimum it would be necessary to echo Aristotle's observation that, while the polity originates in "the bare needs of life," it continues in existence "for the sake of a good life."[16] Today, the notion of "the good life" has been debased in popular speech until it is synonymous with "the highly pleasurable life," so that a modern reader might take Aristotle to be contrasting the satisfaction of "bare needs" with the provision of luxury. But we would do better to read Aristotle's reference to "the good life" as suggesting a meaningful life: a life that we regard as expressing some fundamentally significant aspect of what it is to be fully human. Nor does the good polity facilitate such a life so much as call it into being, by providing the framework within which its constitutive ideas possess a sense. We transform our nature and importance by the political and juridical practices that we construct.

In an intriguing remark, to be found in his *Doctrine of Virtue*, Kant writes of the tension that exists between the two "great moral forces" of mutual love (which admonishes us to come closer together) and mutual respect (which requires us to keep at a distance one from another). He tells us that "should one of these great moral forces fail" the whole "kingdom of moral beings" would be swallowed, like a drop of water, by the gaping throat of "nothingness."[17] Both values are embodied within the practices of civility and legality that structure our form of association. But this is not simply a matter of human practice successfully enabling us to cope with competing values. For the values here are not simply competing: they also require each other. What is love without respect? And is not respect (with its recognition of the independent reality of the other) itself at least a step towards love? If either one of

15 See the contribution of Glaucon in Plato, *The Republic of Plato* (Allan Bloom tr, Basic Books 1968) 358c–359b.

16 Aristotle, *Politics* 1.2.1252b30. Cf. Plato, *Republic* 369b.

17 Kant, *Metaphysics of Morals*, 6.449.

these "two great moral forces" were to expand its domain at the expense of the other, it would negate its own character. It is their concrete instantiation, within a shared form of life, which constitutes us as moral beings. Without both the contending forces and the resolution that gives them their identity, the "kingdom of moral beings" would cease to exist.

After the intellectual revolution that was brought into being by the Sophists, humanity would no longer be thought of as fully immersed in nature: no longer would the prescriptions of political and ethical life be equated with the laws that dictate the movements of the stars or the cycles of biological growth and decay. But nor would those prescriptions be reduced to the pure subjectivity of individual attitude. Plato and his heirs (including Aristotle, and the central figures of the natural law tradition) saw that, in rejecting a picture of humanity as an undifferentiated part of nature, we by no means abandon as empty the norms and standards that guide our thought and action: the fact that those norms are not akin to the laws of planetary motion does not entail the conclusion that they are mere fictions, or that they lack any genuine authority. Instead, a more subtle account than that offered by the Sophists must be explored. The political community, with its standards of reason and justice, is not a contractual arrangement which aims to overcome conflict between independent self-seeking agents who pursue individually coherent but mutually conflicting goals. For full human flourishing cannot even be conceived of independently of that community.

The forms in which we associate together (such as the family, the market, the state) are significant in ways that go beyond the impact that they inevitably have upon our opportunity to secure desired ends. For those forms of association are also forms of mutual recognition: and, as social beings, there is a sense in which we can fully exist only in the recognition of others.[18] Each form of association depends upon the willingness of every individual to act in accordance with the requirements of the association, and every individual relates to every other individual as the occupant of a socially defined status with duties, rights and responsibilities of its own. No one is regarded as simply a physical object or a locus of desires that compete with, or happily coincide with, my own wishes. The state, or *civitas*, is composed of citizens, as the market is composed of those who own property (perhaps only their own labor). And the facets of recognition are multiple and often interdependent: e.g., property depends upon the state, but the detached public power of the state depends upon its distinctness from the private power of ownership. Individuals move between these distinct statuses, thereby enjoying the possibility in mutuality of a richly flourishing existence that would otherwise be unattainable.

Core political ideas must be understood in this light if they are to be understood at all. Thus freedom is not simply the ability to move through or occupy

18 In many respects, this is the core insight of the tradition that runs through Rousseau, Kant and Hegel.

space in the advancement of one's goals,[19] but consists also in the collective and individual acknowledgment of one's independent, and valued, status. For this reason, to live under domination is to lack freedom even if the dominant party seldom or never intervenes in one's choices: the importance of freedom cannot be reduced to the improbability of an interference with one's currently available options. Being modes of mutual recognition, the forms in which we associate together are frequently oriented towards ideas expressive of that very form of association. This orientation of communal life towards ideas is frequently denied or overlooked; and, in recent times, this has nowhere been more common than within the philosophy of law.

V. The State

The ideas of "law," and of "the state," seem to be poised uncertainly between the prescriptive and the descriptive. On the face of it, they seem to be very real and very evident features of the social worlds that we inhabit. On the other hand, they are remarkably difficult ideas to cash out in terms of observable patterns of conduct or established attitudes. Until very recent times, theories of law and state had a marked tendency to become reflections upon a range of ideal values, so that one modern commentator has even gone so far as to suggest that those theories were concerned with the "advocacy of political and moral ideals within the framework of a convention" that required them to be framed as theories concerning the nature of existing institutions (such as law).[20]

Here we find some of the perennial battles of jurisprudence and political philosophy. These are battles which revolve around the relationship between our values and our descriptive understanding of the social world that we inhabit.

On the one hand are those who wish to treat both "law" and "state" as value-free descriptive categories. The desire is readily understandable, for we tend to think of values as independent standards that are to be employed in the critical assessment of actual practice, and this seems to suggest that the values must be independent of the practices so assessed. Furthermore, we are all familiar with states and systems of law that fall substantially short of what morality requires. If states can be seriously morally deficient, we need a concept of "state" that acknowledges that possibility, and this may seem to necessitate an entirely value-free approach. Such an approach proves hard to carry through, however.

19 For a modern version of this view, see Ian Carter, *A Measure of Freedom* (Oxford University Press 1999); Matthew Kramer, *The Quality of Freedom* (Oxford University Press 2003).

20 Tony Honore, *Making Law Bind* (Clarendon Press 1987) 32.

At first it may seem possible to analyze the notion of "the state" in terms of a claimed monopoly of physical force.[21] But the devil is in the detail and things get problematic when we try to spell that possibility out. Must the state claim a monopoly of force, or a monopoly of *legitimate* force? Does a claim to "legitimacy" not involve an appeal to moral values? Of course, the fact that such an appeal is made is not itself a value. But can a regime plausibly be said to make a moral claim to legitimacy while acting with an undisguised disregard for all moral considerations? When we ascribe a claim to a complex system of institutions, the ascription is unlikely adequately to be justified by reference to some discrete fact, as I might justify my assertion that you claim to be Napoleon by pointing to various letters and emails in which you say just that. It is far more likely that the ascription must be grounded in its ability to make systematic sense of a broad swathe of otherwise puzzling features.[22] A regime's open disregard for moral considerations will therefore count against any ascription to the state of moral claims, whether they be claims of justice or of legitimacy.

Suppose that someone rejects the last argument and insists that the state's claims *can* be an isolated fact detachable from any broader interpretation of its conduct. We must then address some further problems. Must the state (in order *to be* a state) simply *claim* a monopoly or also *possess* it? The former requirement seems too easy to satisfy, for anyone can claim a monopoly of force (just as anyone "can call spirits from the vasty deep"[23]). The latter requirement, by contrast, seems either impossible to satisfy (no state succeeds in *eliminating* the use of force by private citizens) or to return us to a vexing array of moral questions (if it is argued that the violence of the state is alone legitimate).

When Max Weber sought to define the state by reference to its claimed monopoly of physical force, he did so in consequence of his view that "the state cannot be defined in terms of its ends." He argued that there is "scarcely any task that some political association has not taken in hand, and there is no task that one could say has always been exclusive and peculiar to" the state and its historical predecessors.[24] Nevertheless it has struck many as natural to suggest that, when we describe a system of governance or a community as a "state," we view it in the light of certain moral goals, such as the service of justice and the common good. Whether such moral values are "exclusive and peculiar" to the state seems less than decisive. For the idea of the state may involve certain values without the state being definable by sole reference to those values. The governance of the state may, for example, involve a claimed monopoly of

21 Max Weber, "Politics as a Vocation" in H. H. Gerth and C. Wright Mills (eds), *From Max Weber* (Routledge 1948).

22 Cf. N. E. Simmonds, *Law as a Moral Idea* (Oxford University Press 2007) 138–140.

23 Owen Glendower: I can call spirits from the vasty deep.Hotspur: Why, so can I, or so can any man; But will they come when you do call for them? *Henry IV Part I*, Act III Scene I.

24 Weber (n 21) 77.

force while also involving a claim to serve the common good. A state, unlike a robber band, claims to govern justly, and in the interests of all.[25] While all states will fall short of these goals to some extent, states which clearly do no more than pay lip service to the goals are, in a very straightforward sense, not "really" states at all. They are not like broken clocks, which simply fail in their intended purpose, but like decorative clocks (e.g., the painted image of a clock) the function of which is to create an impression of being something which they are not.[26]

It is most certainly true that, as J. N. Figgis put it, "the actual world is the result of men's thoughts."[27] But we must go further than any mere acknowledgment of the shaping influence of thought. For the institutions within which we live cannot be understood except by their orientation towards ideas, and the ideas in question often prove to be ideals. The mundane realities of our daily life point beyond themselves and can properly be understood only when that implicit reference to the ideal is fully acknowledged. We cannot truly understand our practices without a grasp of the values that they seek to express, and towards which they turn their gaze. But equally, we cannot truly understand our values without experience of the practices within which they are embodied.

VI. Law Revisited

Some legal theorists have suggested that the idea of "law" plays no necessary or guiding part in legal thought, but is a fundamentally classificatory notion that simply serves to label a distinctive type of institution.[28] Such a view encourages the assumption that laws derive what authority they may possess, not from their status as law, but from the authority of their creators: perhaps from the lawmaker's expert knowledge and consequent ability wisely to guide conduct into the paths of reason; or perhaps from fact that the lawmaker's decrees serve to coordinate the behavior of the populace in beneficial ways.[29] But this entire approach is back to front. We ordinarily assume that lawmakers derive their authority from the law, not the reverse; and the decrees of officials gain their authority from their status as law, not from the expertise of their authors. Within a polity governed by law, the status of a rule as law is critical to

25 St Augustine, *The City of God* Bk. 4.

26 For this useful analogy (combined, alas, with a questionable application of it) see Scott Shapiro, *Legality* (Harvard University Press 2011) 391. Compare Simmonds, "The Logic of Planning and the Aim of the Law" (2012) 62 *University of Toronto Law Journal* 255.

27 J. N. Figgis, *From Gerson to Grotius* (2nd edn, Cambridge University Press 1916) 2.

28 For criticism of this view, see Simmonds, "Reflexivity and the Idea of Law" (2010) 1 *Jurisprudence* 1–23. Also, Simmonds, "Law as an Idea We Live By" in George Duke and Robert P. George (eds), *The Cambridge Companion to Natural Law Jurisprudence* (Cambridge University Press 2017) 264–268.

29 Joseph Raz, *The Morality of Freedom* (Clarendon Press 1986) Chs. 2–4.

its claim upon our conduct. Thus the conduct of citizens and officials within a polity governed by law is always shaped by reference to the idea of law.

Finnis (describing the view of Max Weber) tells us that,

> authoritative coordination is legal in character when it operates by way not of an attitude of obedience to persons but of a disposition to comply with "the law", a legally established order of consistent, abstract rules (normally established intentionally) and principles to be applied to and followed in particular cases—so that those in authority are regarded as "officials" whose office or authority is defined by these rules, and who are to be obeyed only when they act within their legal powers.[30]

Such an idea of law as a consistent order of rules and principles is a guiding ideal rather than a given reality: it guides judicial decisions, as well as the efforts of treatise writers to render consistent and orderly the often chaotic and fragmentary materials of case and statute; and it is the imperfectly understood vision that underlies the citizen's ascriptions of authority to those who wield lawful power. A legal system exists in so far as people frame their actions, not by reference to decrees or threats or wise prescriptions, but by reference to the idea of law. Here we find the source of philosophical puzzles regarding law (e.g., how does law authorize the very acts whereby law is created?) but also the key to law's moral significance.

Within the ideas that give meaning to political life, law occupies a central but an ambiguous place. Law appears, on the one hand, to be entangled with power and coercion, produced by decree and backed by violence. But, on the other hand, it is quite commonly thought of as an expression of justice and rectitude, a body of standards with which all citizens are expected to comply and to which they may appeal when they seek to defend their rights against the tyrant and the oppressor. Law is thought of as a tool that may be employed for good purposes and for bad and it is for that reason held answerable to standards of justice drawn from outside the law.

Yet law is also thought of as a profoundly significant form of moral association, guided by values that are internal to the character of juridical thought. Similarly, the lawyer is thought of as a technician who designs methods for achieving independently conceived goals, but also as the custodian for a distinct set of values. Thus law seems to be both the antithesis and the perfection of governance by force; both the embodiment of an attainable justice, and the product of sheer power; both a morally neutral instrument and the rich articulation of a moral idea.

30 John Finnis, *Natural Law and Natural Rights* (2nd edn, Oxford University Press 2011) 267. As Finnis points out, Max Weber elsewhere defines "law" by reference to the availability of organized sanctions, but adopts a more subtle and wiser view when he seeks to distinguish the legal type of authoritative coordination from other types.

One way of trying to accommodate the duality of law's appearance is by distinguishing imperfect human law from deeper standards of justice, or of natural law, that institutions should reflect if they are rightly to command our allegiance and fulfil their own pretensions to rectitude. So it is that, in Sophocles' *Antigone*, we find a powerful assertion of the claims of a higher or "natural" law to override the ruler's decrees: a conception of justice and right against which all human enactments must be measured. Recent theories have tended to replace the language of higher law with a language of "normative standards" or "critical morality"; but, in substance, the underlying picture remains the same. Thus we find the claim that law "holds itself subject to certain normative standards," although its success in complying with those standards is a variable and contingent matter.[31]

We are encouraged to conclude that those who see moral authority as somehow integral to the status of law are making an all-too-obvious error: they simply confuse what may sometimes be the case (the requirements of law may sometimes correspond with the relevant "normative standards" of justice and the good) with what must necessarily be the case. Or they conflate the idea that law makes a "claim" to moral authority (or to justice) with the assumption that such claims are soundly based. Law, we are told, is necessarily bound up with certain structures of power, but it has moral force only in so far as it mirrors standards derived from elsewhere. It claims a moral authority that it may not possess.

Jurisprudential thought has often seemed overly concerned with this supposed relationship between positive law (the laws created by human lawmakers) and a "higher law," or "natural law," or "normative standards" from which positive law derives its legitimacy and moral force. Such a focus, if unqualified by an acknowledgment of law's transformative significance, can become a source of impoverishment. But, in recent times, it has become still more narrowing, as questions concerning the status of such normative standards have been largely shunted out of jurisprudence into the supposedly separate disciplines of moral or political philosophy. The constricted outlook that results from this too easily suggests that the core questions for jurisprudence concern the way in which we choose to extend or apply the label "law." Should we think of law as truly law only when it more-or-less satisfies the standards to which it is answerable? Or should we employ the concept of "law" in a morally neutral way, so that it applies to all institutions with certain characteristic features quite independently of the normative standards, or natural laws, which could lend moral authority to the law? Such questions are not without their importance, but they capture only the most superficial aspect of law's problematic status.

It is often assumed that the notion of a "higher law," to which positive law is answerable, serves to distinguish the tradition of natural law thought

31 Joseph Raz, *Between Authority and Interpretation* (Oxford University Press 2009) 2.

from the tradition of legal positivism: legal positivists are assumed to deny the existence of any such higher law. But this is really a confusion. The most influential strands of thought within *both* traditions emphasize the answerability of positive law to critical moral standards which are independent of positive law. Legal positivists might be less likely to speak of those moral standards as a "higher law" but this terminological difference is of uncertain import at best. In the case of both traditions, the emphasis upon law's answerability to independent values has tended to obscure the way in which certain values are conceivable only as facets of the form of human association that is constituted by the development of law. Though a human product, and an all-too-fallible institution, law does not merely import or reflect (or stand answerable to) values from elsewhere, values with which it may at best achieve a contingent convergence. Rather, by its very nature, law transforms the relations of those it governs, and opens up new possibilities for human flourishing. In creating a distinctive form of association, the governance of law also gives rise to distinctive critical values to which the law is itself answerable. Those values can be said to be internal to the idea of law itself. To investigate the nature of law is not to contribute to a taxonomy of institutions, but to seek an improved understanding of the good by reflecting upon this aspect of our shared project of endeavoring to realize the good.

Something of the transformation wrought by legal institutions can be seen, for example, in Aeschylus's play *The Eumenides*, when the Furies are renamed the "kindly" or "gracious" ones on agreeing to accept and be bound by the decision of a lawful Athenian jury. Once disciplined by the requirements of legal process, vengeance is transfigured into the justice that obtains between fellow citizens, thereby creating the domain of public concern that is the state. This might at first be thought of simply as an improvement in the circumstances of social existence, replacing disorderly violence with orderly standards and regularity. It might even be portrayed as enabling people better to comply with reasons that applied to them quite independently of, and prior to, the law.[32] But it is hardly enlightening to approach the matter in this way. Law ultimately derives its authority, not simply from its capacity to coordinate conduct, or from its deployment of expert knowledge, but from the way in which it calls into being a distinctive and valuable form of moral association. That form of association is one in which reflection upon the nature of law plays a key part.

Those who are friends will from time to time need to reflect upon the nature of friendship. For friendship, while based in the slowly acquired bonds of memory and attachment, is structured and formed by an ideal of friendship towards which we aspire while inevitably falling short.[33] However much their conduct may be shaped by unreflective affection and spontaneity,

32 Raz (n 29) Chs. 2–4.

33 See Kant's remarks on this, discussed in Simmonds, "Law as an Idea We Live By" (n 28) 265.

it is always the case that friends may from time to time need to ask themselves what is required of them by the very idea of friendship. They then ask "What would a true friend do, in these circumstances?" Those who could never need to ask such a question are clearly not friends. Something similar is true of communities governed by law, for law is a principal expression of civic friendship. To be governed by law, rather than by the dictats of the powerful, we must reflect upon the idea of law. Forms of legal thought which seek to eschew such reflection simply confuse law with technocracy and power. For a community that espouses law, the jurisprudential debate concerning law's nature must be central.

Part I

Natural Law Tradition

2 God, Nature, and Human Law

An Introduction to Natural Law Tradition

Mir Ahmad Murtiza

I. Introduction

Natural law theory, both as a theory of morality and as a theory of law, is a critical reflection on human actions and institutions. It seeks to scrutinise these actions and institutions to identify deficiencies that preclude them from realising their true ends. Such scrutiny is made possible by its purported grasp of principles of goodness in actions and of the right order and form of human institutions. Natural law theory claims to discover these standards of goodness or rightness in the very nature of humans and the place they occupy within the cosmic order.[1] Therefore, these standards are, as Cicero affirms, 'constant [and] everlasting.'[2] The existence of these universal and unchanging standards allows the possibility of putting even the most ubiquitously practised norms of a particular society (including its positively constituted legal system) to moral judgment.

Natural law jurisprudence is intrinsically linked to certain positions in moral philosophy. It is acknowledged that many of the natural law positions in modern analytical jurisprudence can be formulated without reference to moral philosophy. However, a complete theory of natural law jurisprudence requires an adequate account of practical rationality that underpins moral judgments and makes normative evaluation of positive law possible.[3] A complete theory of natural law ethics must entail philosophical beliefs about human moral responsibility, an account of natural human well-being and its constitutive elements, an epistemology of these constitutive elements, principles guiding the pursuit of these constitutive elements in the ordinary moral reasoning, and, ultimately, the supra-human source (whether it be theistic God as ordinarily

1 Jonathan Crowe, 'Metaphysical Foundations of Natural Law Theories' in George Duke and Robert P. George (eds), *The Cambridge Companion to Natural Law Jurisprudence* (Cambridge University Press 2017) 104.

2 Marcus Tullius Cicero, *On the Republic and on the Laws* (David Fott tr, Cornell University Press 2014) 98.

3 Mark C. Murphy, 'Natural Law Jurisprudence' (2003) 6 *Legal Theory* 241; John Finnis, *Natural Law and Natural Rights* (Oxford University Press 2011) 18 (henceforth *NLNR*).

DOI: 10.4324/9781003728603-3

understood or any other conception of the divine) of natural order that provides meaning to any notion of objective good or evil. Furthermore, natural law jurisprudence aims to explain the essential nature of legal reality, the relation between positive law and moral norms, the obligatoriness of legal rules, the extent of the public sphere, and other issues of similar ilk.

Given the diversity of views associated with natural law jurisprudence, one is readily confronted with the problem of how to capture the unity underlying these ideas and to give an exposition of natural law jurisprudence as such. This chapter attempts to briefly survey the opinions of major thinkers associated with natural law tradition in chronological order. By giving a brief description of the central ideas of these major philosophers, it seeks to reach an understanding of the fundamental beliefs that underpin the whole enterprise of natural law jurisprudence. However, the present study does not intend to be exhaustive and excludes many classical and contemporary thinkers.

II. Natural Law in Greek Thought

Any attempt to discuss the thoughts of classical philosophers as forming part of a particular school comes with specific difficulties. One may easily be duped by the temptation of reading certain ideas into their works that had never been the concern of these philosophers.[4] Another problem that besets the interpretation of classical philosophical texts is that their composition often allows the possibility of multiple interpretations, obscuring the doctrinal identity of the concerned thinker. Mindful of the risk that such an exercise entails, we will venture to briefly discuss the natural law reading of the texts of Plato and Aristotle as representative of Greek thought.

A. *Plato*

Even before Plato, the idea of the cosmic order that was to be obeyed even by the mightiest of powers (e.g., Zeus) was common among Greeks.[5] Some philosophers even referred to a common law that can be rationally known and should be the basis of the political law of the community.[6] It was in Plato that we find the most expensive engagement with the ideas that were to become the cardinal themes of the natural law tradition. In *Euthyphro*, Plato asked a question that was to command the attention of generations of thinkers and

4 Brian Bix, 'Natural Law Theory' in Dennis Patterson (ed), *A Companion to Philosophy of Law and Legal Theory* (Wiley-Blackwell 2010) 215.

5 Bertrand Russell, *History of Western Philosophy* (Routledge 2015) 116.

6 John M. Finnis, 'Natural Law Theory: Its Past and Its Present' (2012) 57 *American Journal of Jurisprudence* 81.

responses to which can help determine one's allegiance to the idea of natural law. Leibniz describes the question thus:

> It is agreed that whatever God wills is good and just. But there remains the question whether it is good and just because God wills it or whether God wills it because it is good and just: in other words, whether justice and goodness are arbitrary or whether they belong to the necessary and eternal truths about the nature of things, as do numbers and proportions.[7]

Plato himself held[8] that God wills something because it is good and just and that the ideas of goodness and justice do 'belong to the necessary and eternal truths about the nature of things.' On this account, the goodness of any act or thing is independent of the fact that it is issued from the will of God, and God wills justice and goodness because He is just and good. The separation of the goodness of something from the will of any power is one of the principal tenets of natural law tradition and can also be recognised in natural law positions in modern analytical jurisprudence.

The platonic metaphysics of morals is grounded in a distinctive theological view of the harmony between humans and the cosmos. The objectivity of moral values is a consequence of the governance of the cosmos by a rational soul whose inherent rationality and friendship with creation bestows objectivity not only to moral values but to anything that exists. In *Gorgias*, Plato writes:

> [H]eaven and earth, gods and men are held together by community (*koinonia*) and friendship (*philia*), and orderliness, temperance and justice.[9]

Another central idea of the natural law theory is that rational deliberations upon the nature of humans and their place in the cosmic hierarchy of being can yield norms for ordering human conduct. Plato's conception of nature and its relationship with positive law, which is essential to any theory of natural law, is to be understood from his disputations with his main philosophical opponents, the sophists, and the views he vehemently opposed. For sophists, nature and positive law are incompatible with each other, for laws restrain the desires and tendencies fostered by nature. *Callicles* affirmed that 'convention

7 Gottfried Wilhelm Leibniz, 'Meditation on the Common Concept of Justice (c. 1702–3)' in Patrick Riley (ed), *Leibniz: Political Writings* (Cambridge University Press 1988) 45–65.

8 Terence Irwin, *Plato's Ethics* (Oxford University Press 1995) 152.

9 Richard F. Stalley, 'Platonic Philosophy of Law' in Fred D. Miller Jr. and Carrie-Ann Biondi (eds), *A Treatise of Legal Philosophy and General Jurisprudence* (Vol. 6, Springer 2015) 61, quoting Plato, *Gorgias* 507e–508a.

and nature are generally in variance with one another'[10] and laws are nothing but 'agreements contrary to nature,'[11] which may be trampled underfoot by any naturally superior person.[12] Moreover, for sophists, it is shown by nature that the superior rules over the weaker and that conquerors, like Xerces, acted 'according to nature . . . and according to the law of nature: not, perhaps, according to that artificial law, which we invent and impose upon our fellows. . . .'[13] *Thrasymachus* espoused, '[J]ust is nothing other than the advantage of the stronger,'[14] and *Hippias* proclaimed, '[L]aw is the tyrant of mankind, and often compels us to do many things which are against nature.[15] A perfunctory glance at these selective excerpts reveals that for sophists, nature stood for the brute fact of human physical existence, from which springs those sub-rational passions and inclinations that demand immediate gratification. Positive laws and conventions are restrictive of these sub-rational passions and are, therefore, inharmonious with nature as conceptualised by sophists. A natural life, for sophists, is 'a life pursuing passionate satisfactions such as power, sex, and other bodily and emotional interests (today often conceived as psychological or "subconscious" drives or "complexes").'[16] Such a conception of nature is incompatible with any notion of objective moral standards that can guide law-making. Hence, natural law is impossible.

In contrast, Plato conceived nature as a cosmic order that was at once 'moral, purposeful, rational, [and] divine.'[17] Plato rejects the moral relativism of the sophists and presents an alternative conception of objective morality.[18] For Plato, 'according to nature' meant 'according to reason.'[19] Humans'

10 Jerome Hall, 'Plato's Legal Philosophy' (1956) 31 *Indiana Law Journal* 171, quoting *Gorgias* 482e.
11 Ibid. 203, quoting *Gorgias* 492c.
12 Ibid., quoting *Gorgias* 484a.
13 Ibid., quoting *Gorgias* 483e.
14 Plato, *The Republic of Plato* (Allan Bloom tr, Basic Books 1968) 338c (henceforth *Republic*).
15 Hall (n 10) 203, quoting *Protagoras* 337d.
16 Finnis (n 6) 81.
17 M. T. McClure, 'The Greek Conception of Nature' (1934) 46 *Philosophical Review* 109.
18 The distinction between *phusis* (nature) and *nomos* (laws or conventions) is considered the hallmark of sophistic ethics. Sophists distinguished nature from laws or conventions and referred to the former for the ethical justification of action. Plato agreed with sophists in holding that nature is the source of moral standards; however, his concept of nature was markedly opposed to theirs. He bridged the gap between nature and laws and prepared the philosophical ground for setting the latter in the former. Brenner M. Fissell, 'The Justification of Positive Law in Plato' (2011) 56 *American Journal of Jurisprudence* 89. Commenting on Plato's *Laws*, Richard F. Stalley writes, 'one way of interpreting . . . the whole of the Laws would be to see it as a systematic attack on the nomos-phusis distinction.' Richard F. Stalley, *An Introduction to Plato's Laws* (Basil Blackwell 1983) 29.
19 V. Bradley Lewis, '"Reason Striving to Become Law": Nature and Law in Plato's Laws' (2009) 54 *American Journal of Jurisprudence* 67.

faculty of reason, which is an 'immortal element'[20] in them, has the ability to grasp the intelligible goods, which ought to be the object of human actions not because they have the function of maximising utility or are instrumental in the pursuit of any other hedonistic end but for their own sake. Through dialectical interactions with his opponents, Plato comes to the knowledge of the objectivity of goods, such as life, knowledge, friendship, etc., because these intelligible goods are involved in any meaningful dialogue concerning human actions.[21] These goods are not grounded in human nature in the sense that nature directly determines them.[22] However, they can still be called natural in at least four senses. Firstly, human nature defines the possibilities of human achievement[23] that condition the pursuit of these goods. Secondly, humans have a natural capacity to grasp these goods as worthy objects of pursuit.[24] Thirdly, the objectivity of these goods is much like the objectivity of natural objects, for they exist 'quite independently of human thought, contrivance, and action.'[25] Fourthly, these goods, as Finnis interprets them, are good for humans because of their nature, and the knowledge of these goods enriches our knowledge of human nature.[26]

Because of its ability to perceive the objective good, reason ought to be the guiding principle of human actions. Thus, Plato calls for subjecting lower elements, both in the soul and the polity, to the authority of reason.[27] According to Plato, the law, when ideally defined, is the 'offspring of reason';[28] in other words, the law is a tool whose proper end is to rationally guide its subjects to live a life that leads them to perfection unique to their natures. However, it does not follow that each and every positive law is perfectly rational; rather, actual positive laws may fall short of the standards set by the principle of reason. It allows reason to serve as a 'higher standard' on the basis of which the justice of human laws can be judged, and if any human law fails to satisfy the standard of justice, it is not obligatory for the subjects.[29] However, can

20 Plato, *The Laws of Plato* (A. E. Taylor tr, J. M. Dent & Sons Ltd. 1934) 714a (henceforth *Laws*).

21 Finnis (n 6) 83; Germain Grisez, Joseph Boyle, and John Finnis, 'Practical Principles, Moral Truth, and Ultimate Ends' (1987) 32 *American Journal of Jurisprudence* 99 ('Dialectical arguments relate a proposition to be defended to other knowledge, and show that denying it has unacceptable consequences. The dialectical defense of the basic goods is a theoretical project . . . Attempts to add candidates to the list of basic goods can be dealt with dialectically.').

22 Mark Murphy, 'The Natural Law Tradition in Ethics' in Edward N. Zalta (ed), *Stanford Encyclopedia of Philosophy* (Summer 2019 edn), https://plato.stanford.edu/archives/sum2019/entries/natural-law-ethics/ accessed March 18, 2025.

23 Ibid.

24 Finnis (n 6) 84.

25 Ibid.

26 Ibid.

27 *Republic* 442d.

28 Stalley (n 9) 71, quoting *Laws* 890d.

29 *Laws* 715b.

the laws that fall short of this standard be rightly called laws? It is to ask whether or not Plato agrees with the classical dictum of *lex iniusta non est lex* (An unjust law is no law at all) as popularly understood. As per Richard F. Stalley, three passages in the Platonic oeuvre expressly argue that unjust laws should not be called laws; however, none of them can be reasonably interpreted to imply Plato's own philosophical belief.[30] Nonetheless, if one looks at the Platonic corpus as a whole, one may be convinced that Plato agreed with what is referred to as 'weak reading' in modern jurisprudence. Weak reading in natural law jurisprudence claims that unjust laws are laws, but their injustice precludes them from creating valid moral obligations, though they still are *intrasystemically* valid.[31] For instance, when in *Apology*, Socrates is asked why he disobeyed the orders issued by the Thirty Tyrants, he calls their orders a 'specimen of the sort of commands which they were always giving . . . . [T]he strong arm of that oppressive power did not frighten me into doing wrong.'[32] Here, Plato seems to be defending Socrates' refusal to obey the unjust commands of positively appointed rulers. Plato considers positive law essential for realising the principles of natural law in a particular polity, and the laws that fail to effectively realise these principles are considered defective and, hence, impotent in creating valid moral obligations for their subjects.

B. Aristotle

Unlike Plato, Aristotle's connection to the natural law tradition is less contested, though not completely uncontroversial. Aristotle is often apotheosised as the 'father of the natural law,'[33] and the influence of his teachings in later discourses in the tradition is more palpable.[34] According to Aristotle, law is 'intellect without desire,'[35] and the science of law-making is the 'master science'[36] of the human good. Aristotle regards legislative science as a kind of

30 Stalley (n 9) 81.

31 Murphy (n 3) 254.

32 Hall (n 10) 172, quoting *Apology* 32cd.

33 Max Salomon Shellens, 'Aristotle on Natural Law' (1959) 4 *American Journal of Jurisprudence* 72.

34 It is not to claim that Aristotle's conception of natural law is similar to the later Stoic, Roman, or Christian natural law thought; rather, Aristotle presented ideas that later came to be considered part of the natural law tradition, and there were key elements in the development of later natural law thought that developed under characteristically Aristotelian influences. Ernest Barker, *The Politics of Aristotle* (Oxford University Press 1946) 336; Carl J. Friedrich, *The Philosophy of Law in Historical Perspective* (University of Chicago Press 1958) 22–23; Michael B. Crowe, *The Changing Profile of Natural Law* (Nijhoff 1977) 19.

35 George Duke, 'Aristotle and Natural Law' (2020) 82 *Review of Politics* 21, quoting *Politics* 3.16 1287a33.

36 Fred D. Miller Jr, 'Aristotle's Philosophy of Law' in Fred D. Miller, Jr. and Carrie-Ann Biondi (eds), *A Treatise of Legal Philosophy and General Jurisprudence* (Vol. 6, Springer 2015) 86.

practical science,[37] a science that is concerned with the knowledge of making rational judgments about the goodness or badness of human actions based not on any extraneous factor but for their own sake. Moreover, for Aristotle, the primary source of law is the practical rationality of a human legislator who is capable of grasping ethical truths.[38] Hence, for Aristotle, law-making is essentially an ethical activity. In this aspect, Aristotle's concept of law is somewhat similar to the Platonic conception, for Aristotle also lays much emphasis on the rational content of positive law. In *Rhetoric to Alexander*, a later Aristotelian treatise, law is defined in the following words:

> Law, simply described, is reason [*logos*] defined according to the common agreement [*homologia*] of the city-state, regulating action of every kind.[39]

Any discussion of the natural law in Aristotle's thought must take account of the distinction he draws between common law and particular law in *Rhetoric* and his examination of the constituent parts of political justice in *Nicomachean Ethics*. In *Rhetoric*, Aristotle talks about two kinds of laws: one common and the other particular. The text reads:

> By the two kinds of law, I mean particular law and universal law. Particular law is that which each community lays down and applies to its own members: this is partly unwritten and partly written; universal law is the law of nature. For there really is, as everyone to some extent divines, a natural justice and injustice that is common to all, even to those who have no association or covenant with each other. It is this that Sophocles' Antigone clearly means when she says that the burial of Polyneices was a just act in spite of the prohibition: she means that it was just by nature,
> Not of today or yesterday it is,
> but lives eternal: none can date its birth.[40]

Particular law can be read as positive law because a particular community lays it, and it regulates the affairs of its members. It may be written in the case of statutes, or it may be unwritten in the case of conventions or customs. In contrast to particular law, common law is always unwritten, is the same everywhere, and is said to be eternal. It is interesting to note that Aristotle equates it with the law of nature. Here, Aristotle seems to reject the subjectivism of

37 Ibid. 85.
38 Ibid. 82.
39 Ibid. 83.
40 Christoph Horn, 'Aristotle on the Legal and Moral Aspects of Law' in Maria Liatsi (ed), *Ethics in Ancient Greek Literature: Aspects of Ethical Reasoning from Homer to Aristotle and Beyond* (De Gruyter 2020) 84, quoting *Rhetoric* I.13 (1373b1–18).

sophists, and this concept of natural law accommodates many of the elements of later-developed natural law theories.[41] For Aristotle, goodness is inextricably related to nature. Something is good because it is perfective of a being, and this idea of perfection is dependent on the nature of that being.[42] A good law is one that is perfective of a political community whose function is the perfection of its members. Common law is normatively superior to a particular law and prevails in case of conflict between the two. To illustrate this, Aristotle gives the example of Antigone's burial of her brother in defiance of the tyrant of Thebes.

The relation between natural law and positive law in Aristotelian legal thought is a point of great controversy[43] and has led some even to deny Aristotle's natural law credentials.[44] The debate mainly revolves around the interpretation of an excerpt from *Nicomachean Ethics*, which reads:

> Of political justice part is natural, part legal—natural, that which everywhere has the same force and does not exist by people's thinking this or that; legal, that which is originally indifferent, but when it has been laid down is not indifferent, e.g., that a prisoner's ransom shall be a mina, or that a goat and not two sheep be sacrificed, and again all the laws that are passed for particular cases, e.g., that sacrifice shall be made in honor of Brasidas, and the provisions of decrees.[45]

In this excerpt, Aristotle partitions political justice into two distinct yet connected components: natural and legal. The natural component is said to be necessarily the same everywhere and is not a product of human decision. Later, to further illustrate the necessity inherent in the idea of natural justice, he gives the example of a fire that burns everywhere in the same way. The second part is legal or conventional, which concerns particular matters and is not the same everywhere. It is illuminating to note that the legal part concerns particular enactments and is said to be insignificant before it is laid down, but it attains significance only after it has been laid down. It echoes Aquinas's concept of *determinatio*—the idea that certain rules in the civil law of a particular political community can only be reasons for actions for the members of that

41 Ibid. 83.

42 Murphy (n 22).

43 Weirnick discusses various ways in which this relation has been viewed. Darren Weirnick, *Law in Aristotle's Ethical-Political Thought* (PhD dissertation, Rice University 1998) 102, Rice Research Repository.

44 David G. Ritchie, *Natural Rights: A Criticism of Some Political and Ethical Conceptions* (S. Sonnenschein 1895); Hans Kelsen, 'Aristotle's Doctrine of Justice' in Hans Kelsen (ed), *What Is Justice?* (University of California Press 1957) 128; Bernard Yack, 'Natural Right and Aristotle's Understanding of Justice' (1990) 18 *Political Theory* 216.

45 Aristotle, *Nicomachean Ethics* (W. D. Ross tr, Batoche Books 1999) Book V, Ch. 7, 1134b–1135a.

community if they are posited by the positive ruler. The ruler is free to choose one option from a range of alternatives made available by natural law to serve the common good of the community.[46] For example, it is in the very nature of political communities to regulate economic or sexual relations, though different communities may have different laws concerning contractual relations, property ownership, marriage, etc. By making natural and legal parts of the same political justice, Aristotle seeks to emphasise the manner in which these two are interwoven[47] in the positive law of the particular political communities. In each law of a political community, one can discern natural and legal parts, but no law would be possible without the union of these two parts.

In the given excerpt, the relation between the natural and legal parts is horizontal rather than vertical,[48] but still, the natural part can be said to be prior to the legal part and can serve as a ground for the normative evaluation of the latter.[49] Natural justice is described as having the same force for all political communities and is not dependent on being adopted by a particular legal system for its continued existence. Natural justice is obligatory without being made part of any political justice, for it is contrasted with legal justice, which is 'originally indifferent' and only becomes significant (or obligatory) when it is laid down. It may also be argued that natural justice is that part of political justice (or positive law) that is directly derived from the universal law of nature referred to by Aristotle in *Rhetoric*. As political justice is the product of practical deliberations of a legislator who is capable of grasping objective truths of natural law,[50] it contains rules that are directly derived from natural law and those rules that are particular specifications of the general principles of natural law. Such an interpretation is plausible, for the given text does not exclude the possibility of natural law that exists independently of the political law of the community. On this account, the goodness of a particular system of positive law can be evaluated on the basis of how perfectly it incorporates the law of nature; however, the specification of particular rules of positive law (legal justice) may differ depending upon varying circumstances.[51]

The argument for the normative potential of natural justice is further bolstered when one takes into account the general normative naturalism of Aristotle's political philosophy.[52] Aristotle claims that there is only one kind of

46 John Finnis, *Aquinas: Moral, Political, and Legal Theory* (Oxford University Press 1998) 267–274.
47 Tony Burns, 'Aristotle and Natural Law' (1998) 19 *History of Political Thought* 142.
48 Ibid. 148.
49 Duke (n 35) 7.
50 Ibid. 6.
51 Ibid. 7.
52 Christoph Horn, 'Normative Naturalism in Aristotle's Political Philosophy?' in Peter Adamson and Christof Rapp (eds), *State and Nature: Studies in Ancient and Medieval Philosophy* (De Gruyter 2021) 59–80.

constitution that is just by nature[53] and that the natural constitution can be recognised by its direction toward the common good.[54] These claims provide a ground for normative evaluation of particular constitutions. A constitution that is more capable of realising the common good is naturally better than the one that fails to do so.

III. The Centrality of St. Thomas Aquinas

Aquinas is a central figure in the history of Western moral philosophy. In his thought, one finds what may be called the flowering of natural law tradition. In Thomistic thought, the classical wisdom of Greeks and Romans is synthesised with Christian revelation in an attempt to develop an understanding of moral objectivity set in the context of a larger theological framework. Aquinas heavily draws upon writings of early fathers of the Church, who are copiously cited throughout his works; however, the primary influence on his ethics and politics is that of Aristotle, to whom Aquinas refers as 'the Philosopher.' The centrality of Aquinas in natural law tradition can be evidenced by the fact that many of the controversies within the modern natural law jurisprudence mainly revolve around the interpretations of his texts, particularly *Treatise on Law* in *Summa Theologica*. We will attempt to give a brief account of Aquinas's theory of natural law, a theory that has been termed the 'central case of natural law position.'[55]

Aquinas defines law as 'an ordinance of reason for the common good, made by him who has care of the community, and promulgated.'[56] The given definition reveals four conditions that must be satisfied by any rule to be 'Law' in the fullest sense. Firstly, law is an ordinance of reason, for it reasonably directs its subjects towards an end. Law is concerned with practical reason rather than speculative reason, for it is the province of practical reason to direct human acts.[57] Secondly, the end to which law is directed is the happiness or good of the community. Law is not directed towards the good of particular persons or classes of persons but the good of the community conceived as a whole. It is the law's claim of promoting the common good that makes it legally and morally obligatory for the subjects.[58] Thirdly, law is made by the one who has the care of the community. Law-making, which is aimed at the common

53 Ibid. 75.
54 Ibid. 76.
55 Murphy (n 22).
56 St. Thomas Aquinas, *Summa Theologiae* (Fathers of the English Dominican Province tr, New Advent 2000) pt. I–II, q. 90, art. 4 (henceforth *ST*).
57 Ibid. pt. I–II, q. 90, art. 1, rep. obj. 2.
58 John Finnis, 'Aquinas' Moral, Political, and Legal Philosophy' in Edward N. Zalta (ed), *Stanford Encyclopedia of Philosophy* (Spring 2021 edn), https://plato.stanford.edu/archives/spr2021/entries/aquinas-moral-political/ accessed March 18, 2025.

good, belongs to either the whole people or viceregent of the whole people[59] because 'in all other matters the directing of anything to the end concerns him to whom the end belongs.'[60] In other words, since the law is directed to the good of the whole people, it is to be made by the whole people or their duly appointed representative. Finally, promulgation is essential to law, for it must be notified to those whom it is to rule and measure.

Furthermore, Aquinas identifies four kinds or, in a sense, levels of law: (1) the eternal law, (2) the natural law, (3) the divine law, and (4) the human law. All four kinds satisfy the conditions laid out in the aforementioned definition. Eternal law is the divine reason by which the community of the universe is governed.[61] By the concept of eternal law, Aquinas seeks to accentuate the lack of arbitrariness in the divine governance of the universe. Eternal law is God's rational plan for the whole creation, and eternal law determines its natural order. Though humans participate in the eternal law, the complete comprehension of the eternal law is beyond the reach of human understanding. We must agree with John Finnis that it is 'quite unknown to us.'[62] All things under the divine providence are ruled by the eternal law from which they derive their 'respective inclinations to proper acts and ends.'[63] However, rational creatures like humans are ruled more perfectly by eternal law, for they also have a share of the divine providence and reason that enables them to partake in the eternal law in a rational manner.[64] Humans can naturally know the first principles of good and evil by virtue of possessing reason and free will that ultimately come from divine origins. By rooting the human capacity for discerning good and evil in divine providence, Aquinas aims to stress the pivotal role of God in moral reasoning. Aquinas writes:

> [T]he light of natural reason, whereby we discern what is good and what is evil, which is the function of the natural law, is nothing else than an imprint on us of the Divine light. It is therefore evident that the natural law is nothing else than the rational creature's participation of the eternal law.[65]

Murphy claims that there are two features of Aquinas's understanding of natural law.[66] Firstly, natural law may be viewed as an aspect of divine providence. In this view, God's role as the bestower of natural law and the continuity between eternal law and natural law are emphasised. Secondly, natural law may

59 *ST* pt. I–II, q. 90, art. 3.
60 Ibid.
61 Ibid. pt. I–II, q. 91, art. 1.
62 *NLNR* 391.
63 *ST* pt. I–II, q. 91, art. 2.
64 Ibid.
65 Ibid.
66 Murphy (n 22).

be viewed as constituting an essential part of the theory of practical rationality, a theory of what is reasonable to do in a given situation considering all the circumstances involved.

The self-evident precepts of natural law constitute the first principles of practical reason from which conclusions as to particular matters may be drawn, for 'the precepts of natural law are to the practical reason, what the first principles of demonstrations are to the speculative reason; because both are self-evident principles.'[67] Emphasising the fundamentality of the notion of good to practical reason, Aquinas compares it to the notion of existence. He affirms that just as the first thing that is universally apprehended is 'Being' and the first principle thus grasped is that 'the same thing cannot be affirmed and denied at the same time,' the first thing that is apprehended by practical reason is 'good'; therefore, the first principle of practical reason is based on the notion that 'good is that which all things seek after.' Consequently, we attain the knowledge of the first principle of natural law that 'good is to be done and pursued, evil is to be avoided.'[68] Thus, anything that is apprehended by human reason to be good for humans belongs to natural law. Humans have a natural inclination to pursue certain objects that are 'naturally apprehended by reason as being good'[69] and the order of precepts of natural law is in accordance with the order of these natural inclinations.[70] The knowledge of the general precepts of natural law is common to all, but people may differ in the application of these general precepts in certain matters.[71]

In addition to natural law, humans also need divine law to reach perfection. Divine law corrects human understanding in the application of general precepts of natural law to particular situations. Divine law is essential for man to pursue the end of eternal heavenly happiness that may otherwise be unattainable because it is 'inproportionate to man's natural faculty.'[72] A precept of divine law cannot conflict with a true determination of natural law.

After providing an account of the divine origins of the human capacity for moral reasoning, Aquinas moves to discuss human law (or positive law) and its relation with natural law. This part of Aquinas's thought can properly be categorised as part of legal philosophy as understood today and is most pertinent to the contemporary discourses in modern analytical jurisprudence. According to Aquinas, human law is mainly required to desist forcefully those having a propensity for evil and to provide citizens with training in virtue.[73]

67 *ST* pt. I–II, q. 94, art. 2.
68 Ibid.
69 Ibid.
70 Ibid.
71 Ibid. pt. I–II, q. 94, art. 4.
72 Ibid. pt. I–II, q. 91, art. 4.
73 Ibid. pt. I–II, q. 95, art. 1.

For Aquinas, human law is essentially a coercive system of rules legitimised by virtue of having been derived from natural law.[74]

Human law may be derived from natural law in two ways. Firstly, it may be derived from natural law as a 'conclusion from premises.'[75] For instance, the rule against murder may be derived from the premise that 'one should do harm to no man.' Secondly, a rule of human law may be derived from natural law 'by way of determination of certain generalities.'[76] A famous example of this is the determination of the speed limit on a highway. Natural law dictates that there must be some kind of traffic regulation to minimise harm to human life. However, the exact speed limit on a particular road is to be determined by the positively appointed ruler, taking into consideration all the contingencies involved in a particular situation. To emphasise the elements of ingenuity and discretion involved in the making of human laws by way of determination of generalities, Aquinas likens this second method of derivation of legal rules to the art of a craftsman.[77] In a positive legal system, laws are the result of both kinds of derivation. In view of this analysis, one can conclude that, for Aquinas, positive law encompasses two kinds of laws: natural and legal or civil. Commenting on this aspect of Aquinas's legal thought, Finnis argues, '[I]n the Summa he [Aquinas] treats the division between natural and civil as a distinction within positive law.'[78] A certain part of the positive legal system derives its authority both from its derivation from natural law and from the fact that it is positively laid down and can, in a sense, be called part of the natural law. In comparison, the other part derives its entire authority only from the fact that it has been positively laid down and is morally insignificant before being laid down. Aquinas writes:

> [T]hose things which are derived in the first way [as a conclusion from premises], are contained in human law not as emanating therefrom exclusively, but have some force from the natural law also. But those things which are derived in the second way [as determination of generalities] have no other force than that of human law.[79]

In Thomistic legal thought, natural law serves as a criterion for assessing justice and, consequently, the obligatoriness of positive law. According to Aquinas, 'the force of a law depends on the extent of its justice,'[80] and only just laws

74 Finnis (n 58).
75 *ST* pt. I–II, q. 95, art. 2.
76 Ibid.
77 Ibid.
78 John Finnis, 'The Truth in Legal Positivism' in Robert P. George (ed), *The Autonomy of Law* (Clarendon Press 1996) 202. Also see Santiago Legarre, 'Derivation of Positive from Natural Law Revisited' (2012) 57 *American Journal of Jurisprudence* 103.
79 *ST* pt. I–II, q. 95, art. 2.
80 Ibid.

are 'binding in conscience.'[81] Laws can be unjust because of two reasons:[82] (1) for being repugnant to the common good and (2) for being in contradiction with the divine good. For Aquinas, natural justice is essential to the idea of law. He calls unjust laws 'acts of violence rather than laws.'[83] Aquinas writes,

> [E]very human law has so much of the nature of law, as it is derived from the law of nature. But if in any point it deflects from the law of nature, it is no longer a law but a perversion of law.[84]

Though Aquinas contends that unjust laws are not binding in conscience (meaning that they fail to create valid moral obligation), he advises obedience to unjust laws 'in order to avoid scandal or disturbance'[85] and goes on to say that in such a case, one 'should even yield his right.'[86]

Aquinas heavily influences the dominant strains in modern natural law theory, and many important contemporary thinkers present themselves as the faithful interpreters of his thought. However, few agree with each other. Disagreements have recently been flamed up by the proponents of the so-called new natural law theory and their critics. The debate mainly centres on the question of how much moral goods are grounded in human nature and how much they are the product of practical reasoning.

IV. Natural Law in Modern Legal Thought: Lon L. Fuller and John Finnis

After the classic statement of natural law by St. Thomas Aquinas, the influence of natural law experienced many ups and downs. However, it has recovered some of its influence in the modern era owing to several factors.[87] Nonetheless, the concept of natural law has also been subject to various reinterpretations or, at times, misinterpretations. It was made to confront new ideas and incorporate new concerns. This chapter discusses only the ideas of Lon L. Fuller and John Finnis.

81 Ibid. pt. I–II, q. 96, art. 4. For understanding the concept of conscience in Aquinas' thought, see Cajetan Cuddy, O.P., 'St. Thomas Aquinas on Conscience' in Jeffrey B. Hammond and Helen M. Alvare (eds), *Christianity and the Laws of Conscience* (Cambridge University Press 2021).

82 *ST* pt. I–II, q. 96, art. 4.

83 Ibid.

84 Ibid. pt. I–II, q. 95, art. 2.

85 Ibid. pt. I–II, q. 96, art. 4.

86 Ibid.

87 Raymond Wacks, *Understanding Jurisprudence: An Introduction to Legal Theory* (Oxford University Press 2012) 21–22.

A. *Lon L. Fuller*

The classical natural law tradition is predominantly concerned with the substantive content of legal rules, the consequences of substantive insufficiencies for the nature of these legal rules, and the obligatoriness of these rules for the subjects. In this sense, the various theories in this tradition may be mainly viewed as the 'substantive theories of natural law.' It is not that the classical natural law tradition is unconcerned with legal forms or the institutional aspects of law. Rather, it is only after extensively engaging with abstract questions about the nature of law and the substantive requirements of the legal obligation that it turns to the question of legal forms. On the contrary, Fuller is primarily interested in legal forms and the institutionality of law and describes his theory as a 'procedural version of natural law,'[88] though he is not oblivious to the substantive concerns.

For Fuller, law is 'the enterprise of subjecting human conduct to the governance of rules.'[89] However, this enterprise should not be viewed as a 'one-way projection of authority, originating with government and imposing itself upon the citizen.'[90] It needs to be seen as 'the product of an interplay of purposive orientations between the citizen and his government.'[91] Hence, it is to be contrasted with mere managerial direction. Fuller conceptualises law as an ongoing activity[92] with the purpose of solving problems of communication and coordination between fellow individuals.[93] Moreover, certain requirements are to be fulfilled by any legal system to be properly called law. In *Morality of Law*, Fuller outlines these requirements as 'eight ways to fail to make law'[94] and equates these requirements with the 'inner morality of law.' Following are requirements or virtues of 'inner morality of law':

1. The law should consist of general rules.
2. The law should be publicised to the people whose conduct it is to regulate.
3. The law should not be retrospective.
4. The law should be comprehensible.
5. The law should not consist of contradictory rules.
6. Law should not require conduct that is beyond the power of addressees to comply.
7. The law should not change so frequently as to make it difficult for addressees to align their conduct with it.

88 Lon L. Fuller, *The Morality of Law* (Yale University Press 1969) 96.
89 Ibid.
90 Ibid. 204.
91 Ibid.
92 Ibid.
93 Charles L. Palms, 'The Natural Law Philosophy of Lon L. Fuller' (1965) 11 *Catholic Lawyer* 94.
94 Fuller (n 88) 33–91.

8. There should be no discrepancy between promulgated rules and their actual administration.

Various legal systems may embody these virtues to various degrees, and the extent to which any purported legal system fails to incorporate these virtues of inner morality, it fails to be law to that extent. There may be a social arrangement that is so devoid of these virtues that it is no longer correct to call it a governance through law.[95] Therefore, satisfying these requirements is necessary for even creating an otherwise unjust law.[96] The key feature of Fuller's argument—which is also the most criticised part of his theory[97]—is his attribution of moral value to these procedural requirements because they contribute to the construction of an efficient and ordered legal system. For Fuller, the very 'notion of order itself contains what may be called a moral element.'[98] Law and good order (hence, law and morality) are inextricably linked. He writes:

> Law may be said to represent order simpliciter. Good order is law that corresponds to the demands of justice, or morality, or men's notions of what ought to be.[99]

Again, he affirms:

> Law, considered merely as order, contains, then, its own implicit morality. This morality of order must be respected if we are to create anything that can be called law, even bad law.[100]

Furthermore, Fuller is also concerned with the substantive content of legal rules and calls it 'external morality of law.' It is the moral quality of law that justifies its claim upon the subject's fidelity to it.[101] What connection do the external and inner moralities of law have with each other? Fuller acknowledges that the internal morality of law is 'indifferent towards the substantive aims of

95 Sean Coyle, *Modern Jurisprudence: A Philosophical Guide* (Hart 2022) 210.

96 Lon L. Fuller, 'Positivism and Fidelity to Law: A Reply to Professor Hart' (1958) 71 *Harvard Law Review* 630.

97 H. L. A. Hart censures Fuller for confusing efficiency with morality. His animadversion is founded on the argument that Fuller's proposed 'inner morality of law' is nothing more than principles of 'good legal craftsmanship' and may be employed to produce grossly iniquitous laws. H. L. A. Hart, *The Concept of Law* (Clarendon Press 1961) 207; H. L. A. Hart, *Essays in Jurisprudence and Philosophy* (Clarendon Press 1983) 350. For more criticisms, see 'The Morality of Law: A Symposium' (1965) 10 *Villanova Law Review* 631.

98 Fuller (n 96) 645.

99 Ibid. 644.

100 Ibid. 645.

101 Suri Ratnapala, *Jurisprudence* (Cambridge University Press 2009) 167.

law and is ready to serve a variety of such aims with equal efficacy,'[102] but he rejects Hart's claim that it is 'compatible with great iniquity.'[103] Fuller avers that 'law is a precondition for good law'[104] and finds the idea that a 'faithful adherence to internal morality of law'[105] can be combined with 'a brutal indifference to justice and human welfare'[106] uncorroborated by evidence. Here, the main point of Fuller's argument is that adherence to the principles of legality obstructs the objectives of a tyrannical regime. Both kinds of morality invigorate each other, and one's deterioration leads to the other's deterioration. Elsewhere, he writes:

> In the life of a nation these external and internal moralities of law reciprocally influence one another; a deterioration of the one will almost inevitably produce a deterioration in the other.[107]

The core of Fuller's argument is that moral value is inherent in the very idea of a fully consistent and efficient legal system and that the pursuit of principles of legality that make such a legal system possible is itself a moral good.[108] The requirements of the inner morality of law are 'intrinsically and specifically promotive of good order'[109] and contribute to the construction of a substantially just legal system. When fully realised in a legal system, these principles inhibit the pursuit of the ends of an unjust regime by curbing the illegal or extra-legal use of political power.[110] Moreover, values of reciprocity and autonomy are developed in a legal system that embodies these virtues.[111] A legal system founded on the principle of reciprocity between the government and the citizens protects the dignity of citizens and allows them to live their lives under the minimum moral requirements upheld by the law and follow their moral aspirations freely.

B. *John Finnis*

In contemporary times, John Finnis has restated or reconstructed the natural law tradition. Finnis's reconstruction of natural law tradition has received bitter

102 Fuller (n 88) 153.
103 Hart, *The Concept of Law* (n 97) 207.
104 Fuller (n 88) 157.
105 Ibid. 154.
106 Ibid.
107 Fuller (n 96) 645.
108 Bix (n 4) 221.
109 Coyle (n 95) 209.
110 Colleen Murphy, 'Lon Fuller and the Moral Value of the Rule of Law' (2005) 24 *Law and Philosophy* 239.
111 Ibid. 239.

opprobrium,[112] which he attributes to his decision to take out things from their 'traditional orders of treatments'[113] and critics' haste to read 'occasional programmatic declarations more or less in isolation from contexts, endnotes, and later argumentation.'[114] Two main aims structure Finnis's philosophical project. Firstly, he aims to defend the traditional natural law tradition against the accusation of the naturalistic fallacy[115] of deriving 'ought' from 'is' and accuses legal positivists of committing the said fallacy.[116] Secondly, he seeks to clarify the long-standing confusion concerning natural law jurisprudence's view on the status of unjust laws.

Finnis's legal theory is informed by his ethical theory. Finnis defends the objectivity of the seven basic goods that are the foundation of morality. These basic goods are aspects of human flourishing that contribute to the constitution of a good life. These basic goods are (1) life, (2) knowledge, (3) play, (4) aesthetic experience, (5) friendship or sociability, (6) religion, and (7) practical reasonableness.[117] Later, Finnis added marriage to the list of basic goods.[118] These goods or principles are *basic* for any attempt to derive them involves affirming these very principles, and they are grasped as good *per se nota* (known through itself) by any competent reasonable person.[119] These goods are not worthy because they are instrumental in the pursuit of any further good but because they are to be pursued for their own sake. Moreover, these basic goods are incommensurable for Finnis because 'no basic good considered precisely as such can be meaningfully said to be better than another.'[120]

At this stage, these basic goods are only 'incipiently moral.'[121] According to Finnis, these goods only take on a moral force when applied 'upon definite ranges of project, disposition, or action, or upon particular projects,

112 For some criticisms of Finnis, see Lloyd L. Weinreb, *Natural Law and Justice* (Harvard University Press 1987); Russell Hittinger, *A Critique of the New Natural Law Theory* (University of Notre Dame Press 1987); Steven A. Long, 'Fundamental Errors of the New Natural Law Theory' (2013) 13 *National Catholic Bioethics Quarterly* 105; Sean Coyle, 'Natural Law Theory, "New" and Old' (2023) 68 *American Journal of Jurisprudence* 33. For defense against some of the major criticisms, see Robert P. George, 'Recent Criticism of Natural Law Theory' (1988) 55 *University of Chicago Law Review* 1371.

113 *NLNR* 416.

114 Ibid.

115 David Hume accused all moral systems developed until his time of being guilty of fallaciously deriving 'ought' propositions from 'is' propositions. David Hume, *A Treatise of Human Nature* (David Fate Norton and Marry J. Norton eds, Oxford University Press 2007) 302.

116 John Finnis, 'On the Incoherence of Legal Positivism' (2000) 75 *Notre Dame Law Review* 1597.

117 *NLNR* 81–90.

118 John Finnis, 'Marriage: A Basic and Exigent Good' (2008) 91 *Monist* 388.

119 *NLNR* 33.

120 Grisez, Boyle, and Finnis (n 21) 110.

121 John Finnis, 'Natural Law Theories' in Edward N. Zalta (ed), *Stanford Encyclopedia of Philosophy* (Summer 2024 edn), https://plato.stanford.edu/archives/sum2024/entries/natural-law-theories/ accessed March 18, 2025.

dispositions, or actions.'[122] In other words, these basic principles take on a moral force when moral rules concerning particular instances of actions are derived from them under the guidance of the requirements of practical reason. Finnis enlists requirements of practical reasonableness:[123] (1) a coherent plan of life, (2) no arbitrary preferences among values, (3) no arbitrary preferences among persons, (4) detachment, (5) commitment, (6) efficiency within reason, (7) respect for every basic value in every act, (8) requirements of the common good, and (9) following one's conscience. Under the guidance of these requirements, basic goods are given specificity, and decisions as to appropriate moral action can be made. In this process, basic goods are not considered 'one by one but in their united ("integral") directiveness.'[124] Finnis considers an adequate account of the way fundamental principles of morality are to be given specificity essential to a complete natural law moral theory.[125]

It is crucial to note that the fundamental principles (basic goods) of natural law are not logically derived from any prior empirical or theoretical knowledge about human nature. Finnis agrees with neo-Thomists that basic goods are grounded in human nature. However, he disagrees with their account of the epistemology of these goods. These goods are grounded in human nature because their goodness for humans is the result of the nature humans have. On the other hand, the knowledge of these goods is not obtained from any examination of human nature but is the result of the immediate grasp of the first principles of practical reason, which are known *per se nota*.[126] Seemingly, this account does not fall prey to naturalistic fallacy.

Practical reason requires that one pay due regard to the requirements of the common good in calibrating one's actions and that the basic goods can only be fully and effectively pursued in common with others.[127] Each of the basic goods is itself a common good and is to be pursued with others in a political community.[128] Finnis defines the common good as

> a set of conditions which enables the members of a community to attain for themselves reasonable objectives, or to realise reasonably for

122 *NLNR* 101.
123 Ibid. 100–126.
124 Finnis (n 121).
125 Finnis laments the lacunae in Aquinas's account of the first principles of practical reason and how these 'first moral principles are given specificity in less fundamental principles and norms.' 'This failure,' he complains, 'contributed significantly to the spread of voluntaristic and fideistic currents which virtually overwhelmed the tradition of natural law theory, as a living school of thought.' John Finnis, 'Natural Law' in *Reason in Action* (Vol. 1 of *Collected Essays*, Oxford University Press 2011) 208.
126 Ibid.
127 *NLNR* 155.
128 Ibid.

themselves the value(s), for the sake of which they have reason to collaborate with each other (positively and/or negatively) in a community.[129]

However, there is a 'luxuriant variety of appropriate but competing choices of "means"'[130] to pursue the common good, which gives rise to problems of coordination as different members of the community may choose different means to realise the common good. Resolving such problems of coordination necessitates the existence of a recognised legal authority[131] that provides the most effective 'common path for pursuing the common good.'[132] Therefore, the law is justified for Finnis because it is the most effective instrument for pursuing the common good, and its authority depends 'on its justice or at least its ability to secure justice.'[133] Law's directiveness towards the common good creates a generic and presumptive moral obligation for the participants of the legal system, which may only be outweighed by the considerations of extreme injustice.[134]

For Finnis, positive law, in its focal sense, is the most effective instrument for pursuing the common good and maintaining conditions of justice in society. However, palpable instances of law may not always satisfy this standard and may even be specimens of gross inequity. It raises questions about the extent to which these unjust laws create valid obligations for the subjects of a given legal system. Finnis explores four senses in which such questions of obligation can be raised.[135] Firstly, an obligation may be said to arise in the sense of the possibility of being subjected to sanction in case of non-compliance with a positive demand. Finnis considers it a 'theoretically banal point of view' and 'least likely, in practice, to be intended by anyone raising the question.'[136] Secondly, one may talk of legal obligation in the *intrasystemic* sense. It is to ask whether a particular rule is obligatory according to the formal criteria of an internally complete and consistent legal system. It is the most usual sense employed in legal practice, and Finnis regards such inquiries as worthwhile. Thirdly, one may ask whether one has any moral obligation to obey an unjust law given that the legal obligation also entails a presumptive moral obligation and the legal system is largely just. In response to this question, Finnis affirms that immoral or unjust laws may lose their obligatory force even if they are intrasystemically valid. Legal positivists would banish such inquiries from the province of jurisprudence, but Finnis considers such inquiries essential to any

129 Ibid.
130 Ibid. 289.
131 Ibid. 231–222.
132 Ibid. 262.
133 Ibid. 260.
134 George Duke, 'Finnis on the Authority of Law and the Common Good' (2013) 19 *Legal Theory* 44.
135 *NLNR* 354–361.
136 Ibid. 355.

project of jurisprudence that 'aspires to be more than the lexicography of a particular culture.'[137] Finally, an obligation from a 'collateral source' may arise to obey an unjust law that is not morally obligatory. Obligation in this sense may arise from the fact that one's repeated non-compliance with an unjust law may promote contempt for just parts of the legal system and render the whole legal system ineffective. It is not a 'legal obligation in the moral sense,'[138] and one is only required to comply with an unjust law as may be necessary 'to avoid bringing "the law" (as a whole) "into contempt."'[139]

The dictum of *lex iniusta non est lex* is often claimed as the principal tenet of the natural law tradition, and one does find somewhat similar averments in the works of masters of the natural law tradition, such as Plato, Aristotle, Cicero, Augustine, and Aquinas. The said dictum is often taken to deny legal validity to unjust laws and is criticised severely by legal positivists for disregarding the facticity of the law. Finnis strongly rejects the meaning associated with this dictum by the critics as 'pure nonsense' and affirms that natural law tradition has never denied legal validity to unjust laws but rather counsels obedience to these laws in certain circumstances.[140] Finnis writes:

> Far from 'denying legal validity to iniquitous rules,' the tradition explicitly (by speaking of 'unjust laws') accords to iniquitous rules legal validity, whether on the ground and in the sense that these rules are accepted in the courts as guides to judicial decision, or on the ground and in the sense that, in the judgment of the speaker, they satisfy the criteria of validity laid down by constitutional or other legal rules, or on both these grounds and in both these senses.[141]

What the natural law tradition is genuinely concerned with is distinguishing 'primary' or 'central' cases of law from the 'secondary' or 'peripheral' ones. According to Finnis, unjust laws are valid laws, but they are not laws in the 'focal sense,' for they lack the elements of justice that are essential to the 'central case' of law.[142] For example, one may call a friendship based purely on selfish motives a friendship, but it cannot be a friendship in the focal sense of the term. Hence, Finnis agrees with the legal positivists in maintaining the distinction between the existence or validity of a legal rule and the moral quality of its content.[143]

137 Ibid. 358.
138 Ibid. 361.
139 Ibid.
140 Ibid. 364.
141 Ibid. 365.
142 Ibid. 9–11, 354.
143 Michael Baur, 'In Defense of Finnis on Natural Law Legal Theory' (2005) 6 *Vera Lex* 35.

V. Natural Law Thought and Islamic Tradition

Natural law thought in Islamic tradition is popularly associated with the schools of *Mu'tazila* and *Imāmiyya*. Legal positivism or scriptural positivism is associated with the school of Ash'ariyya, a school that has dominated the Sunni orthodoxy for much of history and still holds significant sway over traditional scholarly circles.[144] *Mu'tazila*'s influence gradually declined after the 5th/11th century, and their main ideas are represented in *Imāmiyya* theology.[145] Our discussion of natural law in Islamic tradition will mainly centre on two issues: (1) the question of divine justice and (2) the question of the authority of human reason to derive legal rule (*hukm*) in the absence of textual evidence (*nass*).

Classical Muslim jurists and theologians grappled with challenges posed by Plato's *Euthyphro Dilemma*. All Muslims agree that God is just, but it remains to be answered whether something is just because God enjoins it or God enjoins it because it is just. On this issue, they disagreed ferociously. *Mu'tazila* and *Imāmiyya* agreed with the second option and contend that God is essentially just and His acts are always just according to the notion of justice, which is comprehendible by human reason. In other words, divine justice is rationally intelligible.[146] In their view, God does not act arbitrarily and does not commit or command any wrong.[147] To substantiate this claim, *Imāmiyya* quotes the following verses:

> Verily, God wrongeth not even the weight of an atom. (Sura al-Nisa: 40)

Again:

> Verily, God wrongeth not mankind in anything . . . . (Sura Yunus: 44)

In addition to several textual evidences, they also provide intellectual arguments to substantiate their belief and argue that God's justice is a necessary consequence of His absolute perfection. Ja'far Sobhani argues:

> [T]he intellect can discern the justice of God with utmost clarity. For justice is an attribute of perfection (*Kamal*), while injustice is an attribute of imperfection; and the human intellect perceives that God possesses all possible perfections and that He is exalted beyond any possibility of imperfection or deficiency, both as regards His Essence and His actions.[148]

144 Wael B. Hallaq, *Sharī'a: Theory, Practice, Transformations* (Cambridge University Press 2009) 502.

145 Muhammad Ammar Khan Nasir, '*Husn Wa Qubh Ka Tasawar Aur Aql Wa Shara ka Bahmi Taluq: Qadi Abd al-Jabbar Ki Tuzihat Ki Roshni Main*' (2020) 3 *Tajdeed* 11.

146 Najam Haider, *Shi'i Islam: An Introduction* (Cambridge University Press 2014) 18.

147 Ayatollah Ja'far Sobhani, *Doctrines of Shi'i Islam: A Compendium of Imami Beliefs and Practices* (Reza Shah-Kazemi tr, I. B. Tauris 2001) 48.

148 Ibid.

Belief in the ability of human reason to have access to the notion of justice that is upheld by God in all of His acts, including that of prescribing Shari'ah, allowed *Mu'tazila* and *Imāmiyya* to bestow human reason with the authority to derive rules (*ahkam*) of Shari'ah in the absence of textual sources.

For both *Mu'tazila*[149] and *Imāmiyya*,[150] God's justice meant that He created the world to benefit humanity. According to some *Mu'tazila*, this infuses natural creation with a purpose and value and makes possible the rational deliberations about good (*husn*) and bad (*qubh*).[151] Such an endowing of value on the facts of the natural world bridges the gap between 'is' and 'ought' and allows human reason to develop norms of conduct by reflecting on the benefits discerned in the creation, which is purposely created to facilitate human fulfilment.[152] The purposefully beneficial nature of the creation also entails a presumption of *permissibility* in favour of all acts, but this presumption can be rebutted by subsequent recourse to textual or rational evidence.[153] *Mu'tazila* also abundantly employed human reason to classify acts under five categories of legal value (*al-ahkam al-khamsa*).[154]

Furthermore, *Mu'tazila* believed that God's justice entails punishing those whose actions or omissions are repugnant to these rationally derived rules. *Ash'arite* jurists condemned *Mu'tazila* for replacing divine will with reason as the source of obligation.[155] Later, Shihab al-Din al-Qarafi, an *Ash'arite* jurist, clarified how the rationalist theology of *Mu'tazila* allowed them to attribute divine obligation to rationally derived rules.[156] God's absolute justice and rationality entail that whatever is rationally known to be prohibited is prohibited by God, and whatever is rationally known to be commanded is commanded by God. In this way, *Mu'tazila* maintained a congruence between the will of an absolutely just God and a rationally derived Shari'ah.

Though the influence of traditionalists (*Akhbari*) was quite strong at times in Shi'i history,[157] the now dominant school of Shi'i jurisprudence, the *Usulis*, accord considerable authority to reason to derive legal rules in the absence of textual evidence and to evaluate the validity and relevance of textual evidence itself.[158] Both Shias and Sunnis have four main sources (*adillat ul-arba'ah*) of law. For Sunnis, these are (1) the *Quran*, (2) *Sunnah* (the normative practice

149 Anver Emon, 'Natural Law in Islam' in Tom Angier (ed), *The Cambridge Companion to Natural Law Ethics* (Cambridge University Press 2019) 186.

150 Haider (n 146) 25.

151 Anver M. Emon, *Islamic Natural Law Theories* (Oxford University Press 2010) 26.

152 Anver M. Emon, 'Natural Law and Natural Rights in Islamic Law' (2005) 20 *Journal of Law and Religion* 351.

153 Ibid. 357.

154 Ibid. 359–360.

155 Ibid. 358.

156 Ibid.

157 Hossein Modarressi, 'Rationalism and Traditionalism in Shi'i Jurisprudence: A Preliminary Survey' (1984) 59 *Studia Islamica* 141.

158 Mohammad Soltani Renani, 'The Principle of Divine Justice and its Effect on Islamic Jurisprudence' (2019) 11 *Contemporary Comparative Legal Studies* 125.

of the Prophet), (3) *Ijma* (consensus), and (4) *Qiyas* (analogical reasoning).[159] Shi'i jurists agree with the first three with some differences but reject the *Qiyas* for being inexact and replace it with *aql* (intellectual reasoning).[160] *Aql* is the reason, both pure and practical, which can be used to derive legal rules in case no evidence is found in the previous three sources.[161] Murtadha Mutahhari argues that Shari'ah aims to serve the best interests of subjects.[162] Whatever is against the interests of subjects is prohibited or discouraged by Shari'ah, and whatever serves the interests of subjects is commanded or encouraged by Shari'ah. In cases in which the law-giver has provided no direction, we can presume that the law-giver prescribes the pursuit of basic human interests.[163] Human reason has the capacity to know the basic interests of human subjects, and the rules of Shari'ah can be derived on the basis of these interests. For this reason, the Shi'i theologians and jurists emphasise the correlation between Shari'ah and reason (*aql*). In Shi'i *usul-e fiqh*, this position is referred to as the principle of *mulāzama* (concomitance). It holds:

> كل ما حكم به العقل حكم به الشرع وكل ما حكم به الشرع حكم به العقل[164]
>
> Whatsoever the intellect decreeth, the Shari'ah decreeth likewise; and whatsoever the Shari'ah decreeth, the intellect decreeth likewise.

It is interesting to note that despite the existence of such strong rationalist beliefs in Shi'i theology and jurisprudence, the use of *aql* in the actual practice of driving legal rules has remained marginal.[165]

Shi'i jurists also employ reason to evaluate textual evidence. Al-Shaykh al-Mufid held that if any hadith (a tradition from the Prophet or any of the Imams) is opposed to judgment of reason, it is not to be relied upon,[166] and Al-Sayyid al-Murtada maintained that if any verse of the Quran appears to be inconsistent with intellectual certainties, it is to be symbolically interpreted (*ta'wīl*).[167]

The methodology developed by Islamic rationalist jurists not only allows them to speak on behalf of God in matters that are not covered by scriptural

159 Imran Ahsan Khan Nyazee, *Islamic Jurisprudence* (3rd edn, Federal Law House 2016) 160.

160 Muhammad Baqir As-Sadr, *Lessons in Islamic Jurisprudence* (Roy Parviz Mottahedeh tr, Oneworld 2003) 20.

161 Haider (n 146) 24.

162 Murtadha Mutahhari, *Jurisprudence and Its Principles* (Mohammad Salman Tawhidi tr, Tahrike Tarsile Qur'an 1983), https://www.al-islam.org/jurisprudence-and-its-principles-murtadha-mutahhari.

163 Ibid.

164 *Kullu mā ḥakama bihi al-'aqlu ḥakama bihi al-shar'u, wa kullu mā ḥakama bihi al-shar'u ḥakama bihi al-'aqlu.*

165 Ali-Reza Bhojani, *Moral Rationalism and Shari'a: Independent rationality in modern Shi'i usul al-Fiqh* (Routledge 2015) 1–2.

166 Renani (n 158) 130.

167 Ibid. 131.

evidence but also explains the rational foundations of obligation created by Shari'ah. The natural law methodology can also help distinguish the fundamental values of Shari'ah from their particular determinations and make legal reasoning more appreciative of the legal relevance of contingent circumstances. If further explored, such an approach can open new possibilities for reform in Islamic law and make it more prepared to deal with problems unleashed by modernity.

VI. Conclusion

A survey of the opinions of major thinkers in the natural law tradition reveals that, despite the diversity of the ways the concept of natural law has been conceived, certain beliefs are shared by most, if not all, thinkers. These beliefs may be summarised as follows: (1) there is a rational order in the creation of the universe (given by God); (2) humans have an innate rational capacity to grasp the fundamental elements of their natural well-being; (3) these fundamental elements of human well-being or basic human goods are somehow grounded in human nature; (4) these goods can provide objective moral guidance concerning particular human actions; (5) there is no necessary connection between rightness and the act of will; (6) human persons are the proper point of positive legal or political systems, and it is regard for the well-being of human persons that affords legitimacy to these systems; (7) there are certain forms of legal institutions that are more appropriate to the pursuit of human well-being; (8) the laws that fail to pursue these goods effectively are defective and are normatively inferior to the laws that effectively realise these goods in human communal life; and (9) any law that fails to meet the standards of justice and morality is deprived of any moral obligation for the subjects.

In contemporary jurisprudence, natural law theory is mainly viewed in opposition to legal positivists. Contemporary natural law philosophers are busy criticising positivist views on the separation of law and morality and their disregard for the moral foundation of legal obligation. Among themselves, they disagree mainly on the details of the manner in which goods are grounded in human nature and the precise status of unjust laws in the legal system. In ethics, there are a variety of natural law positions on abortion, euthanasia, homosexuality, sex or gender transition, etc.

3 The Origins of the Concept of Natural Law in Ancient Greece

Tony Burns

Introduction

There is a commonly held view that the concept of natural law, or the idea of a philosophy of law that is based on this concept, emerged clearly for the first time only in the philosophy of the Stoics,[1] as represented in the writings of Cicero.[2] However, a number of commentators have attempted to trace the origins of the concept of natural law back, beyond the Stoics, to classical Athens in the fourth century BCE.[3] One group has argued that it emerged in the writings of Plato,[4] whereas another group maintains that the origins of

1 For the Stoic conception of natural law see Philipp Brüllmann, 'The Stoics' in Tom Angier (ed), *The Cambridge Companion to Natural Law Ethics* (Cambridge University Press 2019); Gisela Striker, 'Origins of the Concept of Natural Law' (1986) 2 *Proceedings of the Boston Area Colloquium in Ancient Philosophy* 79; Gerald Watson, 'The Early History of Natural Law' (1966) 33 *Irish Theological Quarterly* 65; Gerald Watson, 'The Natural Law and Stoicism' in A. A. Long (ed), *Problems in Stoicism* (Athlone Press 1996).

2 Fernando H. Llano Alonso, 'Cicero and Natural Law' (2012) 92(2) *ARSP: Archiv für Rechts und Sozialphilosophie/Archives for Philosophy of Law and Social Philosophy* 157; Julia Annas, 'Cicero on Natural Law and Ideal Laws' in Julia Annas (ed), *Virtue and Law in Plato and Beyond* (Oxford University Press 2017); Elizabeth Asmis, 'Cicero on Natural Law and the Laws of the State' (2008) 27(1) *Classical Antiquity* 1.

3 See Howard P. Kainz, 'Concepts of Natural Law in Ancient Greece and Rome' in Howard P. Kainz (ed), *Natural Law: An Introduction and Re-Examination* (Open Court 2004); John R. Kroger, 'The Philosophical Foundations of Roman Law: Aristotle, the Stoics, and Roman Theories of Natural Law' (2004) 3 *Wisconsin Law Review* 905; A. A. Long, 'Law and Nature in Greek Thought' in Michael Gagarin and David Cohen (eds), *The Cambridge Companion to Ancient Greek Law* (Cambridge University Press 2005); Paul E. Sigmund, 'Natural Law in Greek Thought' in Paul E. Sigmund (ed), *Natural Law in Political Thought* (Winthrop 1971); Ákos Tussay, 'Natural Law and Unwritten Law in Classical Greek Thought' (2024) 65 *Hungarian Journal of Legal Studies* 114.

4 For Plato and natural law see Julia Annas, 'Plato on Law-Abidance and a Path to Natural Law' (2018) 9(1) *Jurisprudence: An International Journal of Legal and Political Thought* 19; Jed W. Atkins, 'Zeno's *Republic*, Plato's *Laws*, and the Early Development of Stoic Natural Law Theory' (2015) 32 *Polis: The Journal for Ancient Greek Political Thought* 166; Hans Kelsen, 'Plato and the Doctrine of Natural Law' (1960) 14(1) *Vanderbilt Law Review* 23; G. P. Maguire, 'Plato's Theory of Natural Law' (1947) X *Yale Classical Studies* 51; Glenn R. Morrow, 'Plato

DOI: 10.4324/9781003728603-4

the concept can be found in the works of Aristotle.[5] The discussion that follows has four parts. In Part One, I say something about Cicero and the Stoic conception of natural law. In Part Two, I consider Plato's views on the subject. In Part Three, I do the same for Aristotle. In Part Four, I draw attention to the significance of a number of relatively minor figures among the Sophists in fifth-century BCE Athens, who appear to have embraced the idea of natural law, and whose views were criticized by both Plato and Aristotle because of their egalitarian political implications. My conclusion is that the origins of the concept of natural law are to be found, not in the Stoics, nor in the works of either Plato or of Aristotle, but in those of the Sophists. These include the anonymous opponents of slavery who are referred to by Aristotle in Book I of his *Politics*.

Part One: Cicero and the Stoic Conception of Natural Law

Although Cicero (106 BCE–43 BCE) was not a Stoic, the classic formulation of this way of thinking about natural law theory is often thought to be found in his writings. The following well-known passage from Cicero's *De Republica* (54 BCE–51 BCE) is often cited in this regard:

> True law is right reason in agreement with nature (*vera lex recta ratio naturae congruens*). It is of universal application, unchanging and everlasting . . . [I]t is a sin to try to alter this law, nor is it allowable to attempt to repeal any part of it, and it is impossible to abolish it entirely. We cannot be freed from its obligations by senate or people, and we need not look outside of ourselves for an expounder or interpreter of it. And there will not be different laws at Rome and Athens, or different laws now and in the future, but one eternal and unchangeable law will be valid for all nations and all times.[6]

The passage above expresses very well the Stoic conception of natural law. In it the concept of natural law and of natural law theory is associated (either

and the Law of Nature' in Milton R. Konvitz and Arthur E. Murphy (eds), *Essays in Political Theory: Presented to George H. Sabine* (Cornell University Press 1948); John Wild, *Plato's Modern Enemies and the Theory of Natural Law* (University of Chicago Press 1953).

5 For Aristotle and natural law see R. Bodéüs, 'The Natural Foundations of Right and Aristotelian Philosophy' in R. C. Bartlett and S. D. Collins (eds), *Action and Contemplation. Studies in the Moral and Political Thought of Aristotle* (SUNY Press 1999); Tony Burns, *Aristotle and Natural Law* (Continuum Books 2011); Ross J. Corbett, 'The Question of Natural Law in Aristotle' (2009) 30(2) *History of Political Thought* 229; George Duke, 'Aristotle and Natural Law' (2020) 82 *Review of Politics* 1; Fred D. Miller Jr., 'Aristotle on Natural Law and Justice' in David Keyt and Fred D. Miller Jr. (eds), *A Companion to Aristotle's 'Politics'* (Oxford University Press 1991); Max Salomon Shellens, 'Aristotle on Natural Law' (1959) 4 *Natural Law Forum* 72.

6 Cicero, *De Republica* (Clinton Walker Keyes tr, Harvard University Press 1928) III, XXII, 211.

explicitly or implicitly) with the following assumptions. Acting rightly or justly involves obedience to certain moral rules or laws. These rules or laws are natural. The validity of these moral rules is universal. They apply or should apply in all societies everywhere. Hence they should be recognized by or incorporated into their systems of law. For this reason natural law theory may be associated with cosmopolitanism. The validity of these moral rules is eternal, that is to say, timeless or unchanging. It is not therefore conventional, or relative to any particular society, time or place. The moral rules associated with natural law are discoverable by the faculty of reason (*recta ratio, orthos logos*). This is the reason of individual moral agents. There is therefore no need for any authentic or authoritative interpretation of the requirements of the natural law from a source other than the faculty of reason of the individual agent. The principles of natural law constitute a higher standard of justice to which the civil laws of particular societies ought to conform. Civil laws ought to copy, mirror or reflect the precepts of natural law exactly. Any civil law which conflicts with the requirements of the natural law is unjust and cannot be regarded as 'true law' (*vera lex*). Although this is not stated explicitly in the passage quoted, some later thinkers took this to imply that, according to Cicero and the Stoics, disobedience to an unjust law might in certain circumstances be justified.

The Stoic approach to thinking about natural law and natural law theory had a considerable influence on the later history of political thought. For example, in eighteenth-century France, the passage from Cicero's *De Republica* cited above is referred to frequently in the articles dealing with the subject of natural law in the grand *Encyclopédie* of Denis Diderot and Jean D'Alembert (1751–1780). Of particular interest, in this connection, is the Marquis de Condorcet's observation, made in his *Observations on the 29th Book of the Spirit of Laws* (1780), that 'as truth, reason, justice, the rights of man, the interests of property, of liberty, of security, are in all places the same,' he could not see why 'all the provinces of a state, or even all states, should not have the same civil and criminal laws,' given that 'a good law should be good for all men,' just as 'a true proposition is true everywhere.'[7]

It has sometimes been suggested that a significant difference between the modern and the pre-modern conceptions of natural law is that the former is rigid and inflexible, whereas the latter is not. For example, E. K. Lewis has claimed that 'the flexibility of medieval natural law theory' contrasts sharply with 'the rigidity of natural law in eighteenth century thought.'[8] Similarly, J. L. Montrose has argued that it is only 'eighteenth century rationalists' such as

7 Marie-Jean-Antoine-Nicholas Caritat, Marquis de Condorcet, *Observations on the 29th Book of the Spirit of Laws*, Thomas Jefferson (tr), in Antoine Louis Claude, Comte Destutt de Tracy, *A Commentary and Review of Montesquieu's Spirit of Laws, to which are Annexed, Observations on the 29th Book of the Spirit of Laws, by the Late M. Condorcet* (William Duane 1811) XVIII, 274.

8 E. K. Lewis, *Medieval Political Ideas* (Routledge & Kegan Paul 1954) 11; see also E. K. Lewis, 'Natural Law and Expediency in Medieval Political Theory' (1946) 50 *Ethics* 144.

Condorcet who 'thought that detailed rules, valid for all times and all places, could be deduced with certitude from basic principles.'[9] As an account of the assumptions which are associated with pre-modern natural law theory, this view seems to me to be imprecise. It is true of course that some versions of natural law theory in the ancient world might be said to be flexible. As we shall see, that of Aristotle is a case in point. However, the cast of mind which Lewis and Montrose associate with rigidity, and which is certainly present in the writings of Condorcet, can also be found in the Stoic conception of natural law, as represented by the passage from Cicero cited above. It cannot therefore be said to be peculiarly modern.

Part Two: Plato and the Concept of Natural Law

Discussion of the question of Plato's attitude towards the concept of natural law must refer to the nature versus convention debate in classical Athens in the late fifth and early fourth centuries BCE, in which he was one of the participants. Leo Strauss has claimed this is a 'basic controversy in political philosophy' because the participants within it are addressing (and disagreeing with one another) about a fundamentally important question, namely: 'Is there any natural right?' or law.[10] Perhaps the most important sources for Plato's views here are his *Gorgias*[11] and *Laws*.[12]

At one point in the *Gorgias*, when considering the beliefs of those nihilists or immoralists whose conduct is devoted entirely to the pursuit of their own self-interest as they understand it, Plato has his character Callicles say that such men 'follow nature—the nature of right—in acting thus; yes, on my soul, and follow the law of nature' (*nomos fuseos*).[13] A number of commentators have claimed that, so far as we know, this is the very first time that the phrase *nomos tes physeos*, or 'law of nature,' is used in the history of Western philosophy. W. K. C. Guthrie, for example, has maintained that in ancient Greek political thought 'a verbal association of 'unwritten laws' with *physis* only occurs, among extant sources, in Fourth Century authors,' and that 'the first use of the actual term' is in Plato's *Gorgias*.[14] A. E. Taylor has argued that it is here in Plato's *Gorgias* that we find 'the first occurrence' in the 'extant literature'

9 J. L. Montrose, 'Review of Peter J. Stanlis, *Edmund Burke and the Natural Law*' (1961) 6(1) *Natural Law Forum* 214. See also Philip Selznick, 'Sociology and Natural Law' (1961) 6(1) *Natural Law Forum* 81, 91–92, 103.

10 Leo Strauss, *Natural Right and History* (University of Chicago Press 1974 [1953]) 93.

11 Plato, *Gorgias*, Donald J. Zeyl (tr), in John M. Cooper (ed), intro. and notes, *Complete Works* (Hackett 1996).

12 Plato, *Laws*, Trevor J. Saunders (tr), in *Complete Works*.

13 Plato, *Gorgias* 483e, 828.

14 W. K. C. Guthrie, *The Sophists, A History of Greek Philosophy* (Cambridge University Press 1971) Vol. 3, Part I, 18–19.

of 'the ominous phrase "Law of Nature".'[15] And Glenn R. Morrow has also claimed that no phrase which 'implies a connection between *nomos* and *physis*, is clearly attested in the extant literature of the Fifth and early Fourth Centuries, outside the writings of Plato.'[16]

It is clear, however, that Plato's Callicles (and presumably, therefore, also Plato himself) does not mean by the expression 'law of nature' what the later Stoic thinkers or indeed perhaps any natural law theorist properly so called means by it. As E. R. Dodds has noted, the doctrine advocated by Callicles ought 'not to be confused with "natural law"' in anything like 'the Stoic sense.' It is not a moral rule. For 'as Socrates shows later it amounts to domination by instinctive appetites.'[17] Nevertheless, there might be other reasons for thinking that Plato's political thought could legitimately be said to rest upon a commitment to the concept of natural law. As John Wild has observed, 'even though the terms used' by Plato when expressing his own views 'may be different,' nevertheless 'the concept could be present' although it is expressed in a different way.[18]

A more satisfactory source for those interested in Plato's attitude towards the concept of natural law, understood in an ethical sense, is the *Laws*. There Plato refers at one point to a school of thought in ancient Athens, by which he meant his opponents the Sophists, which maintained that government 'has very little to do with nature' and is 'artificial' or 'largely a matter of art.' According to Plato's account, this group of thinkers maintained that laws in general are like 'the gods,' namely 'fictions' or 'artificial concepts corresponding to nothing in nature.' Consequently the laws of different societies 'vary very widely, according to the different conventions' which as a matter of fact people happen to 'agree on.' According to the Sophists as Plato understood their views, therefore, 'there is no natural standard of justice at all,' given that men [*sic*] 'are always wrangling about their moral standards and changing them,' and in their view 'every change introduced becomes binding from the moment it's made, regardless of the fact that it is entirely artificial, and based on convention, not nature in the slightest degree.'[19]

In the *Laws*, Plato associates Sophism with conventionalism. He explicitly rejected what he took to be this Sophist view. Not surprisingly, therefore, a number of commentators have concluded that he endorsed the notion of a law of nature, understood in the ethical sense of the term. Glenn R. Morrow, for example, has argued that 'it is plausible to suppose' that 'Plato's philosophy was an important factor in the formulation of the Stoic doctrine of the Law of

15 A. E. Taylor, *Plato: The Man and His Work* (Methuen 1949 [1908]) 17.

16 Morrow (n 4) 19; see also 20–28.

17 E. R. Dodds, 'Commentary,' in Plato, *Gorgias*, E. R. Dodds (ed and tr) (Oxford University Press 1959) 268; also Guthrie (n 14) 104.

18 Wild (n 4) 135.

19 Plato, *Laws* X, 889a–890a, 1546–1547.

Nature,' and indeed that it was Plato who 'laid the foundations for the Stoic conception of natural justice.'[20] John Wild has also claimed that it was Plato rather than the Stoics who was the founder of the natural law tradition.[21] Similarly, Michael Bertram Crowe has maintained that we find in Plato's writings 'almost all the elements of the fully formed theory of natural law as it was to appear in the Stoics and those who came after them.' According to Crowe, 'it has been argued by some commentators that the natural law really begins with Plato, rather than with the Stoics, who are usually given the credit of having been the first to formulate the doctrine.'[22]

There are four features of Plato's version of natural law theory which are worth emphasizing. The first is Plato's enthusiasm for the ideas of the mathematician Pythagoras. In his critique of Callicles and immoralism in the *Gorgias*, Plato's Socrates agrees with Pythagoras and his followers that justice is a cosmic principle inhering within the order of the universe as a whole, including therefore inanimate nature, rather than something which is solely a human phenomenon. It is a constituent of what Arthur O. Lovejoy has referred to as 'the great chain of being.'[23] Hence, it is a component part of the natural order of things, which is structured rationally in accordance with the principles of mathematics, especially those of geometry. Socrates argues that it is justice, understood in this way, which 'hold[s] together heaven and earth, and gods and men, and that is why they call this universe a world-order, my friend, and not an undisciplined world-disorder.'[24] Socrates claims that Callicles overlooks this because 'you neglect geometry,' together with the notion of 'proportionate equality' with which it is associated.[25]

Plato's association of the concept of justice with that of proportionate equality in the *Gorgias* reflects his view that the universe as a whole is imbued with the principles of order, hierarchy and authority. Plato also thinks in this way about the lives of human beings who live together in a political society or *polis* under its system of law. Here too, he suggests, we can discern a system of order which might properly be characterized as natural.

In the *Laws*, Plato emphasizes that justice in society, like justice in nature [*sic*], is associated with the notion of equality. He points out, however, that there are 'two concepts of "equality",' which, he says, are 'virtual opposites' of one another. The first of these is arithmetical equality, or the kind of equality which 'measures weights and numbers.' The second is geometrical equality, or the proportionate equality that is referred to by Socrates in the *Gorgias*.

20 Morrow (n 4) 17, 29.
21 Wild (n 4) 38, 62, 103, 134–136.
22 Michael Bertram Crowe, *The Changing Profile of Natural Law* (Martinus Nijhoff 1977) 17.
23 Arthur O. Lovejoy, *The Great Chain of Being: A Study of the History of an Idea* (Transaction Books 2010 [1936]).
24 Plato, *Gorgias* 507e–508a, 852, *Laws*, X, 903b–d, 1560.
25 Plato, *Gorgias* 508a, 852.

This, the Athenian Stranger argues, is 'the most genuine equality.'[26] It is, he suggests, respect for the notion of justice understood in this way, by reference to the principle of geometrical equality, that is required by the law of nature.

Whether this aspect of Plato's doctrine of natural law, with its emphasis on the notion of geometrical equality, is a similarity between his views and those of the Stoics as presented earlier or a difference is a matter for debate. At least some commentators associate Stoic political thought with a commitment to the notion of equality, understood in what Plato refers to as the arithmetical sense. In their opinion, therefore, this should be regarded as a significant difference between his version of natural law theory and that of the Stoics.

The second point to note about Plato's version of natural law theory is that Plato's political thought generally rests on the belief that that a life of justice under law is an expression of our essential nature as human beings. In his debate with the Sophists, Plato is more concerned with the nature of justice than he is with natural justice. He does not talk about natural justice as such. However, to argue that a life of justice is something that is natural to man, as Plato does, is evidently but a very short step from arguing that there is indeed such a thing as natural justice. Glenn R. Morrow has observed that for Plato the nature of justice and natural justice are one and the same thing. In Plato's view, 'natural justice *is* the Idea Justice.' In Plato's political thought, therefore, the expressions '"justice itself" and "natural justice" mean the same thing.'[27]

As a number of commentators have noted, there is a difference between asking the question 'what is the nature of law?' on the one hand, and asking the very different question, 'what is the law of nature?' on the other. Georgio del Vecchio, for example, has argued that the 'need for a logical determination of law' must be kept 'distinctly separate from the deduction of a system of natural or rational law.'[28] In his opinion, there is a persistent tendency in the history of political thought for certain authors to confuse 'logical and ethical or deontological demands,' or 'the purely logical concept of law' with 'other elements' of the theory of law. These authors have tried to solve these two distinct problems by a single doctrine.' Hence in seeking 'the logical qualities of law' they have at the same time attempted 'to establish its ideal paradigm.'[29] The tendency identified by del Vecchio arguably begins with the writings of Plato.

The third point of interest has to do with the issue of whether Plato thinks that natural law constitutes a higher standard of justice which might be used to critically evaluate the laws of a *polis*. At first sight, one of the implications of Plato's belief that all justice is natural is that in his opinion natural law should not be thought of in this way. Plato appears to be committed to the idea that

26 Plato, *Laws* VI, 757b, 1433.
27 Morrow (n 4) 31.
28 Georgio del Vecchio, *Philosophy of Law* (J. Lisle tr, New York 1921 [1914]) 19–20.
29 Ibid. 86–87.

there is no ideal system of law or justice. Rather, the systems of law of all *poleis* everywhere must be regarded as just. One problem with this conclusion, however, is that it is not consistent with how Plato argues in his *Republic* and *Laws*. For in these works Plato does arguably offer his readers a blueprint for an ideally just society which might perform such a critical function. It might be argued that this is a similarity which exists between his theory of natural law and that of the Stoics and not a difference.

Some commentators have claimed that Plato's *Republic*, with its other-worldly vision of an ideal or perfect society, is the first major work of utopian literature. Lyman Tower Sargent has observed that Plato's *Republic* has often been 'treated as the fount of Western utopianism.'[30] It has been claimed that Plato's text had a significant influence on Sir Thomas More's *Utopia* (1516), which in a number of respects resembles closely the political vision of Plato, in both the *Republic* and the *Laws*. This is significant for a discussion of Plato's attitude towards the concept of natural law because, as R. W. Chambers has argued, there is a connection between the form of utopianism which he associates with both Plato's *Republic* and More's *Utopia* and the concept of natural law. Commenting on More's *Utopia*, Chambers states that there is a significant difference between 'men who merely obey the laws of the state,' no matter what those laws tell them that they ought to do, and 'the men who have, as every citizen of Utopia was bound to have, a belief that there is an ultimate standard of right and wrong, beyond what the state may at any moment command.'[31] When making these remarks Chambers invokes the idea that More's utopianism rests upon a commitment to a Platonic, transcendent idea (or ideal) of justice that is assumed to be valid for all societies everywhere, in all times and all places, and which might be used to criticize existing political arrangements and laws. This is an idea which, as we have seen, has traditionally been associated not only with Plato's *Republic* and *Laws*, but also with the Stoic conception of natural law.

The fourth point of interest to note about Plato's version of natural law theory has to do with the emphasis which he places on the desirability of mathematical precision in politics. In the *Laws* Plato maintains that 'no single branch of a child's education has such an enormous range of applications as mathematics.' He refers there to 'the mathematical framework' which he thinks should be borne in mind by those planners who are seeking to provide a constitution for his ideal society in Magnesia. This framework is based on the assumption that 'as a general rule' mathematics or 'numerical division' can be 'usefully applied to every field of conduct.' It is this mathematical framework which, Plato argues, will provide the detailed guidance required for creating

30 Lyman Tower Sargent, *Utopianism: A Very Short Introduction* (Oxford University Press 2010) 17; see also J. O. Hertzler, 'The *Republic* of Plato' in J. O. Hertzler (ed), *The History of Utopian Thought* (Allen & Unwin 1922).

31 R. W. Chambers, *Thomas More* (Penguin Books 1963 [1935]) 380.

the best possible constitution. In his opinion, 'the legislator should not be afraid of appearing to give undue attention to detail.' Plato insists that 'the law must regulate all these details so that the proper proportions and correspondences are observed.'[32]

It is remarks like this which have led some commentators and critics to associate Plato not only with utopianism, but with utopianism is a very specific sense, namely that he is somebody who offers his readers a detailed account, with mathematical precision, of the *minutiae* of how an ideal society should be organized. There are a number of references in the *Laws* to 'blue-prints,' understood in that way.[33] The significance of this in the present context is that Plato's political thought in general, and his theory of natural law in particular, might be and has been criticized for being rigid or inflexible. It is, as it were, a 'one-size-fits-all' approach which, according to Plato's critics, does not pay sufficient attention, or indeed any attention at all, to the historical specificities which justifiably exist between different societies. We saw earlier that this is the type of thinking which was indulged in by Condorcet in eighteenth-century France. We also saw that a somewhat similar view is advanced by Cicero in his remarks on the Stoic conception of natural law in his *De Republica*.

Part Three: Aristotle and the Concept of Natural Law

Some commentators have claimed that it was not Plato, or the Stoics, but Aristotle who was the founder of the natural law tradition. Max Salomon Shellens, for example, has claimed, that 'philosophers and historians almost invariably claim that Aristotle is the father of natural law.'[34] This is an exaggeration, possibly due to the fact that Aristotle's ideas were such a strong influence in the medieval period on the natural law theorizing of Saint Thomas Aquinas (1225–1274) and others. One reason for thinking it is an exaggeration is because natural law thinking can also be found in the writings of Plato. Another is because, as Aristotle himself acknowledges in his *Rhetoric*, it can also be found in the writings of a number of the Sophists in the late fifth century BCE.

For the subject of Aristotle's attitude towards the concept of natural law two works are particularly significant, the *Rhetoric*[35] and the *Nicomachean Ethics*.[36] It is fruitful to compare and contrast what Aristotle has to say about this subject in these texts with the views of both Plato and the Stoics. In his *Rhetoric*

32 Plato, *Laws* V, 746d–747b, 1426–1427.

33 Plato, *Laws* IV, 711a–c, 1397–1398; IV, 713a–b, 1399; V, 745e–746b, 1426.

34 Shellens (n 5) 72. See also Crowe (n 22) 19; Wolfgang Friedmann, *Legal Theory* (5th edn, Columbia University Press 1967) 10; Carl Joachim Friedrich, *Philosophy of Law in Historical Perspective* (University of Chicago Press 1963 [1958]) 22–23.

35 Aristotle, *Rhetoric*, W. Rhys Roberts (tr), in *The Complete Works of Aristotle*, in 2 Volumes, Jonathan Barnes (ed) (Princeton University Press 1984).

36 Aristotle, *Nicomachean Ethics*, W. D. Ross and J. O. Urmson (trs), in *Complete Works*, 2.

Aristotle distinguishes between the concept of 'special' or 'particular' law (*nomos idios*) and that of 'general' or 'universal' law (*nomos koinos*). He associates the former with 'that written law under which each community lives' and the latter with 'those unwritten ordinances, which seem to be acknowledged on all hands.'[37] He suggests that this general or universal law is 'the law of nature,' whereas special or particular law is that 'which each community lays down and applies to its own members.'[38] He also suggests that this general or universal law is a higher law than special or particular law. It is associated with the principles of a 'greater equity and justice.' This higher law is 'permanent and changeless,' simply because 'it is the law of nature.' As opposed to this, he says of written laws that they 'often do change.'[39]

In order to illustrate what he means by the concept of natural law, Aristotle refers to the writings of Sophocles (497 BCE–406 BCE), Empedocles (494 BCE–434 BCE) and Alcidamas (399 BCE–300 BCE?). The characteristic features which, according to Aristotle, were associated with the concept of natural law by his contemporaries and immediate predecessors are apparent from what he says about their views. There are three such features. First, it is maintained that the principles of natural law are universal, in the sense that they apply to all human beings, in all societies everywhere. Second, it is argued that the principles of natural law are timeless or eternal. They remain valid at all times, no matter what the circumstances. The fundamental principles of ethics are not conventional, to be associated with a particular society and time. Third, these authors take the view that the principles of natural law provide a yardstick for the critical evaluation of existing social and political institutions. Aristotle argues that it is for these reasons that they might be thought to have employed the concept of natural law in their writings.

The three features which Aristotle associates with the concept of natural law in the *Rhetoric* are evidently the same as those which Cicero associates with the Stoic conception of natural law in the passage from his *De Republica* cited earlier. One question here is whether or not Aristotle was sympathetic to the type of natural law theorizing which he claims to have discerned in these writings. Opinion on this subject is divided. Some commentators have argued that he was, and that it is for this reason that he might be said to have himself endorsed the concept of natural law in something like the Stoic sense. Other commentators, however, are of the opposite opinion. They argue that when Aristotle introduces his readers to these ideas, the point of doing so was not to endorse them but to criticize them. My own view is that, although Aristotle did not reject the concept of natural law outright, he did reject this way of thinking about it. However, for present purposes, what matters is that,

37 Aristotle, *Rhetoric* I, §10, 2178.
38 Aristotle, *Rhetoric* I, §10, 2178.
39 Aristotle, *Rhetoric* I, §15, 2190.

whether or not Aristotle agreed with it, this understanding of the concept of natural law can indeed be found in his *Rhetoric*.

I turn now to consider what Aristotle has to say about natural justice or law in the *Nicomachean Ethics*. In Book V of the *Ethics* Aristotle defines the concept of justice in general in such a way that it involves obedience to law.[40] Like Plato in his *Gorgias*, Aristotle endorses the Pythagorean idea that there is a divine principle of cosmic order which may be detected throughout the universe. In his *Politics* Aristotle states that 'law is order, and good law is good order.'[41] To introduce order into the world 'is the work of a divine power' which 'holds together the universe.'[42] Aristotle agreed with Plato and the Pythagoreans that the universe as a whole is an ordered, rational and harmonious system, the organization of which is based on the mathematical principle of proportionality or geometrical equality.

Aristotle states in the *Ethics* that the idea of justice in particular is associated with the notion of equality.[43] Following Plato and the Pythagoreans, he states in the *Politics* that there are two different senses of that concept, namely arithmetical equality and geometrical or proportional equality.[44] He also maintains that there is an overarching principle of particular justice which connects these two notions together. This is the principle of equity, which stipulates that likes should be treated alike, or that equals should be treated equally and unequals unequally, though proportionately. Aristotle assumes that the principle of equity is the most fundamental precept of natural justice.

Aristotle's principle of equity possesses a purely formal character. It is an empty concept, devoid of any substantive content. This is so because it does not specify who exactly should be regarded as equals, nor how exactly they ought to treat one another and be treated by the laws of the *polis*. An important question here is what ought to be the source for this content? Aristotle's answer to this question is that the source should be legal justice or positive law. To adapt a phrase of Immanuel Kant's, we might say that for Aristotle whereas law without justice is blind, justice without law is empty.

In the *Ethics* Aristotle identifies two different spheres of justice, namely distributive justice and rectificatory or corrective justice.[45] In distributive justice it is assumed that those concerned are unequals, and that the notion of geometrical or proportional equality ought to apply, whereas in the sphere of rectificatory justice it is assumed that they are equals and that it is the idea of arithmetical equality which ought to apply. As Georgio del Vecchio has noted, in the case of rectificatory or corrective justice, Aristotle holds that the

40 Aristotle, *Nicomachean Ethics* V, §1, 1782.
41 Aristotle, *Politics*, Benjamin Jowett (tr), *Complete Works* 2, VII, §4, 2105.
42 Aristotle, *Politics* VII, §4, 2105.
43 Aristotle, *Nicomachean Ethics* V, §1, 1782.
44 Aristotle, *Politics* V, §1, 2067.
45 Aristotle, *Nicomachean Ethics* V, §2, 1784–1785.

principle of equity reduces to that of simple reciprocity, or the golden rule for all citizens of doing as you would be done by.[46] Aristotle regards certain actions as being wrong or unjust because they contravene this principle of simple reciprocity. He suggests that such actions disturb an initial balance or equilibrium which exists between two citizens as equal individuals. Once such an action has been performed, the law steps in to rectify or correct this imbalance.

Like Plato, Aristotle assumes that justice involves the rule of law, that is to say, respect for the principle of order, hierarchy, inequality and authority. He agrees with Plato's view that social order is a good thing in and of itself. He contrasts this with disorder, social conflict, anarchy and chaos. Also like Plato, he celebrates the rule of law wherever it is to be found and is a critic of lawlessness, for example the moral nihilism of Plato's Callicles in the *Gorgias*. In the *Ethics*, he too associates lawlessness with egoism and with the idea of reason losing control of the passions.[47]

According to one reading of Aristotle's thought, he agrees with the opinion that is occasionally suggested by Plato, for example in the *Gorgias,* that all law should be regarded as just. For example he observes in the *Ethics* that 'all lawful acts are in a sense just acts.'[48] Aristotle maintains therefore that there is no higher law which might be used to critically evaluate the laws of a *polis* and declare them to be unjust. On this reading of his views, he believes that law is prior to justice, and not justice to law,[49] and that the idea of an unjust law is a contradiction in terms. It is for this reason that some commentators, for example Hans Kelsen, have associated Aristotle with legal positivism, a doctrine which they consider to be incompatible with the assumptions of natural law theory of any kind.[50] This reading overlooks the possibility that some versions of natural law theory, including that of Aristotle, do not associate the notion of natural justice with that of a higher law. This is a significant difference between Aristotle's conception of natural law in the *Ethics* and that of both Plato (at times) and the Stoics.

When Aristotle says that justice in general involves obedience to law, he assumes that the laws in question are those of a *polis.* He refers to these as principles of political justice.[51] He states that a principle of political justice is composed of two parts. It is a principle of natural justice combined with a principle of legal justice. The principles of natural justice state that a particular

46 Georgio del Vecchio, *Justice* (A. H. Campbell ed, Edinburgh University Press 1952) 87–88.

47 Aristotle, *Nicomachean Ethics* II, §2, 1743; III, §5, 1760; III, §11, 1766; V, §11, 1796; VI, §1, 1797–1798; VI, §13, 1808; VII, §8, 1818–1819.

48 Aristotle, *Nicomachean Ethics* V, §1, 1782.

49 See Lester G. Crocker, 'The Priority of Justice or Law' (1961) 28 *Yale French Studies* 34.

50 Hans Kelsen, 'The Foundation of the Theory of Natural Law' in Hans Kelsen (ed), *Essays in Legal and Moral Philosophy* (Reidel 1973) 127, 131–132, 135; Hans Kelsen, 'Aristotle's Doctrine of Justice' in Hans Kelsen (ed), *What Is Justice? Justice, Law and Politics in the Mirror of Science, Collected Essays by Hans Kelsen* (Lawbook Exchange 2013 [1957]) 125–136.

51 Aristotle, *Nicomachean Ethics* V, §7, 1790.

type of action is wrong or unjust. Those of legal justice identify which acts are to be regarded by the laws of a *polis* as being actions of that type.

As an example we might take the act of theft. Aristotle considered the precept of law which forbids the act of theft to be a principle of natural justice. He assumes that it is possible to deduce from the principle of equity, together with certain assumptions about human nature, that actions such as theft are necessarily wrong or unjust, and ought not to be performed. This is so because they conflict with the requirements of simple reciprocity or the golden rule of doing as you would be done by. Aristotle argues that, like the principle of equity itself, the precepts which forbid such actions are also principles of natural justice or law. Aristotle's views on this subject had a considerable influence on medieval scholastic natural law theory, for example that of Saint Thomas Aquinas. In that theory precepts forbidding acts such as theft and murder are regarded as secondary precepts of natural law.[52]

Aristotle maintains that 'in the case of actions' such as 'adultery, theft, murder,' their names alone imply that 'they are themselves bad, and not the excesses or deficiencies of them.' Moreover, this is something that cannot be changed. 'It is not possible,' Aristotle argues, 'ever to be right with regard to them; one must always be wrong.'[53] Their performance could never be justified. In the case of prohibitions, the actions which they forbid are assumed by Aristotle to be necessarily wrong or unjust, in and of themselves (*mala in se*). Like the Stoics who came after him, Aristotle maintains that the precepts of law which forbid their performance are valid and apply always, in all societies everywhere.

Nevertheless, Aristotle also maintains that in any particular society what is to be regarded as an act of theft is an open question. In the terminology of the scholastic natural law theory of a later age, the precept of natural law forbidding theft requires a specific determination. Aristotle holds that this task can and should be carried out by the principles of legal justice or the positive laws of a *polis.* It is this which specifies the content of the principle of natural law which prohibits theft, thereby incorporating that principle into the civil laws, or the system of political justice, of a particular society.[54]

Aristotle argues that the principles of legal justice of a *polis* can legitimately vary or be altered, because they relate to matters which are indifferent morally speaking. Hence different societies will hold different, though equally legitimate, views about them. In any particular society, actions which have to do with legal justice are not forbidden because they are thought to be

52 R. A. Armstrong, *Primary and Secondary Precepts in Thomistic Natural Law* (Martinus Nijhoff 1966).

53 Aristotle, *Nicomachean Ethics* II, §6, 1748; see also Aristotle, *Eudemian Ethics*, J. Solomon (tr), *Complete Works* 2, II, §3, 1934.

54 For this issue see Tony Burns, 'Aquinas's Two Doctrines of Natural Law' (2000) 48(5) *Political Studies* 929.

inherently wrong or unjust. Rather, they are thought to be wrong or unjust simply because they are forbidden (*mala prohibitiva*).

It follows from this that in Aristotle's view the laws or systems of political justice of different *poleis* can (and do) also vary legitimately. Like the principles of legal justice, they too are changeable, in at least one sense of the term. Aristotle therefore builds into his version of natural law theory a certain flexibility. He insists that it is necessary to be flexible when applying the formal principles of natural law to the circumstances of particular societies. The principles of legal justice of one society may not be appropriate for another, if it has very different customs and traditions. This is a significant difference between his views and those of both Plato and the Stoics, as represented by the passage from Cicero cited above and repeated by Condorcet in the eighteenth century.

Aristotle criticizes Plato in the *Nicomachean Ethics* precisely because he considered Plato's approach to questions of ethics and politics to be rigid and inflexible. In response to Plato's belief in the possibility and desirability of mathematical precision, he maintains that 'we must be content' to 'indicate the truth' only 'roughly and in outline.'[55] It is, Aristotle insists, 'the mark of an educated man to look for precision in each class of things just so far as the nature of the subject admits,' and no further.[56] If this attitude of mind is associated with utopianism, and if it is plausible to regard Plato as a utopian thinker, then we might say that Aristotle was one of the first critics of that form of utopianism in politics.

In the modern era, a number of thinkers maintain that the propositions of ethics constitute a deductive system similar to that of arithmetic or geometry. For example, Hugo Grotius (1583–1645) argued in his *De Jure Belli ac Pacis* (1625) that the proposition that murder is wrong has the same logical status as the proposition that 2 + 2 = 4.[57] For in the case of both of these propositions to deny the truth of the proposition would be to contradict oneself. There is a sense in which Grotius's views on this subject might be said to be following in the footsteps of Aristotle, Aquinas and a number of other scholastic thinkers of the medieval period. However, this is true only up to a point. Aristotle is very clear that one should not take a good idea too far. He maintains that, from the standpoint of ethics, what the specific determination of the formal principles of natural law ought to be is a matter of indifference. In the case of ethics, unlike that of mathematics, there is no single correct answer to that question. On this issue Aristotle parts company with what he took to be the rigid inflexibility of Plato. This is a significant difference between Aristotle's natural law theory and that of Cicero and the Stoics.

55 Aristotle, *Nicomachean Ethics* I, §3, 1730.

56 Aristotle, *Nicomachean Ethics* I, §3, 1730; also I, §2, 1729.

57 Hugo Grotius, *The Rights of War and Peace* (Richard Tuck ed, Liberty Fund 2005 [1625]) Preliminary Discourse, 89; and Book I, Chapter 1, §5, 155.

The relevance of this for our understanding of Aristotle's views regarding the relationship which exists between natural law, positive law and civil law, is readily apparent. For as we have seen Aristotle holds that it is for the laws of the *polis*, and in the final analysis therefore also for its courts of law, to decide whether an action does or does not constitute murder or theft, and whether or not therefore it is contrary to the requirements of natural justice or law. In Aristotle's political thought, and in that of a number of his followers in the medieval period, the appeal to the precepts of natural justice or law, which is undoubtedly made by them, is used to legitimate existing civil law rather than to establish the possibility of criticizing it. This too is a significant difference between Aristotle's conception of natural law and that of Plato and the Stoics.

Part Four: The Sophists and the Concept of Natural Law

It is well known that in his *Politics* Aristotle offers a defence of slavery.[58] It is, he says, clear 'that some men are by nature free, and others slaves, and that for these latter slavery is both expedient and right.'[59] At the same time, however, Aristotle also observes that there are at least some people 'who take the opposite view' to his own. He concedes that amongst his contemporaries and immediate predecessors there were those who maintained that there is no one who is by nature a slave and who insisted that slavery is unjust.[60] According to Aristotle, this group of thinkers affirmed 'that the rule of a master over slaves is contrary to nature, and that the distinction between slave and freeman exists by convention only, and not by nature; and being an interference with nature is therefore unjust.'[61]

Aristotle does not name these anonymous opponents of slavery and establishing their identity is by no means an easy task. However, possible candidates include Euripides (485 BCE–406 BCE?), Antiphon (480 BCE–411 BCE), Hippias (460 BCE–390 BCE) and Alcidamas (late fifth to early fourth century BCE). Euripides, for example, puts into the mouths of one of the characters in his *Phoenician Women* the view that 'nature gave to men the law of equal rights.'[62] And in his play *Ion* he has another character state that 'it's only the name of

58 Aristotle, *Politics* I, §§3–6, 1989–1992.

59 Aristotle, *Politics* I, §5, 1991.

60 For discussion of this ancient debate on slavery, and of who Aristotle's opponents within it might have been, see Guiseppe Cambiano, 'Aristotle and the Anonymous Opponents of Slavery' in Moses I. Finley (ed), *Classical Slavery* (Frank Cass 1987); and Trevor J. Saunders, 'The Controversy About Slavery Reported in Aristotle, *Politics* I vi, 1255 a 4ff,' in Ann Moffatt (ed), *Maistor: Classical, Byzantine and Renaissance Studies for Robert Browning* (Brill 2017 [1984]).

61 Aristotle, *Politics* I, §3, 1989.

62 Euripides, *Phoenician Women*, in P. Vellacott (tr), *Orestes and Other Plays* (Penguin 1972) Line 538, 254.

slave that carries disgrace with it; in every other point a loyal slave is as good as a free man.'[63]

There is disagreement over the issue of how the views of Antiphon should be understood. However, according to Gerard Pendrick, the ethical natural law reading of Antiphon represents 'the consensus view' amongst modern commentators.[64] Antiphon is recorded as having made the remarkable assertion that 'by nature there is nothing at all in our constitutions to differentiate foreigners and Greeks.' For if we 'consider those natural qualities which are essential to all human beings and with which we are all equally endowed,' then it is clear that 'in the case of all these qualities there is nothing to tell any of us apart as foreigner or Greek,' given that 'we all breathe the air through our mouths and nostrils, laugh when our minds feel pleasure or cry when we are distressed,' and that we all 'hear sounds with our ears' and 'see with our eyes,' as well as 'work with our hands, and walk with our feet.'[65] In short, in disagreement with both Plato and Aristotle, Antiphon appears to have maintained that all human beings are by nature equal in at least some fundamentally important and ethically significant respects, and that it is for that reason that slavery should be regarded as unjust.

It might be argued that it is precisely because Antiphon thought that certain existing laws and conventions, including slavery, conflicted with the requirements of this principle of natural equality that he maintained that 'most things that are just according to law' are in fact 'inimical to nature,' and therefore also in a different sense unjust.[66] Given these remarks, it is not too surprising that Robin Waterfield has argued that Antiphon was a fifth-century Athenian radical who championed the claims of nature over those of law and convention. According to Waterfield, Antiphon's views 'would have seemed highly shocking and unusual' to 'his contemporaries,' especially of course to Plato and Aristotle.[67]

Similar views have also been attributed to Hippias. According to Plato in his *Protagoras,* Hippias was of the opinion that although 'like is akin to like by nature,' nevertheless 'convention, which tyrannizes the human race, often constrains us contrary to nature.' Plato attributes to Hippias the view that 'I regard all of you here present as kinsmen, intimates, and fellow citizens.'

63 Euripides, *Ion*, in *Orestes and Other Plays* Line 854, 61.

64 Gerard J. Pendrick (ed), intro and commentary, *Antiphon of Athens: The Fragments/Antiphon the Sophist*, with introduction, translation and commentary (Cambridge University Press 2002) 61.

65 See Robin Waterfield (ed), *The First Philosophers: The Presocratics and the Sophists* (Oxford University Press 2000) 264; also Michael Gagarin and Paul Woodruff (eds), *Early Greek Political Thought from Homer to the Sophists* (Cambridge University Press 1995) 245.

66 Gagarin and Woodruff (n 65) 245–246.

67 Waterfield (ed) (n 65) 259.

However, he goes on, this is so 'by nature' and 'not by convention.'[68] Xenophon in his *Memorabilia* presents his readers with a dialogue between Hippias and Socrates in which Socrates defends the traditional view that justice is a matter of following the laws or *nomoi* of one's own *polis.* Hippias responds by suggesting, to the contrary, that justice is a matter of obeying the 'unwritten laws' (*agraphoi nomoi*) of the Gods. This remark has led Joseph Vogt to the conclusion that Hippias 'postulated the existence of natural justice, and declared that it was contrary to such natural justice for one man to be the master of another.'[69]

It is true that in Xenophon's representation of his views Hippias does not connect the notion of an unwritten law with the idea of a law of nature, as Aristotle does in his *Rhetoric.*[70] Nor does Aristotle name Hippias in the *Rhetoric* as being one of his predecessors who employed the concept of natural law. Nevertheless, given what Plato and Xenophon say about Hippias and his beliefs, it is not at all surprising that some modern commentators have concluded that he was indeed an early advocate of the notion of a law of nature, construed in an ethical sense. W. K. C. Guthrie, for example, has claimed that Hippias was one of those 'fifth century supporters of the unwritten laws' who were 'on the side of *physis* against the limitations and errors of positive *nomoi.*'[71]

What about Alcidamas? Aristotle does not mention Alcidamas by name when referring to the anonymous opponents of slavery in the *Politics.* However, as noted earlier, he does refer to him explicitly in his remarks on the concept of natural law in the *Rhetoric.* Here we are extremely fortunate because a later scholiast, commenting on the *Rhetoric,* tells us that the original words of Alcidamas which Aristotle must have had in mind state that 'God has left all men free; nature has made no man a slave.'[72] E. R. Dodds once claimed that these remarks of Alcidamas, alluded to by Aristotle, constitute 'the first explicit condemnation of slavery' for being unjust 'which has come down to us' from the ancient world.[73] For present purposes, what is most interesting is the argument which Alcidamas employed when criticizing slavery. The testimony provided by the *Rhetoric* suggests that, as Aristotle understood him, Alcidamas maintained that there is a moral law which asserts that all human

68 Plato, *Protagoras*, in *Complete Works* 337c–d, 769–770; see also Waterfield (n 65) 255; Gagarin and Woodruff (n 65) 216.

69 Joseph Vogt, 'Slavery and the Ideal of Man in Classical Greece' in Joseph Vogt (ed), *Ancient Slavery and the Ideal of Man* (Basil Blackwell 1974) 14.

70 For the relationship between unwritten law and natural law see Tussay (n 3).

71 Guthrie (n 14) 118.

72 Aristotle, *Rhetoric* I, §13, 2187.

73 E. R. Dodds, 'The Sophistic Movement and the Failure of Greek Liberalism' in E. R. Dodds (ed), *The Ancient Concept of Progress and Other Essays on Greek Literature* (Oxford University Press 1973) 101; see also R. Schlaifer, 'Greek Theories of Slavery from Homer to Aristotle' in Moses I. Finley (ed), *Slavery in Classical Antiquity* (Heffer 1968 [1936]) 200.

beings are equals, and therefore that they ought to be treated equally. Moreover, Alcidamas also believed that this was a principle of natural law. In his view, an appeal to this law indicates that slavery must stand condemned. It might be regarded as just according to existing legal conventions. However, it is unjust according to the law of nature.

The testimony of Aristotle in the *Politics* and the *Rhetoric* suggests that even if Karl Popper was exaggerating when he claimed that there was an 'anti-slavery movement' in fifth-century Athens,[74] there is nevertheless evidence to support the view that on the issue of the justice or injustice of slavery Alcidamas was not a completely isolated figure. He was not the only one who condemned slavery for being both contrary to nature and unjust, and who based that condemnation on an appeal to the existence of a natural moral law and on the implicit assumption that all human beings are by nature equal. It is the ideas associated with this particular branch of the Sophistic movement which Paul Sigmund presumably had in mind when he claimed that nature was 'regarded as a source of norms' by at least some of the Sophists, and that in the fifth century BCE there was a group of Sophists who challenged 'the prevailing identification of existing laws with justice and nature.'[75] This understanding of the ethical thought of the Sophists contradicts the assumption that in the nature versus convention debate Sophism is to be associated exclusively with conventionalism, and that it is for this reason that the views of the Sophists were opposed by Plato and Aristotle.

Given that this group of Sophists in the fifth century BCE thought that there is a law of nature, or objective ethical principles which are universally and eternally valid, it follows that they adopted a position that is similar in at least some respects to that which was advanced by both Plato and Aristotle somewhat later in the fourth century. However, these early advocates of natural law theory disagreed with their more illustrious successors regarding the question of how the principles of natural justice or law ought to be interpreted and applied, and hence also regarding the practical implications of a commitment to the idea of such a natural law. For example, in the one case an appeal to the notion of natural law was used to criticize slavery, whereas in the other it was used to justify it.

This assessment of the views of Aristotle's anonymous opponents of slavery casts doubt on the claim, made for example by C. H. McIlwain, that 'the idea of the equality of men is the profoundest contribution of the Stoics to political thought.'[76] It implies that it is not with the Stoics that the

74 Karl Popper, *The Open Society and its Enemies*, Vol. II, *The High Tide of Prophecy: Hegel, Marx and the Aftermath* (Routledge 1969 [1945]) 43.

75 Sigmund (n 3) 2–3, 5–6.

76 C. H. McIlwain, *The Growth of Political Theory in the West: From the Greeks to the End of the Middle Ages* (Macmillan 1932) 115.

notion of the natural equality of mankind, or indeed that of natural law theorizing, came into existence. H. C. Baldry has persuasively argued that, so far as slavery is concerned, there were at least 'some thinkers' in the fifth century BCE 'whose views on the subject were more advanced than were those of most Greeks for generations to come.'[77] W. K. C. Guthrie has also pointed out that the critical attitude of this group of Sophists towards the institution of slavery indicates the presence in fifth-century Athens of a universalist, cosmopolitan, rationalist and humanitarian approach to questions of ethics and politics, of the kind which was later to be associated with the natural law theory of the Stoics. According to Guthrie, this group of Sophists maintained that 'distinctions based on race, noble birth, social status or wealth, and institutions such as slavery, had no basis in nature but were only by *nomos*.' These were, in Guthrie's view, 'revolutionary ideas of incalculable potency.'[78] Long ago, Sir Ernest Barker described the proponents of these ideas as a 'radical school' of Sophists which had 'divorced nature from convention' and which, as a result, had 'become revolutionary in its tenets.'[79] Similarly, D. G. Ritchie has also argued that these radical views about the equality of all human beings represented 'an attack on the very basis of ancient society.'[80] It is for this reason, it may be conjectured, that Aristotle in particular was so opposed to them in his *Politics*.

Conclusion

It is not in the writings of the Stoics, or Cicero, or Aristotle, or Plato that the origins of the concept of natural law is to be found but, rather, in those of the Sophistic movement of fifth-century BCE Athens, not least Aristotle's anonymous opponents of slavery. Many of the ideas of these early natural law theorists among the Sophists have unfortunately been lost to us. Those that remain have been preserved and handed down to posterity only partially and in fragments. Their authors have as a result fallen into obscurity or, as Aristotle indicates, into anonymity. Moreover, as E. R. Dodds has noted, because their arguments were unsuccessful, the institution of slavery not being abolished, they might be said to represent one of history's 'failures.'[81] For this

77 H. C. Baldry, *The Unity of Mankind in Greek Thought* (Cambridge University Press 1965) 39–45; see also Peter Garnsey, *Ideas of Slavery from Aristotle to Augustine* (Cambridge University Press 1999) 76–77, 238–239.

78 Guthrie (n 14) 2, 118.

79 Sir Ernest Barker, *Greek Political Theory: Plato and His Predecessors* (Methuen 1960 [1918]) 88.

80 D. G. Ritchie, 'On the History of the Idea of "Nature" in Law and Politics' in D. G. Ritchie (ed), *Natural Rights: A Criticism of Some Political and Ethical Conceptions* (3rd edn, Macmillan 1916 [1894]) 25–26.

81 Dodds (n 73) 102.

reason they have fallen victim to what in a different context E. P. Thompson has referred to as 'the enormous condescension of posterity.'[82] Just like the slaves whose natural or human rights they might plausibly be said to have been defending, they are figures who, in the words of Sheila Rowbotham, remain hidden from history.[83]

82 E. P. Thompson, *The Making of the English Working Class* (Penguin 1975) 13.
83 Sheila Rowbotham, *Hidden From History: Rediscovering Women in History From the Seventeenth Century to the Present* (Penguin 1973).

4 Diachronic Natural Law

The Case of Aquinas

Jonathan Crowe[*]

There are many reasonable ways of capturing the core commitments of the natural law tradition. I have argued elsewhere that a fruitful way of doing so is in terms of what I call the *natural law outlook*.[1] The natural law outlook has two elements: first, there are certain forms of life that are inherently good for humans given their nature, and second, these forms of life are fundamental to explaining the nature and purpose of social, political and legal institutions. These two commitments unite the classical and contemporary writers most prominently associated with the natural law label.

In past work, I have put my own distinctive spin on the natural law outlook, arguing for what I have termed *diachronic natural law*.[2] Natural law, on this view, is hermeneutic and historicised: it is discovered through and shaped by human social practices. This conception of natural law utilises a wide understanding of human nature to situate natural law within both a biological and social context;[3] this wide lens, I argue, offers an explanatorily powerful framework for understanding natural law's sources, content and normativity. Central to this account is the idea that natural law exists in time: it evolves throughout human history, reflecting changes in human practices and environments.

The idea that natural law itself evolves is controversial. John Finnis, the most influential contemporary natural law theorist, flatly denies this. Finnis draws

* This chapter is loosely based on a series of seminars delivered at the Centre for Sino-Christian Studies and Angelicum Thomistic Institute Summer School held at Hong Kong Baptist University in July 2024. I am grateful to James Dominic Rooney and the participants for the illuminating discussion.

1 Jonathan Crowe, *Natural Law and the Nature of Law* (Cambridge University Press 2019) 2; Jonathan Crowe, 'Philosophical Challenges and Prospects for Natural Law Foundations of Human Rights' in Tom Angier, Iain T. Benson, and Mark Retter (eds), *The Cambridge Handbook of Natural Law and Human Rights* (Cambridge University Press 2022) 485. See also Jonathan Crowe and Constance Youngwon Lee, 'The Natural Law Outlook' in Jonathan Crowe and Constance Youngwon Lee (eds), *Research Handbook on Natural Law Theory* (Edward Elgar 2019) 1.

2 Crowe, 'Philosophical Challenges and Prospects' (n 1) 485. See also Crowe, *Natural Law and the Nature of Law* (n 1) 246.

3 Crowe, 'Philosophical Challenges and Prospects' (n 1) 486–489.

DOI: 10.4324/9781003728603-5

a distinction between theories of natural law, which form part of the history of ideas, and natural law itself, which he contends is timeless and unchanging. Natural law, for Finnis, is a set of immutable truths analogous to mathematical principles and, therefore, '[has] no history'.[4] For Finnis, natural law is part of God's plan for human beings; since it exists in the mind of God, and God is outside of time, natural law itself is timeless.[5]

Other natural law authors, including myself, have presented a contrary view. I have argued that natural law does evolve in at least two different senses.[6] First, the core components of natural law—namely, intrinsic human goods and principles of practical reason—reflect what is good and reasonable for humans, given their nature. Human nature, in turn, is a product of both biology and social circumstances. It follows that the precepts of natural law can and do change to the extent that human nature changes. Second, natural law depends importantly on social practices. Intrinsic human goods are expressed in different ways in different societies. Furthermore, social norms play a crucial role in specifying details natural law leaves indeterminate. These specifications, provided they are salient and reasonable, gain normative force for members of the community.

My aim in this chapter is to add further context and support for the diachronic view of natural law through a close reading of some passages from Thomas Aquinas's so-called Treatise on Law in the *Summa Theologica*.[7] Aquinas might seem, to some readers, an unlikely ally for diachronic natural law. After all, Finnis presents his timeless vision of natural law theory as based substantially on Aquinas.[8] However, I will argue that Aquinas's conception of natural law is more dynamic and flexible than it may appear from Finnis's reading. The structure of my discussion will mirror Aquinas's famous distinction between four types of law: eternal, natural, human and divine. We will see that Aquinas emphasises that the content of all types of law (apart from eternal law) can and does change over time; the application of natural law and human law is highly situational; custom counts as a form of law, due to its role in adapting natural law to the needs of human societies; and divine law is not timeless, but is progressively revealed to humans throughout history.

4 John Finnis, *Natural Law and Natural Rights* (Oxford University Press 2011) 24.
5 Ibid. 389–390.
6 Jonathan Crowe, 'The Evolution of Natural Law' in Wojciech Zaluski, Sacha Bourgeois-Gironde, and Adam Dyrda (eds), *Research Handbook on Legal Evolution* (Edward Elgar 2024). See also Jonathan Crowe, 'Is Natural Law Timeless?' (2021) 33 *Bond Law Review* 1; Crowe, *Natural Law and the Nature of Law* (n 1) 6–7; Crowe, 'Philosophical Challenges and Prospects' (n 1) 489–493.
7 Thomas Aquinas, *Summa Theologica* (Dominican Fathers tr, Ave Maria 1948) q 90–108 (hereinafter ST).
8 Finnis (n 4) vi.

Eternal Law

Aquinas prefaces his discussion of the four forms of law in the *Summa Theologica* by considering the nature of law in general. His conception of law is inherently teleological, showing the influence of Aristotle. Aquinas argues that the object of law is the same as the end of human life in general: namely, happiness (or what Aristotle would call *eudaimonia*). The law, for Aquinas, is the 'rule and measure' of human acts, so its guiding principle, like that of human action in general, is identified by reference to practical reason.[9] The object of practical reason, in turn, is 'the last end of human life'—namely 'bliss or happiness'.[10] Consequently, law must principally direct itself to the same end.

Furthermore, Aquinas reasons, the end of law is not the happiness of some individual, but rather the happiness of the whole community. The purpose of each part of a thing is identified by reference to the purpose of the whole. As such, since every person is 'part of the perfect community', the law is properly directed towards 'universal happiness'.[11] Here, Aquinas refers expressly to Aristotle's statement that law is just when it is adapted to achieve happiness for the body politic.[12] Law, Aquinas concludes, is by its nature 'chiefly ordained to the common good'.[13] It follows from this that any law which does not promote the common good, but only the interests of some individuals, 'must needs be devoid of the nature of a law, save in so far as it regards the common good'.[14]

Law's orientation towards the common good helps to shed light on other aspects of its nature. When responding to the question of who has the power to make laws, Aquinas begins by reiterating that '[a] law, properly speaking, regards first and foremost the order to the common good'.[15] He reasons that the task of ordering something to the common good must belong either to the whole people or to someone who is 'the viceregent of the whole people'.[16] Therefore, 'the making of a law belongs either to the whole people or to a public personage who has care of the whole people'.[17] This conclusion, again, serves to distinguish law properly speaking from edicts that serve only a few individuals.

A similar pattern emerges in relation to the question of whether law must be promulgated. Aquinas returns here to his characterisation of law as a 'rule and measure' of human activity.[18] He notes that 'a rule or measure is imposed

9 ST, I–II, q. 90, art. 2.
10 Ibid.
11 Ibid.
12 Ibid.
13 Ibid.
14 Ibid.
15 ST, I–II, q. 90, art. 3.
16 Ibid.
17 Ibid.
18 ST, I–II, q. 90, art. 4.

by being applied to those who are to be ruled and measured by it'.[19] This application, he reasons, occurs when the law is notified by promulgation to those whom it binds. Promulgation, in this sense, 'is necessary for the law to obtain its force'; without it, law could not serve its purpose.[20] Aquinas then arrives at a definition of law incorporating the insights from the previous discussion. Law, he concludes, 'is nothing else than an ordinance of reason for the common good, made by [them] who has care of the community, and promulgated'.[21] This definition, importantly, encompasses not only human (or positive) law but also eternal, natural and divine law.

Aquinas's definition of law in general provides the starting point for his discussion of eternal law. According to that definition, he notes, 'a law is nothing else but a dictate of practical reason emanating from the ruler who governs a perfect community'.[22] The entire world is 'ruled by Divine Providence', while 'the whole community of the universe is governed by Divine Reason'.[23] It follows from this that the ideal form of government can be found in 'God the Ruler of the universe' and God's providence 'has the nature of a law'.[24] God's providential plan for the universe is distinguished from other forms of law by the fact that it 'is not subject to time but is eternal'.[25] Hence, Aquinas calls it eternal law.

The eternal law is timeless and unchanging. It is notable that, for Aquinas, eternal law is the only kind of law with this quality. The other three types of law, as we will see, are temporally situated and subject to change. They are, nonetheless, all derived ultimately from the eternal law. We have seen how law, for Aquinas, is teleological; it 'denotes a kind of plan directing acts towards an end'.[26] If a plan forms part of a larger plan, then the former can be said to be caused by the latter. As Aquinas puts it, 'wherever there are movers ordained to one another, the power of the second mover must needs be derived from the power of the first mover'.[27] The first mover, the deviser of the overarching plan for the world, is God. Since 'the eternal law is the plan of government in the Chief Governor, all the plans of government in the inferior governors must be derived from the eternal law'.[28] Aquinas concludes that 'all laws, in so far as they partake of right reason, are derived from the eternal law'.[29]

19 Ibid.
20 Ibid.
21 Ibid.
22 ST, I–II, q. 91, art. 1.
23 Ibid.
24 Ibid.
25 Ibid.
26 ST, I–II, q. 93, art. 3.
27 Ibid.
28 Ibid.
29 Ibid.

Natural Law

Natural law, for Aquinas, is humanity's mode of participation in the eternal law. It is that part of the eternal law that governs human action and is naturally accessible to humans. '[A]ll things', Aquinas tells us, 'partake somewhat of the eternal law, in so far as, . . . they derive their respective inclinations to their proper acts and ends'.[30] Humans, being rational creatures, partake in eternal law by exercising their intellectual and rational capacities. It is for this reason that the participation in eternal law by humans is 'properly called a law'.[31] The natural law, then, is 'the imprint on us of the Divine light'; it is 'nothing else than the rational creature's participation of the eternal law'.[32]

How can humans, as embodied beings, be subject to eternal law? Aquinas discusses two ways. The first involves 'partaking of the eternal law by way of knowledge', while the second involves 'partaking of the eternal law by way of action or passion'; that is, according to what he terms 'an inward motive principle'.[33] Irrational creatures are subject to the eternal law in the second way, but not the first, since they lack the capacity for knowledge.[34] Humans, by contrast, are 'subject to the eternal law in both ways' because they have both 'some knowledge of the eternal law' and 'a natural inclination to that which is in harmony with the eternal law'.[35] Nonetheless, these capacities in humans are imperfect due to the influence of passions and vicious habits, attributable to humanity's fall from grace.[36]

The core content of the natural law, Aquinas argues, consists of 'self-evident principles'.[37] It is tempting to think that a truly self-evident principle must be immediately knowable to everyone; this would create a puzzle about how humans can fail to know the natural law. However, Aquinas offers a different understanding of self-evidence that avoids this challenge. He clarifies that something can be self-evident in two ways: 'first, in itself; secondly, in relation to us'.[38] Something is self-evident in itself if it is true by definition; for example, it is self-evident that a bachelor is an unmarried man. However, even in this kind of case, a person can only grasp the self-evidence of the proposition if they have some background knowledge about the terms in question. As Aquinas puts it, 'to one who knows not the definition of the subject, it happens that such a proposition is not self-evident'.[39]

30 ST, I–II, q. 91, art. 2.
31 Ibid.
32 Ibid.
33 ST, I–II, q. 93, art. 6.
34 Ibid.
35 Ibid.
36 Ibid. See also ST, I–II, q. 109, art. 2.
37 ST, I–II, q. 94, art. 2.
38 Ibid.
39 Ibid.

Based on this analysis, Aquinas goes on to distinguish those propositions that are 'universally self-evident to all' because the meanings of the terms are known to all and those that are 'self-evident only to the wise, who understand the meaning of the terms of such propositions'.[40] This framework explains how the precepts of natural law may be self-evident, although not everyone understands them to the same extent because a degree of wisdom is necessary to grasp them. Aquinas's analysis of self-evidence also reflects a distinction between divine and human perspectives. Eternal law, as we have seen, is timeless because it exists in the mind of God. Natural law, by contrast, is ***human participation*** in eternal law. It must, therefore, take account of the limitations of the human standpoint.

Practical reason, for Aquinas, is directed towards ends. In reasoning how to act, we identify what objectives we wish to pursue and reason about how to pursue them. By engaging in this type of reasoning, we identify certain objectives as 'good'; that is, as worth pursuing. Aquinas concludes that '"good" is the first thing that falls under the apprehension of the practical reason, which is directed to action: since every agent acts for an end under the aspect of good'.[41] It follows from this that 'the first principle of practical reason is one founded on the notion of good'.[42] From the notion of good as something to be pursued, we can derive 'the first precept of law, that "good is to be done and pursued, and evil is to be avoided."'[43] This forms the basis of '[a]ll other precepts of the natural law'.[44]

How, then, do we identify what exactly is good or worth pursuing? Recall Aquinas's observation that humans partake in eternal law in two ways: by their rational capacity for knowledge and by 'an inward motive principle', also called a 'natural inclination'.[45] Both these ways are involved in accessing natural law. Aquinas posits:

> All those things to which [humans have] a natural inclination, are naturally apprehended by reason as being good, and consequently as objects of pursuit, and their contraries as evil, and objects of avoidance. Wherefore according to the order of natural inclinations, is the order of the precepts of the natural law.[46]

Aquinas identifies three different kinds of natural inclinations that reveal aspects of natural law. First, humans have an inclination to self-preservation, which they share with all substances; 'by reason of this inclination, whatever

40 Ibid.
41 Ibid.
42 Ibid.
43 Ibid.
44 Ibid.
45 ST, I–II, q. 93, art. 6.
46 ST, I–II, q. 94, art. 2.

is a means of preserving human life, and of warding off its obstacles, belongs to the natural law'.[47] Second, humans share inclinations with other animals, according to which natural law includes such goods as 'sexual intercourse, education of offspring and so forth'.[48] Third, humans have inclinations that are special to them by virtue of their rational nature. These include inclinations 'to know the truth about God, and to live in society'.[49] These various examples supply a non-exhaustive list of the goods Aquinas holds to form part of the natural law.

Aquinas discusses some objections to this idea of natural law. One such worry is that the diversity of human nature undermines the link between natural law and human inclinations. As Aquinas notes, 'different [people] are naturally inclined to different things; some to the desire of pleasures, others to the desire of honors, and other [people] to other things'.[50] How can it be said that there is one natural law for everyone?

Aquinas emphasises in response that apparent disagreements about natural law often arise in relation to applications rather than first principles. Practical reason, he notes, is directed to the details of human behaviour, but 'the more we descend to matters of detail, the more frequently we encounter defects'.[51] Furthermore, practical reason is situational, so what appear to be disagreements may actually involve the application of natural law to diverse circumstances.[52] In summary, disagreements about natural law may arise because one party has gone wrong in their reasoning, but they may also arise because the parties are differently situated, meaning natural law yields different outcomes.[53]

A related question for the idea that natural law is revealed by human inclinations concerns whether (and, if so, how) humans can fail to know natural law. Here, Aquinas again distinguishes the general precepts of natural law, which are 'known to all', from the secondary precepts that follow as conclusions from first principles.[54] The general precepts of natural law 'in the abstract, can nowise be blotted out from [human] hearts'.[55] However, people may go wrong when applying natural law to particular circumstances due to 'concupiscence or some other passion'.[56] Furthermore, people may lose sight of the secondary precepts due to 'evil persuasions' or 'vicious customs and corrupt

47 Ibid.
48 Ibid.
49 Ibid.
50 ST, I–II, q. 94, art. 4, obj. 3.
51 ST, I–II, q. 94, art. 4.
52 Ibid.
53 Aquinas's strategy here mirrors responses to the so-called problem of moral disagreement in contemporary metaethics. See generally David O. Brink, 'Moral Realism and the Sceptical Arguments from Disagreement and Queerness' (1984) 62 *Australasian Journal of Philosophy* 111.
54 ST, I–II, q. 94, art. 6.
55 Ibid.
56 Ibid.

habits'.[57] This makes it possible for not only individual humans but also whole communities to make mistakes about the content of natural law. Natural law, then, may be linked to human inclinations without casting doubt on the possibility of either local or pervasive moral errors.

Aquinas's distinction between primary and secondary precepts of natural law is also central to his view on whether natural law changes. He explicitly affirms that natural law can change in two distinct ways.[58] First, natural law can change 'by way of addition' when content is added to it by divine law or human laws.[59] Here, Aquinas recognises the role of other kinds of law in supplementing and thereby shaping the dictates of natural law in ways we will explore further later. Second, natural law may change 'by way of subtraction'.[60] Aquinas emphasises in this context that the first principles of natural law do not change, but the secondary precepts 'may be changed in some particular cases of rare occurrence, through some special causes hindering the observance of such precepts'.[61]

Aquinas's suggestion here seems to be that because natural law is situational, our understanding of its secondary precepts may change when we encounter unusual or novel circumstances. Natural law, as we saw earlier, is human participation in the eternal law and, therefore, reflects humanity's epistemically and temporally bounded standpoint. At the level of secondary precepts, our understanding of natural law advances through application to specific cases. Novel situations can, therefore, bring about changes in natural law. We would not expect this to happen very frequently, especially at our current juncture in human history, but the possibility of such changes is consistent with both the situational character of natural law and its dependence on the human perspective.

Human Law

Human law, for Aquinas, corresponds roughly to the modern category of positive law (although it goes beyond legal enactments to encompass customs, as we will see later). All humans have access to natural law by virtue of their natural inclinations and rational capacities. Why, then, do we need human law to govern us? Aquinas recognises that humans have 'a natural aptitude for virtue', which requires training if it is to be perfected.[62] For young people who have virtuous dispositions and are guided by sound customs, parental training by way of admonitions suffices to lead them towards virtue.[63]

57 Ibid.
58 ST, I–II, q. 94, art. 5.
59 Ibid.
60 Ibid.
61 Ibid.
62 ST, I–II, q. 95, art. 1.
63 Ibid.

Some people, however, are inclined towards vice. It is necessary for these people to be 'restrained from evil by force and fear' so they will leave others in peace.[64] The aim is that, through this mechanism, they will change their habits and ultimately become more virtuous. Law is the means through which this process occurs.[65] In summary, as Aquinas puts it, those 'who are well disposed are led willingly to virtue by being admonished better than by coercion: but [those] who are evilly disposed are not led to virtue unless they are compelled'.[66] This is one reason why human law is needed.

A second rationale for human law is that natural law does not contain all the necessary content to govern human societies. Aquinas notes that 'the force of a law depends on the extent of its justice', quoting with approval Augustine's dictum that 'that which is not just seems to be no law at all'.[67] However, he immediately goes on to clarify that human law may be derived from natural law (and therefore be just) in two different ways. The first way is 'as a conclusion from premises';[68] in this case, human law simply deduces what natural law requires for social governance. The second way is as a 'determination of certain generalities';[69] in this case, human law fills in details of social governance that natural law leaves unspecified and, in so doing, adds to the existing content of natural law.

Human law is needed, on this view, because natural law requires supplementation if it is to effectively guide human action in the context of a community. Aquinas illustrates this idea by reference to punishments for crimes. 'The law of nature', he says, 'has it that the evil-doer should be punished; but that [they] be punished in this or that way, is a determination of the law of nature'.[70] Natural law, in other words, requires that crimes be punished and plausibly that the punishment be proportionate to the crime. However, it does not stipulate whether the punishment should be, say, two months in prison as opposed to a $5,000 fine. Human law exists partly to fill in these kinds of details.

Aquinas's distinction between two ways of deriving human law from natural law is closely related to another distinction he draws between the 'law of nations' and 'civil law'.[71] The law of nations comprises those aspects of human law that are derived from natural law as conclusions from premises. This yields a common core of content in the legal systems of different nations. Civil law, by contrast, consists of local determinations on topics natural law leaves indeterminate, such as specific penalties for criminal offences, tax rates, traffic

64 Ibid.
65 Ibid.
66 ST, I–II, q. 95, art. 1, ad 1.
67 ST, I–II, q. 95, art. 2.
68 Ibid.
69 Ibid.
70 Ibid.
71 ST, I–II, q. 95, art. 4.

regulations and so forth. This aspect of positive law will vary between nations since 'each state decides on what is best for itself'.[72]

Human law, to be just, must be based on natural law in either of the two ways Aquinas discusses. However, Aquinas makes it clear that human law need not reproduce every facet of natural law. The purpose of human law, Aquinas reasons, is not to 'forbid all vices, from which the virtuous abstain, but only the more grievous vices, from which it is possible for the majority to abstain'.[73] In particular, human law focuses on prohibiting those forms of conduct that cause serious harm to others since, without these restrictions, 'human society could not be maintained'.[74] Aquinas comments in this context that '[t]he purpose of human law is to lead [people] to virtue, not suddenly, but gradually'.[75] Laws seeking to impose onerous requirements on its subjects in the name of virtue might prove counterproductive, leading people to disrespect or ignore the law more generally.

Just laws, which are derived from natural law in the ways we have discussed, are binding in conscience because they are ultimately based on eternal law.[76] The situation with respect to unjust laws is more complicated. Aquinas distinguishes two ways that laws may be unjust. The first category of unjust laws encompasses laws that are 'contrary to human good' in the sense of being unnecessarily burdensome, as well as laws that exceed the author's jurisdiction or impose unequal burdens on the community.[77] These unjust standards are 'acts of violence rather than laws'; they do not bind in conscience. Nonetheless, subjects need to weigh the injustice of these laws against the need to 'avoid scandal or disturbance' in the community by encouraging unvirtuous or lawless behaviour.[78] The suggestion seems to be that these types of laws should sometimes be obeyed, despite their injustice, in order to protect social harmony and the legal system as a whole.

The second category of unjust laws is those that are 'opposed to the Divine good'.[79] Aquinas gives the example of laws encouraging idolatry, but this category would also include any other law contradicting God's commands. '[L]aws of this kind', Aquinas says, 'must nowise be observed because, as stated in Acts 5:29, "we ought to obey God rather than [humans]."'[80] Loosely speaking, Aquinas's framework recognises that the question of whether to obey an unjust law involves balancing the degree of injustice against the broader

72 Ibid.
73 ST, I–II, q. 96, art. 2.
74 Ibid.
75 ST, I–II, q. 96, art. 2, ad 2.
76 ST, I–II, q. 96, art. 4.
77 Ibid.
78 Ibid.
79 Ibid.
80 Ibid.

consequences of disobedience. However, there are some laws that are so unjust, being contrary to God's will, that they should never be followed.

Aquinas further acknowledges that some laws may lead to just results in most scenarios while causing injustice in other cases.[81] This is inevitable since lawmakers cannot anticipate every single case; rather, they draft the law 'according to what happens most frequently'.[82] What, then, should we do where a generally just law yields unjust results in a particular case? Aquinas maintains that, in general, when such a case arises, the law should not be observed. However, he adds the caveat that legal authorities are generally more competent to declare exceptions to the law than individuals.[83] If the unjust application of the law does not require an immediate remedy, it should be left to the officials to decide. However, if immediate harm would result from following the unjust law, such that there is no time to consult legal officials, then an individual may decline to apply it.

Human laws, as we have seen, are properly derived from natural law and, therefore, ultimately from eternal law. By filling in details natural law leaves unspecified, they supplement the natural law and change it by addition.[84] Importantly, for Aquinas, the category of human laws is not limited to legal enactments. Aquinas reasons that

> just as human reason and will, in practical matters, may be made manifest by speech, so may they be made known by deeds . . . Wherefore by actions also, especially if they be repeated, so as to make a custom, law can be changed and expounded.[85]

Aquinas appeals here to the way in which custom reflects the 'repeated external actions, the inward movement of the will, and concepts of reason' of diverse humans over time.[86] '[W]hen a thing is done again and again', he observes, 'it seems to proceed from a deliberate judgment of reason';[87] custom may be regarded in this sense as the accreted wisdom of the community. For this reason, Aquinas concludes, 'custom has the force of a law, abolishes law, and is the interpreter of law'.[88]

81 ST, I–II, q. 96, art. 6.
82 Ibid.
83 Ibid.
84 ST, I–II, q. 94, art. 5.
85 ST, I–II, q. 97, art. 3.
86 Ibid.
87 Ibid.
88 Ibid.

Divine Law

So far, we have considered Aquinas's comments on eternal, natural, and human law. Where does divine law fit into this picture? Aquinas gives several reasons why divine law is required in addition to the other types of law. First, human access to natural law is limited by our natural capacities. However, human life is directed by God towards a higher end that transcends our current nature. Divine law is necessary to direct humans in accordance with this higher goal.[89] Second, as discussed previously, humans may reach differing judgments on the implications of natural law. Divine law helps to bring certainty to certain core moral prescriptions.[90] Third, it is not possible for human law to regulate people's internal attitudes, while divine law can govern these areas.[91] Fourth, human law does not prohibit all forms of wrongdoing, but under divine law, no evil goes unpunished.[92]

Divine law comes directly from God. It may be tempting to think that divine law, like eternal law, does not change. After all, 'where there is one king in one kingdom there is but one law'.[93] However, Aquinas warns against this conclusion. According to Christian tradition, 'the Divine law is divided into Old and New';[94] that is, the law of the Hebrew and Greek scriptures, respectively. These two forms of divine law, Aquinas suggests, can be distinguished as 'perfect and imperfect in the same species'.[95] Aquinas follows the Apostle Paul in comparing the state of humanity under the Old Law to that of a child, while humanity under the New Law is like an adult.[96] Just as children require different forms of guidance from adults, humanity at different stages in its history requires different kinds of law.

Eternal law, for Aquinas, does not change. However, natural law can change both when additions are made through human and divine law and when exceptions to its precepts appear through specific cases. Human law also changes, not only when new legal enactments are issued but also through the development of custom. And, perhaps surprisingly to some readers, divine law changes too. God gave humanity one form of law in the Old Testament and another in the New Testament. The Old Law was directed to 'a sensible and earthly good', while the New Law pursues 'an intelligible and heavenly good'.[97] These different forms of law reflected the changing capacities and needs of humanity—what might perhaps be called a change in human nature. As

89 ST, I–II, q. 91, art. 4.
90 Ibid.
91 Ibid.
92 Ibid.
93 ST, I–II, q. 91, art. 5, obj. 1.
94 ST, I–II, q. 91, art. 5.
95 Ibid.
96 Ibid.
97 Ibid.

Aquinas puts it, 'God . . . gave one law to [humans], while they were yet imperfect, and another more perfect law, when, by the preceding law, they had been led to a greater capacity for Divine things'.[98]

Conclusion

The gist of diachronic natural law is that natural law changes in response to social circumstances. This is because both human understanding of natural law and the content of natural law itself depend upon human social environments and practices. I have argued in this chapter that diachronic natural law, thus understood, finds support in Aquinas. Natural law, for Aquinas, is both situational and dynamic. The precepts of natural law are grasped through the development of practical wisdom; the secondary precepts, in particular, are understood and refined through application to cases. Natural law develops over time, not only through application to novel scenarios but also due to additions made through human and divine law. Importantly, here, the category of human law is not limited to formal legal enactments but also includes evolved social customs.

All forms of law, for Aquinas, are based on eternal law. However, eternal law, as its name suggests, is the only type of law that does not change. Not only natural law but also human and divine law may shift in response to human circumstances. God, according to the Christian tradition, chose to reveal divine law progressively to humans throughout history, reflecting their changing environments and capacities. If God chose to reveal divine law in this way, what reason is there to deny that natural law changes as well? Natural law, being human participation in the eternal law, reflects the materially and temporally bounded character of human rationality. Our grasp of natural law develops as our standpoint changes. Furthermore, natural law adapts to the specific scenarios and challenges humans face in their historical and social settings. As Aquinas appreciated, this process represents a kind of change, not merely in our grasp of natural law but in natural law itself.

98 Ibid.

5 Thomas Aquinas's Understanding of Natural Law as Law and as Good

A Close Reading of Passages in *Summa Theologiae* 1–2.94.2

Fr. Kevin Flannery, S.J.

The article in Thomas Aquinas's *Summa Theologiae* that often serves as the basis of explanations of how he understood the natural law is often also interpreted in a way that de-emphasizes natural law's character as law and emphasizes the non-rational or pre-rational character of the natural inclinations mentioned in the article. The chapter begins (section I) by arguing that the title of that article, ST 1–2.94.2, is to be taken seriously.[1] The article is not so much about inclinations as it is about the natural law. Section II makes use of remarks in Aristotle's *Metaphysics* and Thomas's commentary upon them in order to clarify what is meant in ST 1–2.94.2 by the expression "natural inclinations." In section III, examined are a couple of mistranslations of a crucial sentence in ST 1–2.94.2 which in fact speaks positively of the precepts of the natural law, calling them "human goods."

I. Emphasis on the Inclinations

The first thing to notice about ST 1–2.94.2 is its title, which, of course, tells the reader what the article is about; so, this article is about "whether the natural law contains several precepts, or only one."[2] The article, as we shall see, speaks frequently of inclinations—invariably called "natural inclinations"—but

1 "ST 1–2.94.2" stands for *Summa Theologiae* (ST), the first part of the second part (1–2), question 94, article 2. When referring to the second part of the second part, the abbreviation ST 2–2 is used. Thus, *Summa Theologiae*, second part of the second part, question 110, article 1, is referred to as ST 2–2.110.1. In order to reduce the frequency of italicized text, when Latin words or phrases are within quotation marks or indented as a quotation, they will not be italicized.

2 A full translation of ST 1–2.94.2 will not be included in this chapter. The reader can find the translation of ST 1–2.94.2, alongside the Latin text, at https://aquinas.cc/la/en/~ST.I-II.Q94.A2. The translation given at this URL is from the translation of the entire *Summa Theologiae* done by the Fathers of the English Dominican Province and published in three volumes by Benzinger Brothers (New York, NY) in 1948. That same translation was published in five volumes by Christian Classics (Westminster, MD) in 1981 (and subsequently). The present author occasionally employs translations differing from those offered by the Fathers of the English Dominican Province.

DOI: 10.4324/9781003728603-6

it is not about those inclinations. Their existence is merely useful to Thomas in explaining how the natural law can contain just one precept but also, in another sense, several precepts. This, the purpose of ST 1–2.94.2, is often ignored by commentators, several of whom read the article as Thomas's attempt to demonstrate that the precepts of natural law correspond to the inclinations experienced by human beings.

Alan Donagan, for instance, in defending A. J. Price's rejection of "the claim to deduce ethical propositions from ones which are admitted to be non-ethical," criticizes Thomas for "deriving the first precept of the natural law, 'bonum est faciendum et prosequendum, et malum vitandum,' from a non-ethical statement about the nature of good: 'bonum est quod omnia appetunt.'"[3] Donagan refers to Thomas's position that lying is immoral because it is the assertion of something that is "against the mind" ["contra mentem"] of the speaker [ST 2–2.110.1]. Donagan objects: "If speech acts have a natural end, in Aristotle's sense, it is to express whatever thought the speaker chooses to express."[4] In other words, we do have a natural inclination to tell lies and so they, too, contrary to what Thomas maintains, would be in accordance with natural law.

Other authors do not go so far as to assert that Thomas derives the first precept of the natural law from inclinations, and yet they do suppose that Thomas's purpose in ST 1–2.94.2 is to somehow ***ground*** the precepts of the natural law in the inclinations natural to man. According, for instance, to Leo Elders: "Human nature becomes the source of morality of certain acts through the intermediary of man's fundamental natural inclinations"; he then quotes a passage from ST 1–2.94.2.[5]

John Cahalan takes a similar approach:

> Our original, prephilosophic knowledge that choices are morally good or bad comes from the inclinations that are the reasons why we call things good or bad. Without an awareness of those inclinations we could

3 Alan Donagan, "The Scholastic Theory of Moral Law in the Modern World" (1966) 40 *Proceedings of the American Catholic Philosophical Association* 31. The quotation from Donagan, but with the Latin phrases taken from ST 1–2.94.2 translated, would run as follows: "deriving the first precept of the natural law, 'good is to be done and pursued, and evil is to be avoided,' from a non-ethical statement about the nature of good, 'good is that which all things seek after.'" The quotation from Price can be found at A. N. Prior, *Logic and the Basis of Ethics* (OUP 1963) 95. On Donagan's reading of ST 1–2.94.2, see Stephen L. Brock, *The Light that Binds: A Study in Thomas Aquinas's Metaphysics of Natural law* (Pickwick 2020) 107–110.

4 Donagan (n 3) 36.

5 Leo J. Elders, "Nature as the Basis of Moral Actions" (2001) 56 *Sapientia* 576–577. The passage he quotes is the following: "All those things to which man has a natural inclination, are naturally apprehended by reason as being good, and consequently as objects of pursuit, and their contraries as evil, and objects to be avoided. Therefore, the order of the precepts of natural law is according to the order of natural inclinations."

not have our awareness of things as good or bad, since to be good or bad is to be a term to which we are related by such an inclination.[6]

Germain Grisez's interpretation of ST 1–2.94.2 puts even more weight on the inclinations side of the relationship, although he maintains that what is important morally about the inclinations is that they aim at goods and that this orientation towards good then characterizes also the first precept of practical reason ("good is to be done and pursued, and evil is to be avoided").[7]

II. Intellect and Reason

In speaking of our natural inclinations, it is as if Thomas is speaking about an ocean current headed toward a particular end, some of whose molecules are of one type, some of another, some of yet another. Molecules of these types exist also outside of this particular current. Thomas would be interested in these distinct types of "molecules" only because they enable him to show that, although the ocean current is one, within it can be identified (at least) three sectors.

That Thomas is depicting in ST 1–2.94.2 a situation of this sort is evident in some Aristotelian ideas he employs in the main argument (the corpus) of the article. That corpus begins with a discourse regarding what our translation calls "self-evident principles" ["principia per se nota"],[8] in the course of which Thomas speaks of "certain axioms [*dignitates*] or propositions [*propositiones*]"

6 John C. Cahalan, "Natural Obligation: How Rationally Known Truth Determines Ethical Good and Evil" (2002) 66 *Thomist* 126. In a note, Stephen Brock, with reference to this passage, speaks of Cahalan and also Elders as scholars who take the words in ST 1–2.94.2, "omnia illa ad quae homo habet naturalem inclinationem, ratio naturaliter apprehendit ut bona" ["all those things to which man has a natural inclination, are naturally apprehended by reason as being good"], as "presenting us with Thomas's way of grounding the precepts of natural law upon knowledge of human nature. On this reading, the natural way in which a person comes to judge things as human goods—and therefore as due to be pursued, and so forth—would be by his seeing them as the objects of natural human inclinations" [Brock (n 3) 111]. Brock cites also P.-M. Van Overbeke, "La Loi Naturelle et le Droit Naturel Selon S. Thomas" (1957) 57 *Revue Thomiste* 65.

7 Thomas too in ST 1–2.94.2 refers to this principle ("bonum est faciendum et prosequendum, et malum vitandum") as the "primum principium in ratione practica"; he also refers to it as the "primum praeceptum legis." See Germain Grisez, "The First Principle of Practical Reason: A Commentary on the *Summa Theologiae* 1–2, question 94, article 2" (1965) 10 *Natural Law Forum* 176–181, 191–194.

8 On the *per se notum*, see Luca F. Tuninetti, *"Per se notum": Die logische Beschaffenheit des Selbstverständlichen im Denkens des Thomas von Aquin, Studien und Texte zur Geistesgeschichte des Mittelalters* (E. J. Brill 1996). As the title Tuninetti of his book indicates, he prefers as a translation of *per se notum* the term *selbstverständlich*: "understandable in itself." In what follows, however, since it does not impact the present argument, the English Dominican translation "self evident" shall be maintained.

that are "universally self-evident to all."[9] Among these is the proposition that "every whole is greater than its part." He says that "a certain order is to be found in the things that are apprehended universally":

> For that which, before aught else, falls under apprehension, is being, the notion of which is included in all things whatsoever a man apprehends. Wherefore the first indemonstrable principle is that the same thing cannot be affirmed and denied at the same time, which is based on the notion of being and not-being: and on this principle all others are based, as is stated in *Metaph.* iv, text. 9.

The reference here is to *Metaphysics* 4.3.1005b29–34,[10] where Aristotle states first the principle of non-contradiction ("it is impossible for the same man at the same time to believe the same thing to be and not to be") and then remarks: "It is for this reason that all who are carrying out a demonstration refer it to this as an ultimate belief; for this is naturally the starting-point even for all the other axioms."[11]

Thomas's commentary on this passage (which brings in also ideas found elsewhere in Aristotle's *Metaphysics*) sheds light upon what it is to be a natural inclination.[12] Thomas notes, first of all, that "the intellect has a twofold activity: one by which it knows what something is, which is called the understanding of indivisibles, and another by means of which it combines and separates."[13] By the first activity, he means the intellect's ability to grasp what something *is* (a whole, for instance), even before putting that singular grasp into a proposition (into, that is, a proposition combining that thing with some other concept or separating it from some other concept). By the second activity he means propositions, such as "every whole is greater than its part."

Thomas goes on to argue in this same comment that primary [*primum*] with respect to both activities is being. Being's primary character in the first activity is obvious: all thinking begins with "the understanding of indivisibles."[14]

9 The Greek word ἀξίωμα is translated into Latin as *dignitas*. The *dignitates* (or axioms) of which Thomas speaks here are propositions.

10 That is, book 4, chapter 3, lines 1005b29–34.

11 These (and subsequent) translations of Aristotle are taken from Jonathan Barnes (ed), *The Complete Works of Aristotle: The Revised Oxford Translation* (Princeton University Press 1984).

12 Thomas uses ideas set out, for instance, in *Metaphysics* 6.4 and 9.10.

13 "[D]uplex sit operatio intellectus: una, qua cognoscit quod quid est, quae vocatur indivisibilium intelligentia: alia, qua componit et dividitas" [Thomas Aquinas, *In duodecim libros Metaphysicorum Aristotelis expositio* (Marietti 1950) 4.6 §605]. See also Aristotle's *On the Soul* 3.6.430a26-b6.

14 In the ST 1–2.94.2 passage quoted just above, Thomas speaks of such propositions as based "upon the notion of being and not-being" ["supra rationem entis et non entis"] because he knows that that more basic understanding will find its way (as its basis) into the proposition "being is not not-being" (or the principle of non-contradiction). When one knows at that most basic level what a whole is, one also knows what it is not, although one has not yet put

However, in the second operation, being is also primary (or basic): "And so this principle [that is, being] is also by nature primary in the second activity of the intellect, i.e., in the activity of combining and separating."[15] Combining and separating refers to things apprehended in the first activity. Thomas's use here of the expression "by nature" (*naturaliter*) establishes an important link to ST 1–2.94.2. The inclinations of which he speaks there are always referred to as natural inclinations.

The passage in the *Metaphysics* upon which Thomas is commenting is about theoretical reason, whose basis (to repeat) is the principle of non-contradiction and, even farther below, being [*ens*]. In ST 1–2.94.2, he identifies the same sort of alignment in practical reason, although in this case, instead of being and the principle of non-contradiction, he speaks of good and of the "primary precept of law" ["primum praeceptum legis"]—that is, of the practical version of the principle of non-contradiction: "good is to be done and pursued, and evil is to be avoided" ["bonum est faciendum et prosequendum, et malum vitandum"].[16] In order to maintain the parallel with theoretical reason, Thomas continues to use language that puts good and the primary precept of law below everything else in practical reason: he uses, that is, the expressions "founded on" ["fundatur supra"] and "based upon this" ["super hoc fundantur"]. But he combines that language with language that sees good as "an end" ["finem"] and as "what all things seek after" ["quod omnia appetunt"]. To invoke the image employed above, the ocean current goes toward its particular end, which is its good. Good, therefore, is primary, even with respect to the "primary precept of law."

Consideration of the relationship between the primary precept of law, which, like the principle of non-contradiction, involves combining and separating, and good, which is its simple "basis," allows one to see more clearly what Thomas means in ST 1–2.94.2 by the natural inclinations. A natural

---

together a proposition denying, for instance, that a whole is less than one of its parts. It is notable that, although at one point in ST 1–2.94.2 Thomas does speak of the basis as "being and not being," he subsequently returns to speaking simply of being [*ens*].

15 "[I]deo hoc etiam principium est naturaliter primum in secunda operatione intellectus, scilicet componentis et dividentis" [Thomas Aquinas, *In duodecim libros Metaphysicorum Aristotelis expositio* 4.6 §605].

16 As part of his argument against those who would deny the principle of non-contradiction, Aristotle includes some practical applications of the principle: "For why does a man walk to Megara and not stay at home thinking he ought to walk? Why does he not walk early some morning into a well or over a precipice, if one happens to be in his way? Why do we observe him guarding against this, evidently not thinking that falling in is alike good and not good? Evidently he judges one thing to be better and another worse. And if this is so, he must judge one thing to be man and another to be not-man, one thing to be sweet and another to be not-sweet" [*Metaphysics* 4.4.1008b14–20]. In his commentary on the passage, Thomas speaks of "good and not good" ["bonum et non bonum"] [Thomas Aquinas, *In duodecim libros Metaphysicorum Aristotelis expositio* 4.9 §655].

inclination is not just any inclination a person might experience. Another passage in Aristotle is useful in these regards. In *Metaphysics* 9.2, he writes as follows:

> And each of those [potentialities] which are accompanied by reason is alike capable of contrary effects, but one non-rational power produces one effect; e.g. the hot is capable only of heating, but the medical art can produce both disease and health. The reason is that science is a rational formula, and the same rational formula explains a thing and its privation, only not in the same way; and in a sense it applies to both, but in a sense it applies rather to the positive fact [*Metaphysics* 9.2.1046b4–10].

In commenting upon this passage, Thomas remarks:

> And so it is necessary, if a science is a certain understanding [*ratio*] of a thing known in the soul, that it be a science of contraries: of one, indeed, as prior and in itself [*secundum se*] but of the other as secondary. Medicine, for instance, is knowledgeable and operative primarily of health, but secondarily of infirmity, for, as already stated, this is about the understanding [*ratione*] of the thing known in the soul, which [understanding] is in itself [*secundum se*] about one of opposites and about the other accidentally.[17]

Medicine was "invented" in order to bring health to human bodies or to restore it. Had its purpose been ambiguous between pursuing health and pursuing infirmity, it would never have existed. For this reason an act that brings about not health but infirmity or even death to a human body is not the act of a medical doctor, no matter what the credentials might be of the person performing the act. To return briefly to the position of Alan Donagan, the same thing can be said of human language. Its essence consists in its capacity to speak and to communicate truth. Its capacity to speak falsely and to deceive is connected with its being a rational capacity, which is a capacity to combine concepts and to say truly, for instance, that A is B but also—although only accidentally—to separate A from B by saying falsely that A is not B.[18]

Those inclinations (of which rational animals are capable by virtue of being rational) that are not headed toward its good are not part of that "ocean

17 Thomas Aquinas, *In duodecim libros Metaphysicorum Aristotelis expositio* 9.2 §1790. For a fuller account of such ideas as they enter into Thomas's thought, see Kevin Flannery, "Reason and Being, Precepts and Good in Thomas Aquinas's Understanding of the Natural Law," in Maria Silvia Vaccarezza (ed), *Virtù, Legge e Fioritura Umana: Saggi in onore di Angelo Campodonico* (Mimesis 2021) 124–126.

18 Of course, the true statement may be the joining of A and not-B and the false statement their separation, stating that A is not not-B.

current"; only those inclinations that are headed toward that good are what Thomas speaks of repeatedly in ST 1–2.94.2 as "natural inclinations."

III. The Precepts of Natural Law Are Good

All this is confirmation of the idea that ST 1–2.94.2 is primarily about the natural law. In the present section examined are two attempts to read ST 1–2.94.2 in a way that turns one's attention away from its positive regard for natural law as law. Both attempts concern the translation—and so the understanding—of an admittedly dense or compacted sentence in the corpus. A couple of sentences before this sentence (which we can call "the compact sentence"), Thomas makes the point expounded just above: i.e., that good is the basis of all levels of practical reasoning.

> Now as *being* is the first thing that falls under apprehension simply speaking [*in apprehensione simpliciter*], so *good* is the first thing that falls under the apprehension of the practical reason, which is directed to action: since every agent acts for an end under the aspect of good.[19]

He goes on then to associate the first precept of practical reason—"that good is to be done and pursued, and evil is to be avoided"—with good itself, which is its basis:

> Consequently the first principle of practical reason is one founded on the notion of good, viz., that good is that which all things seek after. Hence this is the first precept of law, that good is to be done and pursued, and evil is to be avoided.

It is apparent that Thomas, in this part of the corpus, is interested in associating the first precept of practical reason—which, interestingly, he calls the "first principle of law" [*primum praeceptum legis*]—with good.

This association of good with a precept (and so with a law) does not take Thomas's argument in the direction that certain commentators would like it to go—those commentators, that is, who read ST 1–2.94.2 as primarily about inclinations and/or about the particular goods toward which the inclinations are directed. This line of thought influences their reading of the compact

19 I have altered the English Dominicans' translation slightly, eliminating the word "the" before the first mention of apprehension and translating *simpliciter* as "simply speaking." The apprehension of practical reason is simply a subdivision of apprehension simply speaking.

sentence, which comes immediately after Thomas's mention of the first precept of law. The Latin of the sentence runs as follows:

> Et super hoc fundantur omnia alia praecepta legis naturae, ut scilicet omnia illa facienda vel vitanda pertineant ad praecepta legis naturae, quae ratio practica naturaliter apprehendit esse bona humana.

The present author would translate this sentence in the following manner:

> And on this [the first precept of law] are founded all the other precepts of the law of nature, so that, that is, all those things that are to be done and avoided pertain to the precepts of the law of nature, which [precepts] practical reason apprehends naturally to be human goods.

A number of things might be said about this sentence. First of all, as we have just seen, Thomas has associated just previously the first precept of practical reason with good; here he does the same with respect to the plural precepts of the natural law—something he can do since they, too, are founded upon good. Secondly, Thomas's speaking at the end here of apprehension and good (with no mention of evil) is consistent with his previously articulated association of good with practical reason's apprehension, parallel as it is with his association of being with apprehension simply speaking [*apprehensio simpliciter*]. Apprehension is present before—and is the basis of—the joining and separating engaged in by practical reason.[20] The latter process involves propositions that can go wrong; simple apprehension, the criterion of the naturally good, cannot go wrong.[21] Thirdly, Thomas specifies that these precepts which practical reason "apprehends naturally" are human goods because he will go on to say that some of our inclinations—such as the inclination to preserve ourselves in being—are also found in non-rational beings. It needs to be stated that this does not make those inclinations (and their corresponding laws of nature) any less human, nor does it make those inclinations as present in non-rational beings human.

20 Thomas typically contrasts apprehension with "the operation of the intellect in joining and separating." See, for instance, [Thomas Aquinas, *In Aristotelis librum De anima commentarium* (Marietti 1948) 1.10 §164]: "Sic ergo intelligere, idest simplex apprehensio, et considerare, idest operatio intellectus quae est in componendo et dividendo . . .". In the same work see also, for instance, 2.12 §379, 3.5 §639, and 3.7 §672. In Thomas Aquinas, *In duodecim libros Metaphysicorum Aristotelis expositio*, see, for instance, 1.2 §46, 9.11 §1904 and 9.11 §1907.

21 See ST 1.82.1 and 1.79.12. In the *sed contra* ("On the contrary . . .") section of the latter, citing Aristotle's *Metaphysics* 9.2.1046b4–13, Thomas writes: "According to the Philosopher, rational powers regard opposite things. But synderesis does not regard opposites, but inclines to good only." On *synderesis*, see Kevin Flannery, "*Synderesis, Conscientia* and Human Rights," in Thomas Angier, Iain Benson, and Mark Retter (eds), *The Handbook on Natural Law and Human Rights* (CUP 2022).

The English Dominican translation that we have been using translates the compact sentence in the following manner:

> All other precepts of the natural law are based upon this: so that whatever the practical reason naturally apprehends as man's good (or evil) belongs to the precepts of the natural law as something to be done or avoided.

One notices here a number of things. First of all, and most noticeably, there is the addition in parentheses of the words "or evil," which correspond to nothing in the Latin text. One also notices that the plural bona humana has been rendered in the singular ("man's good"). This interpretation does correspond (more or less) to things that Thomas says elsewhere. As we have seen here in ST 1–2.94.2, when speaking of the most basic level in theoretical reason, he does at one point say that the principle of non-contradiction is "founded upon being and not-being" [*fundatur supra rationem entis et non entis*]. The English Dominicans' translation would, in effect, be saying that "good and not-good" somehow "belongs" to the first precepts of the natural law, which do have to do with what is to be done or avoided. The obvious problem, however, is that *bona humana* is plural and the words "or evil" do not appear in the text. Moreover, this interpretation overlooks the fact that practical reason is said to apprehend naturally that certain things are good. Naturally oriented apprehension looks toward good and not toward not-good, except accidentally. A more reasonable reading of the compact sentence understands Thomas to be saying that practical reason apprehends naturally as human goods the precepts of the law of nature. This idea is consistent with—and nearly equivalent to—saying that the natural law is one, but also plural.

Germain Grisez offers another translation of the compact sentence:

> All other precepts of the law of nature are based on this one [i.e., the first precept of law], in this way that under precepts of the law of nature come all those things-to-be-done or things-to-be-avoided which practical reason naturally grasps as human goods or their opposites.[22]

It is apparent here that Grisez does not want to understand Thomas as saying that precepts of the law of nature are "human goods," an expression Grisez employs later in the same article while speaking of the objects of inclinations.[23]

22 Grisez, "The First Principle of Practical Reason: A Commentary on the *Summa Theologiae* 1–2, question 94, article 2" 170.

23 "Within experience we have tendencies which make themselves felt; they point their way toward appropriate objects. These inclinations are part of ourselves, and so their objects are human goods" [Grisez, "The First Principle of Practical Reason: A Commentary on the *Summa Theologiae* 1–2, question 94, article 2" 180].

Accordingly, in his translation of ST 1–2.94.2, he associates the "which" of the final phrase, "which practical reason naturally grasps as . . .,"[24] with the "things-to-be-done or things-to-be-avoided."[25] This, however, presents a difficulty: "things-to-be-avoided" cannot be human goods. And so, similar to the English Dominicans' translation, he appends to the words "human goods" the words "or their opposites," which correspond to nothing in the text itself.

Conclusion

To conclude, then, as its title suggests, in ST 1–2.94.2, Thomas is primarily interested in showing that the natural law contains plural precepts but is also one. His reference to "natural inclinations," which is a category of inclinations smaller than that of the inclinations that a human being might experience, is in support of this primary concern. Useful in understanding the sense in which some inclinations are natural are a number of passages in Aristotle, especially in his *Metaphysics*. Just as being is at the basis of all theoretical reasoning and of the principle of non-contradiction, so good is at the basis (but also the aim of) all practical reasoning, which is in accordance with natural law and of the first precept of practical reason. It is because of this basis in good (as infallibly apprehended) that Thomas says in ST 1–2.94.2 that the precepts of the natural law (or "the precepts of the law of nature") are human goods.

24 ". . . quae ratio practica naturaliter apprehendit esse . . .".
25 ". . . illa facienda vel vitanda . . .".

6 John Finnis and Natural Law

Christopher Tollefsen

Introduction

John M. Finnis (born 1960) is an Australian legal philosopher who studied under H. L. A. Hart at Oxford, receiving his doctorate there in 1965 as a Rhodes Scholar. In addition to periods of teaching in the United States, England, Australia, and East Africa, he taught at Oxford University for over 40 years, retiring in 2010. In 1996, he began teaching as well at the University of Notre Dame as the Frances and Robert Biolchini Family Professor of Law, moving to emeritus status in 2020.

Finnis is the preeminent theorist of natural law jurisprudence in the late twentieth and early twenty-first centuries. He is also a central collaborator with Germain Grisez and Joseph Boyle in the movement in natural law thought often referred to as the "new natural law theory," though called by Finnis himself the "new classical natural law theory." In general, Finnis is more concerned with normative than descriptive jurisprudential theory. Nevertheless, he has argued for a methodological approach in the philosophy of law that sees "explanatory descriptive general theory of law and the moral justification and critique of law for the guidance of our own conscience [as] . . . radically inter-dependent intellectual enterprises."[1]

This chapter is divided into the following parts. In Part I, I summarize Finnis's methodological argument and approach. Part II presents an account of the "new" natural law ethical and political theory, and Part III gives special attention to Finnis's understanding of rights and the relationship of rights to justice and the common good. In Part IV, I turn to his account of the nature of law and his understanding of positive law and legal positivism. Part V discusses his views on the priority of persons and peoples to legal systems, an understanding of which is central to understanding Finnis's controversial views on a number of disputed moral, political, and legal issues. Part VI concludes with

1 John Finnis, "Positivism and 'Authority'" in *Collected Essays Vol IV Philosophy of Law* (Oxford University Press 2011) 82.

DOI: 10.4324/9781003728603-7

some brief points about Finnis's views on natural (non-revealed) theology, the good of religion, and the claims of the Roman Catholic Church.

I. Method in Philosophy of Law

Finnis's book *Natural Law and Natural Rights*, written at the invitation of Hart for his Clarendon Law Series and published in 1980, is considered a touchstone of the revival of natural law philosophy and natural law jurisprudence in the second half of the twentieth century. Finnis begins that book with a discussion of jurisprudential methodology. There is a difficulty that must be faced by any descriptive philosophical jurisprudence that attempts to answer the question central to analytic jurisprudence, "What is law?"

Much social science aspires to proceed by means of a value-free description of the phenomena under study, phenomena that include, for the social theorist, "human actions, practices, habits, dispositions and . . . human discourse."[2] Finnis argues that such actions, practices, etc., cannot be adequately understood or described without understanding their point, that is, the reasons people have for engaging in these actions, practices, etc. Hart similarly identifies the "internal point of view" of those engaged within the legal system, particularly judges, as methodologically essential for understanding such realities.

However, different people engage in these actions and practices for different reasons, and judges are not the only agents so engaged. A mere catalogue of such differing reasons across all relevant agents would be of little explanatory or theoretical interest. Descriptive social science, in this case, descriptive jurisprudence, is thus faced with the difficulty of identifying the point of view from which the reasons for the social phenomena can be identified.

Finnis argues in *Natural Law and Natural Rights* and elsewhere that the perspective from which law may be descriptively understood most adequately is that of the practically reasonable agent, the agent who, because practically reasonable, recognizes both the genuine needs for the satisfaction of which law is necessary and the central case of what law would be like were it adequately to satisfy those needs.

Thus, according to Finnis, there can be no fully adequate descriptive account of law and no answer to the question "What is law?" in the absence of a fully adequate theory of what it is that practical reason demands of human persons, acting individually and in community. However, such a theory would, in fact, be a theory of natural law, for the natural law is, on Finnis's account, simply the demands of practical reason itself.

Such a theory can, obviously, be pursued primarily for the sake of the "guidance of our own conscience," as those charged with making, following, enforcing, or adjudicating the law, or it can be pursued for the sake of an adequate explanatory understanding of the nature of law. As I have noted, Finnis does

2 John Finnis, *Natural Law and Natural Rights* (2nd edn, Oxford University Press 2011) 3.

not believe the latter project can succeed without the former. However, the former project does not proceed in a vacuum: it also must begin with the reflection on law as it is initially and descriptively known to us and be informed by the efforts of the social sciences to describe law. The two projects are, thus, to reiterate, "radically inter-dependent intellectual enterprises," and as so described, Finnis understands his methodology to be essentially Aristotelian.

II. Natural Law Ethics and Politics

The "new natural law" theory, of which Finnis was an early theorist and defender, holds (following the work of St Thomas Aquinas) that practical reason has its own first principles not known by inference from claims of theoretical reason.[3] These first principles direct agents to the pursuit of a finite number of "basic human goods," goods pursuable for their own sake. In *Natural Law and Natural Rights*, Finnis includes among these goods life, knowledge, play, aesthetic experience, sociability, practical reasonableness, and religion.[4] In subsequent work, Finnis has included marriage among the basic goods.[5]

Any "novelty" in this claim that would be such as to justify the adjective *new* in describing the theory comes by way of contrast with Neo-Scholastic theories of natural law and interpretations of Thomas Aquinas that have asserted an opposing claim about how the foundations of the natural law are known. On such Neo-Scholastic accounts, the principles of the natural law are derived, in the paradigm case, from a theoretical study of human nature. In Chapter II of *Natural Law and Natural Rights*, Finnis argues that any inference from "is" to "ought," such as would be required by the Neo-Scholastic approach, would be illicit and that such an approach is not found in Aquinas.

Rather, for Aquinas, the potentialities of nature are known through their actualizations, and actualizations are known through their objects. Thus, Aquinas directs us to understand human nature by means of understanding the objects—instances of basic goods—towards which we are directed by practical reason. Neo-Scholasticism is correct in holding as a metaphysical claim that our nature grounds our good, but gets wrong the epistemological order by which nature and good are known: our understanding of human nature flows in important part from our understanding of the goods that are the objects of practical reason's understanding.[6]

Additionally, whereas Neo-Scholastic approaches tended to ground the obligatory force of moral precepts on the divine will, Finnis, following his understanding of St. Thomas, holds a non-voluntaristic account of obligation

3 Germain Grisez, Joseph Boyle, and John Finnis, "Practical Principles, Moral Truth, and Ultimate Ends" (1987) 32 *The American Journal of Jurisprudence* 99.

4 Finnis (n 2) 85–90.

5 John Finnis, "Marriage: A Basic and Exigent Good" in *Collected Essays Vol III Human Rights and Common Good* (Oxford University Press 2011) 317–333.

6 John Finnis, *Aquinas: Moral, Political, and Legal Theory* (Oxford University Press 1998) Ch. II.

that is grounded in practical reason's demands. The publication of *Natural Law and Natural Rights* in 1980 thus occasioned considerable controversy among "traditional" defenders of Thomistic natural law theory,[7] controversy not yet entirely quelled.[8]

The basic goods identified by practical reason are incommensurable in goodness, both categorially, in relation to one another, and in the options for action they make possible, even within a category. For example, a physician might present two options to a patient, one of which might extend life at the cost of some increased morbidity, the other of which would diminish morbidity but bring a risk of dying sooner. Each option offers something in goodness and threatens something in the privation of goodness that is not found in the other; they are thus incommensurable in goodness.

This incommensurability of the goodness of options for free choice is central to Finnis's attack on consequentialism as a theory meant to guide choices. Finnis argues in *Natural Law and Natural Rights* that consequentialism is, strictly speaking, "senseless"; it follows that attempts to sum the goodness of options for choice are no more than rationalizations of choices that were made on other grounds. He argues further in *Moral Absolutes* that for Christians who believe in divine providence, the maximizing norm has as its implication "choose anything at all," since one can be confident that whatever one chooses, God will—in the end—bring the greatest possible good from that choice.[9]

While maximization of the good is thus an incoherent project, practical reason nevertheless can guide choice by attending fully to the goodness of the goods at stake in choice and the humanity of all persons affected by choice for the good. Immoral choices are those deflected by unreasonable emotions or preferences; morally upright choices are fully shaped by the normativity of the goods. Thus, in work co-authored with Boyle and Grisez, Finnis argues that the "first principle of morality" should be understood in the following way: "In voluntarily acting for human goods and avoiding what is opposed to them, one ought to choose and otherwise will those and only those possibilities whose willing is compatible with a will toward integral human fulfillment."[10]

Practical reason prescribing without error issues a number of very general prescriptions, which are to be understood as specifications of the even

7 Henry Veatch, "Natural Law and the 'Is-Ought' Question: Queries to Finnis and Grisez" in *Swimming Against the Current in Contemporary Philosophy* (Catholic University of America Press 1990) 293–311; Ralph McInerny, "The Principles of Natural Law" (1980) 25 *American Journal of Jurisprudence* 1.

8 Steven A. Long, "Fundamental Errors of New Natural Law Theory" (2013) 13 *National Catholic Bioethics Quarterly* 105.

9 John Finnis, *Moral Absolutes: Tradition, Revision, and Truth* (Catholic University of America Press 1991).

10 Grisez, Boyle, and Finnis (n 3) 128.

more general first principle of morality. Among these is a norm against ever intending, as a means or an end, harm or damage to an instance of a basic good. The obligations generated by this norm, such as the obligation never to intend the death of another human being, are moral absolutes and ground correlative absolute natural or human rights, such as the right not to be intentionally killed.

Other norms require fairness in the distribution of benefits and burdens in accordance with the Golden Rule, the following of conscience, and an adequate ordering of commitments to both goods and persons.

Because the goods cannot be adequately pursued individualistically, human persons must cooperate in their pursuit, forming communities acting for the sake of common goods that give a shared point to the community's existence and action. A foundational community is the family, but larger forms of community are necessary, as families must work, trade, intermarry, and worship with one another.

Finnis believes that in any community, some form of authority will be necessary when unanimity is not possible if decisions are to be made effectively. For the community formed by groups of overlapping communities, that authority will eventually be political: a plenary form of authority providing exclusionary reasons for action for citizens in order to solve coordination difficulties successfully, provide for common forms of defence, and address certain welfare needs.

That form of authority and the political community for which it is authoritative must be directed to that community's common good. Finnis has a distinctive understanding of the specifically political common good as something both limited and instrumental.[11] Finnis calls this aspect of a community's common good its "public good"; it is to be distinguished from the all-in common good of the society of persons for whom the public good is necessary but far from sufficient for organizing and understanding its common life, as well as from the "common goods" that are constituted by the basic human goods. Finnis's adoption of this more limited form of public good as the common good at which political authority rightly aims has led him to deny the permissibility of "purely paternalistic" morals legislation that aims to restrict purely self-regarding acts of vice. Finnis's student and collaborator, Robert P. George, has argued for a more expansive, paternalistic understanding of the limits of political authority.[12]

11 John Finnis, "Limited Government" in *Collected Essays Vol III Human Rights and Common Good* (Oxford University Press 2011) 83–106.

12 Robert P. George, *Making Men Moral: Civil Liberties and Public Morality* (Oxford University Press 1995).

III. Rights

Prominent among the components of the public good is the securing of justice; the demands of justice, according to Finnis, are, when viewed from the perspective of the recipients of the benefits of justice being done, the rights to which those recipients are entitled. As noted above, the most exigent of the demands of justice, captured in absolute moral norms, are correlative to equally exigent rights, which include the rights not to be intentionally killed, tortured, enslaved, raped, or, as is the case in certain forms of assisted reproduction, made as if a mere product and not a person.

Not every demand of justice is best expressed as a right correlative to a moral absolute. However, Finnis's conception of rights encourages a broader adoption of the language of rights into political discourse, for every relationship of justice imposes a duty on at least one member of a community in relation to another. The community may be narrow (e.g., the community of this seller and that buyer) or broad (e.g., the political community and, in broadest outline, the community of human persons). The duty might be to one person only, to a number of persons, or to all persons. However, in each case, the relationship of justice in which something is owed by the one who has an obligation can also be viewed from the perspective of the beneficiary of that owing. It is from this perspective that what is owed in justice can be understood as a matter of right and of "rights." Thus, in a well-known description from *Natural Law and Natural Rights*, Finnis writes,

> In short, the modern vocabulary and grammar of rights is a many-faceted instrument for reporting and asserting the requirements and other implications of a relationship of justice from the point of view of the person(s) who benefits from that relationship. It provides a way of talking about "what is just" from a special angle: the viewpoint of the "other(s)" to whom something (including inter alia, freedom of choice) is owed or due, and who would be wronged if denied that something.[13]

The process of rational decision-making by which an appeal to rights is made properly action-guiding in a polity is called, by Finnis and others, the *specification* of rights. The essential first step of specification of rights is that two-term rights, such as, for example, a "right to health care," must be translated into three-term rights. Finnis provides further details of what must be accomplished in such a translation. Among other things, the following must be identified, i.e., specified: (1) the identity of the duty holder; (2) the content of the duty; this content must itself be specified, Finnis notes, in regards to the times, circumstances, and conditions in which the duty applies; (3) the identity of the right-holder; (4) the conditions under which the right can be lost or waived;

13 Finnis (n 2) 205.

(5) the remedies—themselves claim rights, liberties, or Hohfeldian powers—in case of non-performance; and (6) the liberties and also associated duties pertaining to the right-holder. However, we can here note: if the specification of a right-holder's claim-right(s) requires an identification of his duties, then that specification, in turn, leads to the specification of the claim rights of *others*. There is perhaps no natural stopping point here; the specification of rights in a polity must be systematic.

The upshot of such systematic specification of rights will be, of necessity, the identification of the limits of each claimable right. The system of specified rights must be coherent, for rights, as understood by Finnis, are dispositive. They are not simply considerations to be assessed by an agent but are rather authoritative reasons for acting in the ways specified by their correlative duties. Thus, in an adequately specified regime of rights, there cannot be a conflict of rights, but there will be limitations on rights claims. The sense of this is captured by the phrase, variations of which are common to the rights "manifesto" tradition, that the exercise of rights is not to be limited (with a qualification to be mentioned shortly) *save by what is necessary* to protect and preserve the exercise of the rights of others. Thus, a properly specified regime of rights will have no room for "conflicts of rights" and no need for "balancing" or "proportionality" between rights claims and other political necessities.

IV. Law

In Chapter X of *Natural Law and Natural Rights*, Finnis acknowledges the need for law to be coercive for human beings as they are. That coercion is exercised both in restoring the "distributively just balance of advantages between the criminal and the law-abiding"[14] and in preventing such imbalances from occurring in the first place. Nevertheless, there would remain a need for law, even in the absence of recalcitrance, as an authoritative yet impersonal and rule-governed and governing form of coordination.

Finnis identifies five features of legal order: (1) the law regulates its own creation, bringing "definition, specificity, clarity, and thus predictability" into human affairs by a system of rules that govern institutions even in those institutions' acts of creating law; (2) the law uses a special method of showing validity by reference to past valid enactments; (3) the law identifies conditions under which individuals can change their legal standing, e.g., by making contracts or sales; (4) the law brings predictability and stability to human affairs by treating past acts as giving now "sufficient and exclusionary" reasons for action; and (5) the law operates on an assumption of "no gaps," presuming that it provides an answer for every practical question.[15]

14 Ibid. 263.
15 Ibid. 266–270.

In keeping with the discussion of the previous two sections, all five features of the law, and especially perhaps (2) and (4), need to be pursued with a view to the public common good: the promotion of justice, the protection of rights, and the maintenance of peace. This raises a question about the relationship between the requirements of the natural law and positive law. Following Aquinas, Finnis argues that some norms of positive law are "derived" from norms of the natural law in a fairly straightforward way. Thus, both the natural law and positive law should track each other closely in regard to, e.g., norms prohibiting various forms of assault.

However, much of the law's coordinative work, much of the statutory work of defining offence regarding the first type of case, and all the law's work defining punishment for the offence is constituted by what Aquinas called *determinatio*. These are acts of, in one sense, sheer positivity on the part of the lawmaker, who must *decide* how the community will be ordered; yet, in another sense, they are acts governed by the natural law since *some* form of order must be chosen if the common good is to be adequately pursued, even if the particular form of order is considerably underdetermined by practical reason. For Aquinas, the relevant comparison is to the construction of a door frame: necessary to make entrance to a house possible and required to be sufficiently, but not too, tall and wide. However, within those parameters, it is a matter of sheer choice on the part of the architect whether to make this door in *this* tall, or *that*, *this* wide or *that*, much less to ornament it in this or that way.

Finnis argues in many places that the emerging picture is one that captures the importance of positive law as possessing *prima facie* both legal and moral authority.[16] Law enacted in the way required by law will be legally binding even if deficient from the standpoint of natural law; yet such law will truly be deficient, not just morally speaking but considered precisely as law. Thus, the sense to be given to the claim often ascribed to natural law theorists that *lex iniusta non est lex* is parallel to that of "an invalid argument is no (real) argument" or "a false friend is no (genuine) friend." There is no contradiction of the sort alleged by some legal positivists (including Hart), who hear the word *law* in the phrases "unjust law" and "no law" as univocal and thus hear *lex iniusta non est lex* as saying, incoherently, "some law is not law."

Having made these points about positivity in law, Finnis is typically impatient with "positivism" as a legal theory:

> Positivism never coherently reaches beyond reporting attitudes and convergent behaviour (perhaps the sophisticated and articulate attitudes that constitute a set of rules of recognition, change and adjudication). It has nothing to say to officials or private citizens who want to judge

16 Finnis (n 1).

> whether, when, and why the authority and obligatoriness claimed and enforced by those who are acting as officials of a legal system, and by their directives, are indeed authoritative reasons for their own conscientious action. Positivism, at this point, does no more than repeat (i) what any competent lawyer—including every legally competent adherent of natural law theory—would say are (or are not) intrasystemically valid laws, imposing "legal requirements" and (ii) what any streetwise observer would warn are the likely consequences of non-compliance. Positivism is . . . redundant.[17]

Finnis thus thinks we should cease talking about positivism as a *legal theory*.

By contrast with a manifestly unjust law, law enacted in the way required by law and serving the common good, at least generally and for the most part, will typically be authoritative for its subjects' deliberations about what may, must, or must not be done in accordance with law. Even when, as is certainly possible, law disfavors some particular individual's interests here and now, such individuals typically have a moral obligation to obey in light of the contribution that the law makes as a whole to the welfare of its subjects.[18] In the 1980s, Finnis engaged in an extended debate with his long-time Oxford colleague Joseph Raz about the authority of law; on Finnis's account, law possesses a general and more extensive authority than is entailed by Raz's "service account."[19]

On Finnis's understanding, law will possess a number of properties when it is in good working order. Those qualities identified in representative discussions of the Rule of Law include prospectivity, compliability, promulgation, clarity, coherence, and so on. A legal order with the virtues of the Rule of Law is thereby one in which individuals are enabled to be selves, to "create a subsisting identity across a 'lifetime.'"[20] This "self-constitution" is a central theme in both of Finnis's ethical and political writings.

17 John Finnis, "On the Incoherence of Legal Positivism" (2000) 75 *Notre Dame Law Review* 1598, 1611.

18 John Finnis, "Law's Authority and Social Theory's Predicament" in *Collected Essays: Volume IV Philosophy of Law* (Oxford University Press 2011) 46–65; Finnis (n 11).

19 John Finnis, "The Authority of Law in the Predicament of Contemporary Social Theory" (1984) 1 *Notre Dame Journal of Law, Ethics, and Public Policy* 115; Joseph Raz, "The Obligation to Obey: Revision and Tradition" (1984) 1 *Notre Dame Journal of Law, Ethics, and Public Policy* 139; John Finnis, "Law as Coordination" in *Collected Essays: Volume IV Philosophy of Law* (Oxford University Press 2011) 66–73.

20 Finnis (n 2) 272.

The Rule of Law has limits on Finnis's account, which I turn to in the next section. I close this section by noting Finnis's lengthy definition of law in its "focal" meaning:[21]

> [T]he term "law" has been used with a focal meaning so as to refer primarily to rules made, in accordance with regulative legal rules, by a determinate and effective authority (itself identified and, standardly, constituted as an institution by legal rules) for a "complete" community, and buttressed by sanctions in accordance with the rule-guided stipulations of adjudicative institutions, this ensemble of rules and institutions being directed to reasonably resolving any of the community's co-ordination problems (and to ratifying, tolerating, regulating, or overriding co-ordination solutions from any other institutions or sources of norms) for the common good of that community.[22]

This definition converges with Aquinas's more concise definition of law as an "ordinance of reason, made by one with authority, promulgated, and serving the common good." Finnis thus identifies his account of law as not simply a natural law account but a more specifically Thomistic natural law account.

V. Priority of Persons and Peoples

In "The Priority of Persons Revisited," Finnis reiterates a point made in an earlier essay, "The Priority of Persons": "[P]ersons are the most important part of law's concerns and law's nature."[23] Thus, the law is for the sake of human persons and their well-being. Five points may be made about this priority.

First, this sense of the priority of persons is lost when law loses sight of some persons: black slaves, for example, or unborn children today. So, the priority of persons for the law requires of law that it take notice of the natural personhood of all human beings and what is necessary, as detailed earlier in this chapter, for their well-being. The guiding importance of persons and their equal dignity has been manifest in Finnis's writings on the rights of unborn human beings and the wrongs of euthanasia, as well as national policies of nuclear deterrence.[24]

Second, the priority of persons requires that the well-known and justified acknowledgement by the law of artificial (e.g., corporate) persons be

21 Ibid. 276.

22 Ibid. 276.

23 John Finnis, "The Priority of Persons Revisited" (2013) 58 *American Journal of Jurisprudence* 45.

24 Finnis, Boyle, and Grisez (n 3); John Finnis, "Euthanasia, Morality, and Law" (1998) 31 *Loyola University of Los Angeles Law Review* 1123; John Finnis, "The Rights and Wrongs of Abortion" in *Collected Essays: Volume III Human Rights and Common Good* (Oxford University Press 2011) 282–306.

understood in terms of the priority of those natural persons and their ends, for, as Finnis quotes Hohfeld, "transacting business under the forms, methods, and procedures pertaining to so-called corporations is simply another mode by which ***individuals*** or ***natural persons*** enjoy their property and engage in business."[25]

Third, the priority of persons enables us to see that the law is founded upon acts of persons. Finnis holds that legal rules should thus ultimately be understood in terms of the person-to-person relationship that exists between those who are subject to and beneficiary of the rules and those whose judicial acts in the past give reason now to those subject to those rules.

Fourth, we can call those natural persons who are bound together by a shared culture, history, sympathies, traditions, etc. *peoples*. Peoples, as a reality, also have a kind of priority for Finnis as an object of concern for the law. That concern warrants, for example, legal rules restricting immigration so as to maintain the bonds of the common culture, history, sympathy, tradition, etc., that Finnis thinks are necessary for maintaining the rule of law.[26]

Fifth, the continued existence of a people makes available an understanding of the continued existence of law across discontinuities, most prominently revolution.[27] Thus, the priority of persons and of peoples bears a significant explanatory role in Finnis's account of the nature of law.

VI. Religion and God

Three of Finnis's four major single-authored books, *Natural Law and Natural Rights*, *Fundamentals of Ethics*, and *Aquinas: Moral, Political and Legal Theory*, conclude with a discussion of the existence of a divine creator and the relationship that human persons should stand in regard to that divine creator. Finnis argues in *Natural Law and Natural Rights* and elsewhere that the contingency of the world's existence coupled with the fact of its existence requires, for an explanation, the existence of a necessarily existing being that, in some sense analogous to human choices, chooses freely to create. Because the being's existence is necessary, it requires no further explanation for its existence; because the being's creativity is freely chosen, the contingency of the created world is respected in the explanation of why it exists.

The existence of such a freely choosing being, whose choice to create could not have emerged from any needs of that being, raises the question of what purpose for us that being might have created and the further question of

25 John Finnis, "The Priority of Persons" in *Collected Essays: Volume II Intention and Identity* (Oxford University Press 2011) 30.

26 John Finnis, "Universality, Personal and Social Identity, and Law" (Oxford Legal Studies Research Paper No 05/2008, 2008), https://papers.ssrn.com/sol3/papers.cfm?abstract_id=1094277.

27 John Finnis, "Revolutions and Continuity of Law" in *Collected Essays: Volume IV Philosophy of Law* (Oxford University Press 2011) 407–435.

whether that being might have communicated the contents of its plan, and further aspects of its nature and character to human beings.

Finnis has argued in a number of places that not only can the existence of this being be known by reason, but that human persons can also judge by reason amongst the various testimonies alleged to report that being's communication. Looking both at the character of the message, of the messenger and of those who offer testimony to the messenger, Finnis has argued that only (Catholic) Christianity plausibly indicates the *full content* of a divine revelation to human persons (see generally Part Two of Finnis's 2011 Collection, *Religion and Public Reasons*). Thus, Finnis continuously objects to any strong contrast between religion and reason or "public reason." The judgments of reason in this domain *precede* submission of mind and will in the act of faith to a revealing God.

At the same time, Finnis has defended a robust conception of religious liberty. That liberty is not a Hohfeldian liberty, i.e., an absence of a duty, for one might very well have a moral duty not to act in accordance with a false religion. It is rather a claim right to immunity from coercion, grounded in the need for religious assent to be free if it is to be meaningful. Is it, then, impermissible for a state to proclaim as true the true religion? Finnis argues, in "Religion and State," that such proclamation could perhaps be permissible so long as it is accompanied by no exclusions from office due to religious or non-religious affiliation and by no attempts at coercion of those who do not follow the true religion.

A final remark: in *Natural Law and Natural Rights*, Finnis asks whether there might be some "further point" to morality and a life lived in accordance with the prescriptions of right reason. Following Plato, Finnis suggests that the divine creation is analogous to human play. "Hence, for one who goes beyond Plato to accept that man is called to a friendship of devotion to God will grant that such friendship takes the form of sharing, in a limited way, in the divine play."[28] Such a form of sharing does give additional reason for, and heightened significance to, the life of practical reasonableness that Finnis believes is desired for us by our divine creator and which must be sought if we are to cooperate with that creator in its purposes adequately.

28 Finnis (n 2) 409.

Part II

Legal Positivism

7 Law as It Is

An Introduction to Legal Positivism

Mir Ahmad Murtiza

I. Introduction

Legal positivism, in its competition with natural law theory,[1] presents an alternative account of the central questions concerning the nature of law. The image of law that legal positivism seeks to offer is essentially social or factual.[2] In other words, it views law as the product of social practice. On this account, the law is a human artefact resulting from human actions conventionally recognised as legally significant. Legal positivism places a significant emphasis on this social or factual character of law. It is the social or positive character of law that legal positivism regards as the most important and distinguishing feature of law, and on which it believes a suitable theory of law must be founded.[3]

For legal positivists, the validity of a legal rule depends on social facts (such as the fact of having been posited by socially constructed institutions like legislatures and courts) and is independent of the quality of its content.[4] Within this framework, the questions of validity or invalidity of a legal rule are settled by the internal logic of the legal system. The legal character of any normative rule is contingent on it having been laid down by any competent body or being part of a practice recognised by the legal system as a valid source of legal norms. Legal positivism insists on distinguishing the law from other categories

1 For a discussion on differences and discourse between natural law theory and legal positivism, see R. D. Lumb, 'Natural Law and Legal Positivism' (1959) 11 *Journal of Legal Education* 503; Deryck Beyleveld and Roger Brownsword, 'The Practical Difference Between Natural-Law Theory and Legal Positivism' (1985) 5 *Oxford Journal of Legal Studies* 1; Barney Reynolds, 'Natural Law Versus Positivism: The Fundamental Conflict' (1993) 13 *Oxford Journal of Legal Studies* 441; Brian Bix, 'On the Dividing Line Between Natural Law Theory and Legal Positivism' (2000) 75 *Notre Dame Law Review* 1615; Mehmet Ruhi Demiray, 'Natural Law Theory, Legal Positivism, and the Normativity of Law' (2015) 20 *European Legacy* 807.

2 Leslie Green and Thomas Adams, 'Legal Positivism' in Edward N. Zalta (ed), *The Stanford Encyclopedia of Philosophy* (Winter 2019 edn), https://plato.stanford.edu/archives/win2019/entries/legal-positivism/ accessed March 7, 2025.

3 Julie Dickson, 'Legal Positivism: Some Contemporary Debates' in Andrei Marmor (ed), *The Routledge Companion to Philosophy of Law* (Routledge 2012).

4 Green and Adams (n 2).

DOI: 10.4324/9781003728603-9

of norms that claim to guide human conduct, i.e., morality, religious tenets, rules of social etiquette, etc. Consequently, it outrightly rejects the claims of those natural law theorists that bind the validity of legal rules with the truth of some corresponding moral prepositions[5] or deny the possibility of any sharp conceptual differentiation between law and morality.[6] The central contention of legal positivism can be summed up in the classic dictum of John Austin:

> The existence of law is one thing; its merit and demerit another. Whether it be or be not is one enquiry; whether it be or be not conformable to an assumed standard, is a different enquiry.[7]

Legal positivism, or similar ways of thinking about law, has a rich historical lineage deeply embedded in the jurisprudential discourse. The early hints of such thinking can be traced back to the writings of various philosophers of Greece and Rome.[8] However, the organised philosophical reflection on the positive character of law began to take shape in the twelfth century among the theological humanists of Paris and Chartres.[9] Some scholars attribute the origins of positivist thinking much later to the figure of Thomas Hobbes (died 1679).[10]

There is a great variety of theses associated with legal positivism, and what constitutes the details of these theses is far from settled. Not only do the central theses of legal positivism remain contentious, but the very way this philosophical enterprise is to be undertaken is also controversial. In this chapter, we will try to stay aloof from the internal disagreements of the legal positivist school and attempt to introduce some of the major themes that dominate the jurisprudential debates (with a focus on English language jurisprudence). Following is such an attempt.

5 Michael S. Moore, 'Law as a Functional Kind' in Robert P. George (eds), *Natural Law Theory: Contemporary Essays* (Clarendon Press 1994). Also see Philip Soper, 'In Defense of Classical Natural Law in Legal Theory: Why Unjust Law Is No Law at All' (2015) 20 *Canadian Journal of Law and Jurisprudence* 201.

6 Philip Soper, 'Some Natural Confusions About Natural Law' (1992) 90 *Michigan Law Review* 2393.

7 John Austin, *The Province of Jurisprudence Determined* (Wilfrid E. Rumble ed, CUP 1995) 157.

8 Gerald J. Postema, 'Legal Positivism: Early Foundations' in Andrei Marmor (ed), *The Routledge Companion to Philosophy of Law* (Routledge 2012).

9 John Finnis, 'Truth in Legal Positivism' in Robert P. George (ed), *The Autonomy of Law: Essays on Legal Positivism* (OUP 1999).

10 Brian H. Bix, 'Legal Positivism' in Martin P. Golding and William A. Edmundson (eds), *The Blackwell Guide to the Philosophy of Law and Legal Theory* (Blackwell 2005).

II. Positivist Concepts of Law: Hart and Kelsen

The primary objective of legal theory is to construct the most accurate concept of law. Concepts are philosophical creations[11] that are constructed to capture the essential features of the objects of which they are concepts. Nevertheless, concepts are not equivalent to objects; they lie, as Raz writes, 'between words and their meanings, in which they are expressed, on the one side, and the nature of things to which they apply, on the other.'[12] The process of concept formation involves a judgment about what is essential to the nature of the object, and this judgment is guided by deeper ontological and epistemological considerations. One way of distinguishing legal positivism from natural law theory may be to see what these theories regard as essential to the nature of their object of study. Natural law theory views law essentially as a subset of practical reasoning delineated from the larger domain of practical reasoning by virtue of having been *promulgated* by a competent positive authority charged with the care of the political community.[13] On the other hand, legal positivism treats law as a fundamentally empirical phenomenon, a factual system of norms that is prevalent in a particular community and holds preeminent significance in people's practical deliberations. For positivists, to have an accurate concept of law is to know how social practices give rise to legal systems. In the following, we briefly discuss the salient features of attempts by H. L. A. Hart and Hans Kelsen to construct a positivist concept of law.

(A) H. L. A. Hart

H. L. A. Hart is one of the most influential thinkers in the history of contemporary legal thought. His magnum opus, *The Concept of Law* (1961), reshaped the entire legal positivist tradition, and the roots of much of what is discussed in contemporary jurisprudential debates trace back to it.[14] Hart regarded this work as 'an essay in descriptive sociology'[15] and called for 'a sharpened awareness of words to sharpen our perception of the phenomena.'[16] Hart espoused a method that emphasised empirical analysis of the social phenomenon of law and deemed the examination of the meaning of words used to talk about this phenomenon crucial to this project. The inquiry into the meanings of

11 Joseph Raz, 'Two Views of the Nature of the Theory of Law: A Partial Comparison' (1998) 4 *Legal Theory* 249.

12 Joseph Raz, 'Can There Be a Theory of Law' in Martin P. Golding and William A. Edmundson (eds), *The Blackwell Guide to the Philosophy of Law and Legal Theory* (Blackwell 2005) 325.

13 Here, 'promulgat[ion] by a competent positive authority' may be taken in a broader sense to include any positive process of laying specific legal rules under the guidance of natural law standards.

14 Bix (n 10) 32.

15 H. L. A. Hart, *The Concept of Law* (Penelope A. Bulloch and Joseph Raz eds, Clarendon Press 1994) Preface (henceforth *CL*).

16 Ibid. Here, Hart is referring to the method of J. L. Austin.

words helps clarify distinctions or similarities between various sorts of social situations or relationships or better appreciate the nuances in the character of the same social situation or relationship.[17] For Hart, a critical examination of the language of legal concepts not only offers linguistic clarifications but also grants valuable insights into the nature of law.

The starting point for Hart's theory of law is his critique of the command theories of Jeremy Bentham and John Austin, particularly of the latter. Command theory provided a simplistic concept of law as a command of the sovereign backed by sanction. Hart criticised the command theory for being 'over-simple' and failing to explain many of the important aspects of the legal system.[18] Notably, Hart took exception to its alleged overlooking of the element of obligation that is essential to the concept of law. He clarified it by distinguishing '*being obliged*' and '*being under obligation*.'[19] Social situations may arise in which one may be obliged to behave or shun certain behaviours without necessarily being under any obligation. For instance, a robber threatens to kill a traveller if he does not hand over his valuables to the robber. The traveller is likely to comply with the command of the robber if he does not have any means at his disposal to ward off the lethal attack of the robber. In this situation, the traveller's likely obedience to the robber's command is motivated by his desire to prevent any kind of harm or unpleasant consequence, but it cannot be said that the traveller is under any obligation to hand over his valuables to the robber. Hart contended that command theory views the legal system as a robber's writ enlarged and, therefore, fails to explain the obligatory character of law adequately.[20]

According to Hart, the obligatory character of law can be satisfactorily explained by viewing it in terms of a rule. The rule involves a 'combination of regular conduct with a distinctive attitude to that conduct as a standard.'[21] Rules are standards of conduct that are held by the community as obligatory and are used to judge those who deviate from them. However, not all rules are necessarily obligatory. For instance, rules of grammar or social etiquette are rules, but they do not carry the sense of obligation commonly attached to legal rules. The obligation arises 'when the general demand for conformity is insistent and the social pressure brought to bear upon those who deviate or threaten to deviate is great.'[22] Different forms of pressure sustain different forms of rules, and for Hart, a rudimentary form of law may be said to arise when social pressure sustaining a rule takes the form of physical sanctions.

17 Ibid.
18 Ibid. 79.
19 Ibid. 82.
20 Ibid.
21 Ibid. 85.
22 Ibid. 86.

Hart's introduction of the concept of *legal rules* was a crucial advancement over the theoretical framework of Bentham and Austin.

Furthermore, Hart censured the command theorists for overlooking the internal aspect of the legal system, which he deemed crucial to appreciate the obligatory character of law fully. A theorist who takes an external point of view on a legal rule merely describes its objective existence. In contrast, one who participates in that legal system and views the law from an internal point of view does not merely recognise its objective existence but accepts it as a standard and a ground for criticism and justification of actions.[23] Hart argues that the challenge for a legal theorist is to 'remember the presence of both these points of view and not to define one of them out of existence,'[24] for to do so would be to 'miss out a whole dimension of social life of those whom he is watching.'[25] Therefore, while describing the empirical existence of legal rules, a theorist should also fully appreciate the view that participants of the legal system take towards these legal rules. This view is called the hermeneutic view.[26]

For Hart, law is essentially a 'union of primary and secondary rules,'[27] and it is in the combination of these two types of rules that the 'key to the science of jurisprudence' is to be found.[28] Primary rules are obligation-imposing rules addressed to individuals to regulate their behaviour. One can imagine a society with only primary rules of obligation sustained by the social pressure of the community. In such a society, if anyone attempts to transgress, they will be met with hostile reactions and criticism and will be disciplined. However, such a situation is only possible in a small community bound by 'ties of kinship, common sentiment, and belief,' which is 'placed in a stable environment' and in which the majority of the inhabitants subscribe to these rules.[29] In larger and more complex societies, maintaining an orderly existence solely by the reign of primary rules will encounter several hurdles. First, the rules of the community will be a set of disparate rules and will not form a system. There will be no common feature or property the possession of which will establish the membership of the rule in the set of primary rules of the community. Such a situation will create much *uncertainty* in the identification of law on any matter. Second, the rules of the community will be *static*. In the absence of any formal legislative authority, a new rule will take much time to be entrenched enough to be followed by all as a standard. Third, it will be difficult to assess

23 Ibid. 98.
24 Ibid. 91.
25 Ibid. 90.
26 For more discussion on 'internal point of view,' see Brian Bix, 'H.L.A. Hart and the Hermeneutic Turn in Legal Theory' (1999) 52 *SMU Law Review* 167; Scott J. Shapiro, 'What Is the Internal Point of View?' (2006) 75 *Fordham Law Review* 1157.
27 *CL* 79.
28 Ibid. 81.
29 Ibid. 92.

whether any rule is violated. It will foster *inefficiency* in the administration of social pressure or other forms of sanctions for maintaining rules.[30]

Hart argued that the remedy to each of these problems lies in supplementing primary rules of obligation with a different kind of rules: secondary rules. Secondary rules are *meta-rules* that resolve the issues of uncertainty, staticity, and inefficiency by identifying, creating, modifying, and adjudicating primary rules. He enumerated three kinds of secondary rules: (1) *rule of recognition*, (2) *rules of change*, and (3) *rules of adjudication*.[31] Rule of recognition is a secondary rule that 'specif[ies] some feature or features possession of which by a suggested rule is taken as a conclusive affirmative indication that it is a rule of the group to be supported by the social pressure it exerts.'[32] Rules of change are secondary rules that cure the rigidity of primary rules by empowering officials to create new rules or modify existing ones. Rules of adjudication are secondary rules that empower officials to issue authoritative determinations concerning any dispute regarding violation of any primary rule. Moreover, it also lays down the procedure that officials follow in the adjudicative processes. Secondary rules bestow *systemicity* to law. For Hart, introducing each of these secondary rules to resolve the issues besetting a community governed solely by primary rules is 'a step from the pre-legal into the legal world.'[33] A fully formed legal system emerges when the citizens generally obey the valid primary rules, and the rule of recognition is upheld in practice by the officials as the standard of official behaviour.[34]

Of the three secondary rules, the rule of recognition holds the most critical position in Hart's concept of law. It lays down the definitive standard that the officials of the legal system follow to judge the validity of any legal rule. It resolves the potential conflicts between various sources of legal rules by establishing an *order of superiority or inferiority* among them.[35] The other two secondary rules—the rule of change and the rule of adjudication—are intrinsically linked with the rule of recognition. The rule of recognition refers to the legislative criteria identified by the rule of change and also recognises the officials' adjudicative powers conferred on them by the rule of adjudication.[36] By identifying the criteria of validity, the rule of recognition engenders a cohesive unity in the structure of the legal system.

30 Ibid. 91–93.
31 Ibid. 94–97.
32 Ibid. 94.
33 Ibid.
34 Suri Ratnapala, *Jurisprudence* (CUP 2009) 53.
35 *CL* 95.
36 Ibid. 96. Also see Matthew H. Kramer, 'The Legal Positivism of H. L. A. Hart' in Torben Spaak and Patricia Mindus (eds), *The Cambridge Companion to Legal Positivism* (CUP 2021) 312–316.

Hart's attempt at the conceptualisation of legal reality reveals some salient features of the positivist enterprise.[37] Hart finds the law dependent on social facts. He insists on making a clear distinction between legal and non-legal norms and rejects the notion that laws must 'reproduce or satisfy certain demands of morality' in order to be valid.[38] He focuses on the empirical reality of law, but this focus is not limited to the mere recording of brute facts; rather, it is an interpretative reflection on how legal standards emerge in societies and are taken as normative guides by the people who are subject to them. In exploring the normative character of law, he is not interested in furnishing justification for any particular arrangement of the legal system but is only concerned with providing a reliable account of the way law actually guides the conduct of its subjects. This strand of legal positivism, with many clarifications, adornments, modifications, and extensions, remains influential in anglophone legal thought.

(B) Hans Kelsen

Hans Kelsen's legal thought represents another strand of legal positivism, though it is largely ignored in English legal literature,[39] which focuses primarily on debates springing from Hart's legal theory. Kelsen's legal theory is built on philosophical foundations entirely distinct from those of Hart and other theorists working in the British or American legal traditions. Nevertheless, this dissimilarity in philosophical underpinnings does not preclude points of intersection between the two strands.

Kelsen offers his 'pure theory of law' as a theory of positive law—one concerned with studying 'how the law is, not how it ought to be.'[40] Like other legal positivists, he rejects the necessity of any specific moral content for the validity of law. He denies the existence of a higher 'true law' that positive law ought to emulate.[41] What distinguishes his theory, however, is its emphasis on *purity*. Kelsen accuses traditional legal theorists of uncritically blending elements of psychology, sociology, ethics, and political theory with the science of law. Therefore, he seeks to purge from legal theory anything 'not strictly law.'[42]

37 For a detailed critical account of HLA Hart's legal and political philosophy, see John M. Finnis, 'H.L.A. Hart: A Twentieth-Century Oxford Political Philosopher' (2009) 54 *American Journal of Jurisprudence* 161; Matthew H. Kramer, *H.L.A Hart: The Nature of Law* (Polity Press 2018).

38 *CL* 186.

39 Iain Stewart, 'Hans Kelsen, Legal Scientist: Review Essay on Thomas Olechowski, Hans Kelsen: Biographie eines Rechtswissenschaftlers (Hans Kelsen: Biography of a Legal Scientist)' (2023) 48 *Journal of Legal Philosophy* 119.

40 Hans Kelsen, *Pure Theory of Law* (Max Knight tr, 2nd rev edn, University of California Press 1967, Lawbook Exchange reprint 2005) 1 (henceforth *PTL*).

41 Hans Kelsen, *General Theory of Law and State* (Harvard University Press 1949, Transaction reprint 2006) 416 (henceforth *GTLS*).

42 *PTL* 1.

This commitment to purity forms the 'methodological basis' of his work.[43] Kelsen writes:

> It is called a 'pure' theory of law because it only describes the law and attempts to eliminate from the object of this description everything that is not strictly law: Its aim is to free the science of law from alien elements.[44]

To maintain the purity of his concept of law, he seeks to distinguish law not only from morality but also from facts.[45] Law is not a fact but a norm. Norm is an interpretation of the legal practice. It exists in the Kantian realm of ideas rather than the empirical realm of facts.[46] Fact is what *is*, but the norm is what *ought to be*. While facts are caused by other facts, norms are validated by other norms. Statements of fact are either true or false, but norms are either valid or invalid. Kelsen's concept of law as a norm is underpinned by his commitment to maintaining the Humean distinction between '*is(fact)*' and '*ought(norm)*.' Physical acts belong to the realms of 'is' and cannot itself give rise to normative meaning. For example, the assembly of elected representatives of people in a specific place to debate and pass a statute or the delivery of judgment by the judge in the courtroom are facts, and their normative significance cannot be comprehended merely by observing these facts.[47] These facts attain normative meaning only when they are normatively interpreted within a particular scheme of interpretation. Similarly, the judgment that any instance of human behaviour is legal or illegal is also an act of interpretation. Kelsen writes:

> The norm functions as a scheme of interpretation. To put it differently: The judgment that an act of human behavior, performed in time and space, is 'legal' (or 'illegal') is the result of a specific, namely normative, interpretation.[48]

Norms create obligations by imputing sanctions to their breach. Kelsen's concept of norms is broad enough to encompass a wide variety of legal forms. A legal norm can command, prohibit, permit, or authorise. Kelsen defines norms as follows:

43 Ibid.
44 Ibid.
45 Ratnapala (n 34) 58.
46 For discussion on the Kantian dimensions of Kelsen's work, see Stanley L. Paulson, 'The Neo-Kantian Dimension of Kelsen's Pure Theory of Law' (1992) 12 *Oxford Journal of Legal Studies* 311; Michael S. Green, 'Hans Kelsen's Non-Reductive Positivism' in Torben Spaak and Patricia Mindus (eds), *The Cambridge Companion to Legal Positivism* (CUP 2021).
47 *PLT* 2–9.
48 Ibid. 4.

> 'Norm is the meaning of an act by which a certain behaviour is commanded, permitted or authorised.'[49]

Also, Kelsen remains faithful to the distinction between 'is' and 'ought' when discussing the validity of legal norms. By validity of legal norms, he means the 'specific existence' of a legal norm.[50] However, the existence of a norm is to be differentiated from the existence of a fact. Norm is not a concrete object to be found in the external world but is a result of the normative interpretation of legally significant facts. Norm is bestowed existence or validated by another higher norm, which is part of the system of norms that is by and large effective. It helps to differentiate the legal system from the robber's writ enlarged. A robber's demand may be coercive like law and may even solicit compliance, but it cannot be a specimen of valid law, for the norms of a legal system do not authorise it. Kelsen writes:

> Now, the question arises: What is the reason of the validity of a definite norm, that is the question: why ought we to behave in conformity with a definite norm? The answer to this question can never be an 'is'-statement, the statement of a fact; it can be only an 'ought'-statement, the statement of a norm. In other words: the reason of the validity of a norm can never be a fact, even not the act of will by which the norm is created; it can be only a norm, another, a higher norm.[51]

Kelsen conceives the legal system as a web of norms in which each norm derives its validity from a higher norm. This chain of validation continues until it reaches a norm that is not validated by any higher norm. This foundational norm, which must be presupposed to make sense of the legal system, is called the *Grundnorm* (basic norm).[52] For example, the norm that murder ought to be punished is a valid norm because it is contained in the criminal statute, which is valid because the parliament makes it through due procedure. The laws made by the parliament are valid because the parliament is authorised to make laws by the constitution. The constitution is valid because it was declared by some kind of constituent assembly (in the case of constitutions having democratic origins) or by a leader wielding effective political power (in the case of constitutions having non-democratic origins). What is the source of the validity of the original constituent act of a constituent assembly or an effective leader? For Kelsen, the validity of this original constituent act is to be presupposed.

49 Ibid. 5.
50 *GTLS* 30.
51 Hans Kelsen, 'On the Basic Norm' (1959) 47 *California Law Review* 107, 107–108.
52 Ibid. 108.

The idea of the basic norm is central to Kelsen's pure theory of law. Most importantly, it helps maintain Kelsen's commitment to the distinction between 'is' and 'ought.' The basic norm provides a non-reductive explanation for the validity of law, which is necessary to avoid conflating 'is' and 'ought.'[53] The validity of legal norms cannot be based on any factual arrangement but must instead depend on validation by a higher norm, which is itself validated by another higher norm. However, this chain of validation cannot continue indefinitely, and at some point, a norm that is not validated by any higher norm must be presupposed. It is presupposed because of the possibility of lower norms ascribing normative meaning to acts and events. In other words, it is presupposed by the assumption of the validity of lower norms.[54] It serves as the foundation of the interpretative framework that assigns objective normative meaning to the factual domain of legal acts and events and allows the law to be viewed as an autonomous normative order distinct from other normative and factual domains. In this sense, Kelsen refers to it as the 'transcendental-logical presupposition' of legal cognition.[55] However, Kelsen's emphasis on is-ought distinction should not be taken to mean that pure theory is oblivious to social practice. *Grundnorm* is not the transcendental-logical presupposition of any order but only of a legal order that is, by and large, effective within a given territory.[56]

Furthermore, like Hart's rule of recognition, the basic norm captures the *systematicity* of the legal system.[57] Pure theory's notion of the systematicity of law can be understood by Kelsen's two postulates.[58]

1. All norms of a system derive their validity from the one basic norm.
2. Two norms belong to the same legal system if they derive their authority from the same basic norm.

Kelsen's pure theory has influenced various areas of legal studies and remains a viable alternative to Hart's legal positivism. It directly engages with one of the most challenging problems for legal positivism: how can a system of facts give rise to valid obligations without recourse to any higher normative order,

53 Andrei Marmor, 'The Pure Theory of Law' in Edward N. Zalta (ed), *The Stanford Encyclopedia of Philosophy* (Fall 2021 edn), https://plato.stanford.edu/archives/fall2021/entries/lawphil-theory/ accessed March 8, 2025.

54 Kelsen (n 51) 108.

55 *PTL* 201.

56 Ibid.

57 *GTLS* 111 ('All norms whose validity may be traced back to one and same basic norm form a system of norms, or an order. This basic norm constitutes, as a common source, the bond between all different norms of which an order consists').

58 For criticism of these postulates, see Joseph Raz, 'Kelsen's Theory of Basic Norm' (1974) 19 *American Journal of Jurisprudence* 84; Andrei Marmor, *Philosophy of Law* (Princeton University Press 2011) 15–20.

such as natural law? However, to what extent it is successful in meeting this challenge is open to doubt.

III. Two Theses on Legal Positivism

Defining the nature of legal positivism is an inherently difficult task because there is a wide variety of claims that are propagated in the name of legal positivism, and there is no uniformity of belief or outlook in the work of those who oppose legal positivism.[59] However, of all the theses associated with the school of legal positivism, two warrant serious attention for at least two reasons. First, these are shared by almost all prominent legal positivists. Second, these theses are considered suitable candidates for a consistent positivist theory of law. These theses are the *social thesis* and the *separability thesis*.[60] Following is a brief elaboration of these two theses.

(A) Social Thesis

Social thesis, stated broadly, means that 'what counts as law in any particular society is fundamentally a matter of social fact or convention.'[61] Joseph Raz coined this term to describe what he claimed has always been at the 'foundation of positivist thinking about the law.'[62] According to the social thesis, law is essentially the product of social facts—a product of socially constructed institutions such as legislatures, courts, etc. Moreover, it implies that the validity and content of legal rules are to be determined by the social facts without any necessary recourse to the moral argument (further discussed in the next section). Therefore, a suitable theory of law must remain committed to a descriptive and neutral analysis of legal institutions without regard to their morality or any other kind of merit.[63] It also excludes from the purview of legal theory the provision of justifications for any particular arrangement of the legal system or the discovery of standards on the basis of which the propriety or impropriety of any law or legal system may be judged.

The social thesis has played a guiding role in the construction of positivist theories. For example, Bentham, Austin, Hart, and Kelsen follow this thesis in their own ways. While Bentham and Austin reduce legality to the fact of having been willed by an effective sovereign, Hart tries to develop a more

59 Joseph Raz, *The Authority of Law* (2nd edn, OUP 2009) 37.

60 Jules L. Coleman and Brian Leiter, 'Legal Positivism' in Dennis Patterson (ed), *A Companion to Philosophy of Law and Legal Theory* (2nd edn, Blackwell 2010). Raz also includes these theses in the list of three theses most commonly associated with legal positivism. He calls them the *social thesis* and the *moral thesis*, respectively. See Raz (n 59) 37.

61 Coleman and Leiter (n 60) 228.

62 Raz (n 59) 41.

63 Andrei Marmor, 'Legal Positivism: Still Descriptive and Morally Neutral' (2006) 26 *Oxford Journal of Legal Studies* 683.

comprehensive account of the complex ways in which legal rules develop out of social practices. Hart's rule of recognition is a social rule. It arises out of the legal officials' treatment of some features or features of the rule as the conclusive criteria of validity.[64] In a sense, Kelsen's basic norm also has a social character. It is derived from the social fact of citizens' treatment of certain acts and events as normative.[65]

(B) Separability Thesis

Legal positivism admits that law is a deeply moral phenomenon. Hart concedes that there are 'many different types of relation between law and morals' and that conventional morality plays a crucial role in the development of law.[66] However, he rejects the idea that 'the criteria of legal validity of particular laws used in a legal system must include, tacitly if not explicitly, a reference to morality or justice.'[67] For Hart, legal positivism means 'the simple contention that it is no sense a necessary truth that laws reproduce or satisfy certain demands of morality, though in fact they have often done so.'[68] This position has been termed the separability thesis of legal positivism. According to the separability thesis, morality or justice is not a necessary element of the criteria of legal validity, and the immorality or injustice of any law does not preclude it from counting as law.[69] For example, Nazi laws in Germany, Jim Crow laws in the United States, or the apartheid laws in South Africa may be grossly unjust, but they were still laws. Moreover, it also seeks to maintain a conceptual differentiation between law and morality. It simply holds that despite many overlaps, law and morality are still *separable*.[70]

The principal insight of the separability thesis is that laws may be bad or good because goodness is not essential to the nature of law. Raz explains:

> [T]he moral value of law (both of a particular law and of a whole legal system) or the moral merit it has is a contingent matter dependent on the content of the law and the circumstances of the society to which it applies.[71]

Recently, some legal positivists have tended to discount the importance of the separability thesis as one of the main theses of legal positivism. However,

64 Bix (n 10) 35.
65 Ibid.
66 *CL* 185.
67 Ibid.
68 Ibid. 185–186.
69 For a classic assertion of this thesis, see H. L. A. Hart, 'Positivism and the Separation of Law and Morals' (1958) 71 *Harvard Law Review* 593.
70 Jules L. Coleman, 'Negative and Positive Positivism' (1982) 11 *Journal of Legal Studies* 139.
71 Raz (n 59) 41.

it may not be very fruitful. This thesis represents an important truth about the nature of positivist thinking and helps distinguish legal positivism from natural law jurisprudence. Natural law theorists may believe in some form of the social thesis,[72] but they cannot truly believe in the separability thesis. The traditional understanding of the main thesis of natural law, *lex iniusta non est lex*, is that unjust laws are not valid laws. Some contemporary theorists offer a somewhat moderate or weak reading of the natural law thesis.[73] In this moderate reading, unjust laws may be *intrasystemically* valid, but they fail to produce valid moral obligations for the subjects. These laws represent *non-central* or *peripheral* cases of law. In other words, these laws lack the essential qualities that make law in the *fullest* sense. Legal positivists may accept that unjust laws are impotent to create valid moral obligations. However, on a legal positivist account, this inability to create valid moral obligations does not degrade their *lawness* in any way.

IV. Inclusive Versus Exclusive Legal Positivism

Contemporary legal positivists are divided into two camps: inclusive legal positivists and exclusive legal positivists. Both of these camps represent positivists' different responses to Ronald Dworkin's criticism of Hart's theory.[74] Dworkin contended that the domain of law is not limited to positive rules but includes *principles of political morality* that do not have a social source.[75] These principles of political morality provide the positive legal material (or 'settled law') with the best possible explanation and moral justification.[76] Simply put, these principles not only help the judges discover the right solution to any legal dispute but also provide moral justification for the solution. Dworkin argued that Hart's positivist legal theory, which emphasises social fact-based rules of recognition for resolving questions of legal validity, cannot explain or accommodate the existence of these moral principles.[77] The core of Dworkin's critique is that legality is not, as legal positivists claim, completely determinable by social facts alone; it also requires recourse to moral facts.[78] Legal reasoning is intrinsically connected with moral reasoning. Dworkin's challenge threatened the very core of legal positivism.

72 John Finnis claims that natural law theory is consistent with the *social thesis*. See John Finnis, 'The Truth in Legal Positivism' in *Philosophy of Law: Collected Essays Volume IV* (OUP 2011).

73 For a summary of these interpretations, see Mark C. Murphy, 'Natural Law Jurisprudence' (2003) 9 *Legal Theory* 241.

74 Scott J. Shapiro, 'The "Hart–Dworkin" Debate: A Short Guide for the Perplexed' in Arthur Ripstein (ed), *Ronald Dworkin* (CUP 2012).

75 Ronald Dworkin, *Taking Rights Seriously* (Harvard University Press 1977) 22.

76 Ronald Dworkin, *Law's Empire* (Harvard University Press 1986) 176–275.

77 Dworkin (n 75) 24.

78 Shapiro (n 74) 23.

Hart did not have the opportunity to respond directly to Dworkin's criticisms in his lifetime. However, his posthumously published postscript to *The Concept of Law* directly engaged with many of them.[79] Even before the postscript was published, Hart's successors had developed diverse responses to the Dworkinian challenge. One group, often referred to as 'inclusive positivists,' 'soft positivists,' or 'incorporationists,' objected to Dworkin's characterisation of legal positivism.[80] They conceded that morality sometimes plays a role in determining the validity of a legal norm but contended that it could be explained within the positivist framework of the social fact-based rule of recognition. They argued that moral standards could play a role in determining binding legal norms, provided that they are *incorporated* into the conventional rule of recognition.[81] For example, many modern constitutions refer to principles of fairness or justice that limit the legislative power of parliaments. However, it is imperative to clarify that such an incorporation of moral standards is not a necessity. Both conceptually and practically, there can be valid legal systems that make no reference to moral standards in their rule of recognition or are even flagrantly iniquitous (e.g., Nazi Germany and apartheid South Africa).[82] In this way, they sought to explain the ubiquitous role of moral principles in legal practice while remaining within the limits set by the social and separability theses.[83]

Another group, often labelled as 'hard' or 'exclusive' legal positivists, disagreed with this explanation. They accepted that judges use or may even be bound in certain cases to apply moral standards to reach judicial verdicts but rejected the notion that this application of moral standards *incorporates* these standards into law in any way.[84] Inclusive legal positivists held that 'legal validity is exhausted by reference to the conventional sources of law: all law is source-based, and anything which is not source-based is not law.'[85] Morality can never serve as the criterion of legal validity because any reference to morality will impinge on positivist legal theory's commitment to the social thesis.[86]

79 In postscript to *The Concept of Law*, Hart stated that his 'doctrine is what has been called "soft positivism" and not as in Dworkin's version of it "plain-fact positivism".' However, even before Dworkin's criticism, Hart recognized the possibility of incorporation of moral principles into rule of recognition. See *CL* 204, 250.

80 W. J. Waluchow, 'The Origins of Inclusive Legal Positivism' in Torben Spaak and Patricia Mindus (eds), *The Cambridge Companion to Legal Positivism* (CUP 2021).

81 Ibid. 494.

82 Coleman (n 70) 141.

83 Coleman and Leiter (n 60) 236.

84 Joseph Raz, 'Dworkin: A New Link in the Chain' (1986) 74 *California Law Review* 1103.

85 Andrei Marmor, 'Exclusive Legal Positivism' in Jules L. Coleman, Kenneth Einar Himma, and Scott J. Shapiro (eds), *The Oxford Handbook of Jurisprudence and Philosophy of Law* (Oxford University Press 2004) 105.

86 Exclusive legal positivists like Raz provides a restrictive definition of social thesis. See Raz (n 59) 39–40.

Joseph Raz argues that the fact that judges are obligated to apply moral standards does not incorporate these standards into law. Judges are often obligated to apply various kinds of *extra-legal* (e.g., foreign laws in *conflict of law* cases) standards to resolve legal disputes, but these extra-legal standards do not become part of the legal system.[87] Raz presents another argument for exclusive legal positivism based on his distinctive conception of legitimate authority. According to Raz, it is the nature of a *legitimate* authority that it provides its subjects with reasons that apply to them in such a way that they would be better able to comply with these reasons by following the authority's directives rather than by acting on them directly, without the *mediating role* of the authority.[88] An authority that cannot provide such *exclusionary or pre-emptive reasons*—reasons that displace any other independent reasons the subjects may have—cannot claim to be legitimate.[89] For Raz, subjects 'can benefit by its[authority's] decisions only if they can establish their existence and content in ways which do not depend on raising the very same issues which the authority is there to settle.'[90] It implies that subjects should be able to determine the content of legal rules without recourse to the moral reasons that motivated the authority's directives. Any alternative would be inconsistent with the function of legitimate authority.

For the exclusive legal positivists, moral considerations in determining legal validity are completely excluded by the law's source-based nature. Andrei Marmor argued that source-based conventions constitute *all law*. Moral standards cannot be law because source-based conventions cannot constitute them. He stated that 'conventions cannot constitute a practice which consists in the expectation that people who engage in the practice do that which they would have reason to do regardless of the practice.'[91] Moreover, the proposition that there are compelling moral reasons for a social convention does not imply that there is actually such a social convention. Similarly, arguing that there are moral reasons for any legal norm does not imply that it is constituted by source-based social convention and, therefore, is part of the positive legal system.[92] However, source-based conventions can constitute the ways

87 Raz (n 59) 46.

88 Raz calls this thesis the *normal justification thesis*, which holds that 'the normal and primary way to establish that a person should be acknowledged to have authority over another person involves showing that the alleged subject is likely better to comply with reasons which apply to him (other than the alleged authoritative directives) if he accepts the directives of the alleged authority as authoritatively binding and tries to follow them, rather than by trying to follow the reasons which apply to him directly.' Joseph Raz, 'Authority and Justification' (1985) 14 *Philosophy and Public Affairs* 3, 18.

89 Ibid. 10.

90 Joseph Raz, *Ethics in Public Domain: Essays in the Morality of Law and Politics* (Clarendon Press 1994) 219.

91 Marmor (n 85) 109.

92 Ibid.

in which moral standards are recognised by the legal system.[93] For example, source-based laws can regulate the ways in which judges may apply moral principles in judicial reasoning.

Interestingly, both camps of legal positivists agree that morality plays a role in the actual practice of legal systems, but they explain its operation in conflicting ways. All of the differences between the two camps stem from their different interpretations of the social and separability theses. While inclusive legal positivists have a broad and liberal interpretation of these theses, exclusive legal positivists espouse a more restrictive interpretation.

V. Conclusion

Despite their numerous differences, legal positivists remain committed to the social character (or artefact nature) of law and its distinction from other normative domains. For them, these commitments are indispensable for achieving conceptual clarity in the study of legal phenomena and, therefore, are necessary elements of any acceptable theory of law. Some even attach normative or ethical significance to their insistence on the separation of law and morality.[94] However, how exactly this distinction should be maintained and what may constitute a betrayal of the social thesis remain subjects of heated debate. Furthermore, the diverse legal theories of Hart and Kelsen illustrate that the legal positivist enterprise is not confined to any particular philosophical tendency but can be conceived in various ways.

In contemporary jurisprudence, legal positivism enjoys an ascendant position. Nevertheless, bitter criticisms persist. The emergence of new classical natural law theories (of John Finnis and others) presents challenges to which adequate responses have not been given. The most pressing challenge for legal positivism is to explain how a descriptive and value-neutral legal theory can account for the normativity of law, that is, how a legal theory can remain morally neutral while explaining an institution that essentially claims to be morally justified.

93 Joseph Raz, 'Legal Principles and the Limits of Law' (1972) 81 *Yale Law Journal* 823.

94 Jeremy Waldron, 'Normative (or Ethical) Positivism' in Jules Coleman (ed), *Hart's Postscript: Essays on the Postscript to 'The Concept of Law'* (OUP 2001).

8 The Pure Theory's Concept of Law[1]

Clemens Jabloner

I. Introduction

We do not find a concise, *one-sentence* definition of his concept of law in Kelsen because the Pure theory of law understands law from various perspectives. The result is a circumscription, which, even in its condensed form in a Kelsen-based Austrian textbook, requires several sentences. At root, it concerns the fact that every effective, codified, coercive system of rules is understood as "positive law" established by people for people. Such a system is regarded as a system of norms founded on an underlying basic norm.

The following comments are an attempt at an analysis of the individual elements of the concept of law, drawing on Kelsen's later theory. Further developments and criticism will only be mentioned selectively. There is no time here to offer more than a brief sketch, which should at least outline the contours of the Kelsenian concept of law.

Let us begin by highlighting some of the fundamental determining features of the Pure theory: *the establishment of the subject "law"* does not derive from a priori inferences or abstract assertions but from an analytical process. For Kelsen, it is a matter of critically illuminating and, as it were, "reconstructing" the subject that legal science has long described as "positive law." A concept of positive law—even if a less precise one—is thus already assumed. One can describe this approach to the subject somewhat colourfully as "***diving into the law***." Alongside this constructive function, the Pure theory, at the same time, exercises a deconstructive function. This consists in the critical analysis of conventional jurisprudence, which Kelsen accuses of "ideologically" distorting positive law under the cover of apparently juridical constructions. The Pure theory is thus not just a methodology for lawyers but also a critique of ideology.

1 Hans Kelsen's oeuvre is very extensive and, in addition to legal theory, also includes political works on democratic theory, ideology-critical writings on legal and religious sociology, work on peacekeeping, and much more. The second edition of "***Reine Rechtslehre***" from 1960 is the main source for the legal theory we are concerned with here: Hans Kelsen, ***Pure Theory of Law*** (Max Knight tr, 2nd rev edn, University of California Press 1967, Lawbook Exchange reprint 2005).

DOI: 10.4324/9781003728603-10

With regard to epistemology, the Pure theory of law is based on the *separation of Is and Ought*: underlying this is the epistemological dualism of facts and values, statements and norms, "to know" and "to will." The assumption of an independent sphere of the "Ought" is not further justified by Kelsen; "we are immediately aware of the difference." The separation of the sphere of the Ought from that of the Is does not exclude interactions. Actual conditions influence the establishment of norms, and norms react on reality. Thus, for example, a prognosis can be made that particular abuses lead to particular counteracting commanding acts, which can perhaps be regarded as norms, and it can be assessed whether the establishment of such norms is adequate to prevent these abuses. The important thing is the logical non-derivability of norms from reality. An Is judgement cannot be derived from an Ought judgement (and vice versa). The order of Is in nature is determined by the principle of causality and described in cause-effect statements; the order of Ought is determined by the principle of imputation and described by statements that express the specific sense in which the condition and consequence, "act" and "sanction" are linked with each other. From a modern perspective, it is a matter of preserving the independent sphere of the Ought as an object of normative science(s). From a historical perspective, however, the establishment of an independent world of the Is that can be described by natural science is only the result of the break-up of the originally normative worldview. As long as reality was regarded as obligatory, there was, for this reason, no place for a "pure" normative science.

Taking all due care regarding the separation of Is and Ought, the Pure theory nevertheless has a dual function: it aims both to be a *normative* theory that describes law in its distinctive nature as an "order of Ought" as well as being a *positivist* theory that seeks to cover only those orders of Ought that display a specific relationship to reality. In this sense, in the following, law will initially be presented as an "*order of Ought*," and then law as an "*effective coercive order*." It should thus initially concern the elements that bring out the normative aspect and then those elements that rather stand for the positivist aspect of the Pure theory. True, at the end we will get back to where we started from, quoting the relevant passage from the mentioned Austrian textbook. If, however, one sees these considerations as superfluous and prefers to go back to the primary sources, then the following outline has also achieved a purpose.

II. The Law as a Normative Order

1. The Pure theory of law understands the law as a system of *Ought rules*—"*Norms*." Norm means that something should be or should happen—in particular, that a person should behave in a particular way. The "Ought" is the objective meaning, the signification of human behaviour. The fact that someone signs a piece of paper is sensually perceptible as a fact, but the legal meaning of his action is the creation—or the participation in the creation—of

a legal norm, for example, the passing of a sentence. The act cannot acquire its legal meaning by itself, and its meaning can also only be claimed by the person carrying it out. Rather, the act receives its legal quality—and thereby, as "*validity*," its specific existence as a norm—through the fact that another norm refers to it and functions as an interpretation *pattern* for it. Only in this way can an act that subjectively has the meaning of an Ought also objectively receive this signification. As the norm is only valid if actual events are interpreted in a normative way—for example, the activity of people in Parliament as the creation of a law on administrative procedure—a progression of conditioning and conditioned norms develops in this way. This recursion necessarily leads to the historically first constitution, whose validity as a legal norm can only be assumed. This assumption is described as the "*basic norm*." For the purpose of legal science, its *epistemological function* consists in the fact that it simultaneously raises and answers the question of validity. With regard to the necessity of the basic norm, that is only hypothetical, but nevertheless, it is possible to speak of the validity of legal norms. Their *unifying function* lies in the fact that a number of norms of the same origin can be interpreted as a norm system.

2. With the interpretation of law as a normative order, the Pure theory of law distances itself from *"realistic" legal sociology theories*, which formulate the subject of "law" without the normative element so that *only* actual human behaviour matters. The impositions of the law are taken into consideration in that, as a psychological motive—as a "normative ideology"—they influence the behaviour of the judge and the other addressees of norms.

   There are above all two arguments in favour of the normativist interpretation by the Pure theory. On the one hand, the normative character of law is absent from the realistic view of law. Now, one could dismiss this as an insignificant objection inasmuch as it is not one of the concerns of legal realism. However, it becomes apparent that this abstention from norms can only be maintained with difficulty. If, for example, the actual issuing of a command on the one hand and, on the other, its effect—thus, in particular, its compliance—are to be meaningfully related to one another (i.e., if we are talking of the norm and compliance with the norm), then this is not possible without reference to the specific Ought character of the command. Even if one qualifies the form of law conceived of in the Ought form as a "normative ideology," one can still not escape the sphere of influence of the Pure theory. Kelsen himself emphasised that law, in the sense of it being the result of a particular interpretation of reality, should also be regarded as "ideology."

3. The assumption of a basic norm lends the legal system the highest, as it were, a free-floating basis of cognition. The basic norm obviously makes no pretence of legal content; in this sense, it is purely "*formal.*" Its neutrality should be emphasised in two directions. With regard to the fundamental separation between Is and Ought, it is impermissible to conclude the validity of norms from their effectiveness. Reference to an

Is phenomenon, such as the decision of a sovereign or recognition by a particular person, is therefore not permitted to be at the top of the norm pyramid. The Pure theory also disapproves of attempts to find the basis of legal validity in norms belonging to another, "higher" order and thereby open the legal concept in the direction of natural law. The axiom of the separation of law and morality, understood as the "separation thesis," is related to Kelsen's value-relativistic fundamental position. According to this, the recognisability of supreme values is denied. The separation thesis not only means that no legal norms can be derived from the norms of morality, of a religion, or of a natural law. The separation thesis also stands in the way of natural law trying to limit positive law and making the validity of positive legal norms dependent on them agreeing with certain highest values.

One must, however, differentiate this legal theory question from the fact that sometimes, within the legal system, reference is made to extra-legal norm systems. Thus, a positive constitutional order can make normative ideas—described as "natural law"—part of the legal order and thus positivise them. We will come back to this again at the end of this chapter.

4. Even though, in the demonstration of the normative interpretation of reality, Kelsen paradigmatically has the normative original-scene of the command in mind, his "Ought"-concept should not be reduced to commandments and prohibitions. Contrary to normal linguistic usage, Kelsen's "Ought" also includes the categories "*may*" and "*can*." Finally, Kelsen adds "*derogating*" as a particular normative function. This is the point of departure for the elaboration of the norm theory of the Pure theory, a task to which the Kelsen school primarily dedicated itself. In the context of a general theory of norms, which does not yet go into the particularities of the concept of the legal norm, the differentiation is mainly concerned with showing the significance of "what one can do with norms." However, we will see that in connection with the introduction of the coercive moment, the question of the kinds of norms and their relationship to one another is shown in a new light.
5. It is not only in the internal normative structure that distinctions are to be made. The sphere of norms that is relevant here should also be demarcated externally: norms are part of the general group of "*directives*." All directives—that is, also advice, requests, and recommendations—are intentionally directed at the behaviour of other people. Norms, however, distinguish themselves through a certain strictness of this intention. To avoid an obvious misunderstanding, this does not yet have anything to do with the question of sanctions but is a reflection with regard to linguistic usage. In this connection, it is not necessary to state the linguistic boundaries of "norms," particularly as this can be an interpretation question relating to specific directives. However, one should not overlook this problem; in international law in particular, it is not unusual for the question to arise of whether a

directive act has a normative character. In this, the self-interpretation of the act, as well as the interpretation on the basis of a creation rule, plays an important role.

6. Even if one can describe the Pure theory of law as also being a "normative" theory of law, according to the theory, the statements of *legal science*—despite possible normative semantics—are *descriptive* and not normative. The legal scientist uses propositions of law to describe a legal situation; his statements may be true or false, but they cannot have "validity." Legal science cannot "create" legal norms.

Two observations should be made on this. A positive legal order, for example, international law, can employ legal science as a source of law. Modern legal orders with specified legal sources do not take this route.

A second problem lies in the relationship between law and logic. In the sense of Kelsen's later theory, no further legal norms can be derived from legal norms by logical operations. However, at the level of legal science, the normative syllogism, for example, can indeed be anticipated. But here, too, the norm is to be set by the person applying the law.

III. The Law as an Effective Coercive Order

1. The basic norm not only has the already mentioned epistemological function of founding validity. It also serves to shape the contours of the normative subject for the purposes of legal science consideration. One can describe this function of the basic norm as *cognitive-economic*. A condition for the assumption of the basic norm is that the *norm system is "by and large"* (that is, relatively) *effective*. The first important positivistic element is thereby introduced into the consideration of the law.

   To start with, it should be borne in mind that the criterion of *relative effectiveness* is essential not only for positive law. If ethics, too, wishes to describe "positive morality" in a norm-scientific way, a corresponding assumption should be made to describe only the effective moral order—and no conceived moral order—as a positive order of Ought. For the sphere of the other norm orders (morality, customs), however—in the absence of an interest in understanding comparable to legal science—the differentiation between the consideration of what "is to be" and what "ought to be" according to conceived rules is not so clear as it is in the consideration of law.

   The relationship between validity and effectiveness expressed in the construction of the basic norm is a particular subject of misunderstanding of the Pure theory. It should, therefore, be stated here that the recourse to effectiveness should be seen as the "*condition of validity*," as the precondition for placing the basic norm only ahead of particular orders of Ought. Neither does this form of accounting for effectiveness mean a breach in the system, nor does it lead to the legitimising of the effective order in question.

The question of which norms have to be effective and how far this effectiveness must go is not analysed in more detail by the Pure theory. This does indeed have its reason in the fact that it understands itself as a *theory for the description of established orders of Ought*. The revolutionary process itself is outside its agenda. It has been variously emphasised in the literature that Hart's legal theory has contributed important elements precisely for the closer examination of the element of "effectiveness."

Finally, it should be mentioned that the criterion of effectiveness also has an effect on the norm structure itself. Effectiveness can, namely, only be spoken of if and for as long as a norm can be *complied with or applied*. The behaviour of the addressee must be ascertained in such a way that he has the choice of behaving according to the norm or not. It is obvious that commands that cannot be complied with—examples are easy to imagine—cannot be norms because they lack directive quality but perhaps have a completely different context, for example, that of humiliation or a joke. It is just as impossible to comply with commands for which non-compliance is impossible, for example, the order not to leave a locked room.

2. For Kelsen, the law is the specific social technique of a *coercive order*. The coercive moment—constituting the legal norm and distinguishing it from other social norms—means the *socially organised, external coercion* that is exercised upon people. Psychological coercion, as a feature of all social orders, should be distinguished from this. This is a form of motivation, i.e., of coercion in a psychological sense. Kelsen differentiates the coercive technique of indirect motivation through punishment from direct motivation as the technique of voluntary compliance with norms. It stands to reason that the effectiveness of a legal order must be based mainly on the coercive threat, that is, on the general norm of compliance with legal norms and not on the exceptional case of the coercive creation of an obligatory state of affairs. Seen from this angle, the law thus has a "regulatory" function and is not simply an apparatus for directing the exercise of coercion. For the following considerations, it is important to keep in mind this difference between the apparatus and its function.
3. The introduction of the coercive element takes place at the normative level. Coercion *"ought" to be exercised*; whether it is "actually" exercised is a question of effectiveness. If one now focuses on the specific characteristic of the legal order, that some people are empowered under closely defined conditions to exercise coercion, and if one sees conditioning elements in the preceding behaviour of those people against whom coercion is now to be exercised, then the legal order appears, as it were, to have "moved away" from the "original" addressees of the norm whose behaviour was to be regulated.

We thereby come to a difficult problem of the Pure theory—the relationship of the *primary to the secondary norm*. By "primary" norm, the already mentioned empowering norm directed at a person "as the executive body" is understood. Can a "secondary" norm, which imposes a particular behaviour on the "original" addressees, be derived from this?

Kelsen adopted a highly nuanced position on this question. Although he was initially guided by the equivalence of the "primary" and the "secondary" norm, in the late work, the secondary norm was dropped: a positive legal order commands a particular behaviour inasmuch as it attaches a coercive act as a sanction on contrary behaviour. *The coercive act is obligatory.* Finally, it is stated that the secondary norm has become superfluous since it is implicit in the norm laying down the sanction. The law commands a certain behaviour "*simply by*" attaching a coercive act as a sanction on the contrary behaviour.

Now, it seems more logical to dispense with the concept of the "secondary" norm altogether than to regard it as being in one form or other implicit in the primary norm. It is sufficient to point out that, for example, in the empowerment of the forced admittance of someone to a psychiatric institution, the derivation of a secondary norm according to which it is forbidden to become mentally ill is obviously pointless. In not a few other constructions—for example, in tax law or sometimes in administrative law—a secondary norm can in no way be derived just like that; furthermore, in these two areas of law, several objectives are often being pursued simultaneously, for example, the direction of behaviour alongside the raising of revenue. From this situation, one could draw the conclusion that the assumption of a secondary norm has simply been carried over into the legal order from outside, corresponding to particular parallel moral conceptions or antecedent considerations. The "secondary" norm would thereby be banished from the concept of law.

Such a reduction of the concept of law to the coercive apparatus corresponds to an economy of thought and the positivist model of the most economical use of terms. One must also see, however, that in this way, one is distancing oneself very much from the concept of the law as a regulator of society. It is arguable whether the fear of sanction on its own is sufficient to steer people's behaviour in the desired direction. On the one hand, it can be said that a legal order has its place in society alongside other orders of Ought, such as morality or customs, which fulfil their respective functions—complementary to law. On the other hand, the emphasis on coercive power threatens the Ought character of the legal order. One could thus, through detours, still end up with a legal realism.

Kelsen's rejection of the secondary norm is also connected with the strict separation of the norm and the (norm) end in the late theory. At several points, Kelsen emphasises that norms cannot be derived from conceived ends, and this is also true in reverse. The end can only be described as a norm if it itself is the content of a—separate legally enacted—act of will. If, however, such an act exists, it thus seems possible to orient oneself on the differentiations of positive law. Ultimately, underlying the problem is a thoroughly philosophical question. Can subjects that have been created by people, among which the law is undoubtedly included, be described without consideration of their ends? An apple can be described without reference to the fact that it can be eaten by people. That it exists to feed people is essentially a religious conception. A description of a hammer can indeed be made without reference to its use, but we feel a marked deficiency in it. The situation is similar in the description of the legal order. So much, therefore, for some provisional remarks on the difficult problem of primary and secondary norms.

4. A particularly striking element in Kelsen's late theory is the consideration of the "*act of will.*" In chapter 8 of his *General Theory of Norms*, Kelsen describes the normative "Original-Scene" of the command. He writes:

> A command, especially a command called a norm, presupposes two human beings: one who commands (or gives the command or posits the norm) and one to whom the command is addressed (or who is commanded to act or whose behaviour is prescribed or decreed to be obligatory). The one who commands (or posits the norm) wills something; the one who is commanded (or whose behaviour is decreed to be obligatory in a norm) ought to do something. The linguistic expression of a command is an imperative. There is a valid principle concerning commands which is usually formulated as "No imperative without imperator." But there is also a valid principle about the person to whom the command is addressed: "No imperative without an imperatus," i.e. a person (or persons) to whom the imperative is addressed. Generally: No norm without a norm-positing authority, and no norm without an addressee.[2]

What is interesting in this description is that an internal-psychological act—belonging to the Is sphere—precedes the communicative process. It is this act of will that gives the norm its positivity. The stratification of the act of will leads to a sharper accentuation of the positivistic aspect of the Pure theory ("*positing positivism*") because the normative world (as something shaped by specific people and thus something that can be changed by them or by others) becomes particularly pronounced. In its extreme form, however, the "imperator thesis" is accompanied by several problems:

a. A first objection concerns the fact that the observability of an internal-psychological act of will is problematic. According to the latest findings, a real event can indeed be empirically verified, but this does not correspond to the "volitional" experience, that is, the conscious "act of will," but precedes it. This does indeed provide a point of contact to the Is world. However, it is questionable whether the measured "readiness

2 Hans Kelsen, *General Theory of Norms* (OUP 1991) 28–29.

potential" as a pre-linguistic element is the appropriate reality for the purpose of the foundation of norms.

In view of the difficulties in discerning the "act of will," it is proposed, drawing on "speech-act theory," to retain the concept that the (subjective) norm is "created" by a fact, namely an act of command, but to dispense with the element of the act of will. In this way, the relevant actual process would be interpreted purely objectively. There would then also still be an imperator, that is, a real person who posits real acts of command, but it would be sufficient to take account only of his external behaviour. One would thereby go from the problematic real-psychological act of will, whose linguistic form is imperative, to the concept of an "act of speech," which does without the "internal factor" and only demands that the speaker knows that his act has the intention of the imperative.

In addition, the following should be considered: The question of the empirical verifiability of the act of will be differentiated from the problem of "free will." There is nevertheless a connection between the phenomena because the expressive act of will is experienced psychologically as being "free." In the tradition of Kant, the problem of free will cannot, in principle, be solved empirically. Free will is not, for example, the naturalistic cause of a normative pattern of interpretation but, much rather, it is its function. If the world is interpreted through a normative pattern—that is, essentially by imputing actions to people—the elements mentioned inevitably come into play. The repeated attempt to establish free will through natural science must, therefore, remain in vain: in a causal pattern of interpretation, it is a concept that cannot occur; however, in a normative pattern of interpretation—which interrupts the chain of causal relations precisely in order to be able to impute effects to people—its adoption is an inescapable necessity.

b. Another objection is that restricting the emergence of norms to the positing of norms by an act of will cannot include the customary norms (customs, customary law). On this, Kelsen believes that after some period of habit individuals developed the will to behave as members of the group habitually did, while also feeling that other members of the group ought to behave in the same manner. In this way, the custom becomes a collective will whose subjective meaning is an Ought. The precise nature of this "collective will" is not quite clear in this explanation. Without deepening this problem here, just two alternatives suggest themselves: either the "imperator theory" is so rigorously maintained that the customary emergence of norms is understood in an ideology-critical way as merely a phenomenon of the internal perspective of people concerned. They suppose always to have done or to do of their own will what "in truth" they have been shown, for example, by the example of "supremators" who hold the real social power. What is meant here can sometimes be clearly recognised if one observes the behaviour of powerful states, among other things, in the emergence of the customary rules of international law. The category of "customary law" would thus, in an ideology-critical way, be revealed as a deception, a consequence that Kelsen ultimately considers. Or the norm concept of the general theory of norms, with its focus on the moment of will, is related only to modern orders of Ought with explicit positing of norms, that is, essentially, to differentiated legal orders.

IV. The Hierarchical Structure of Law

Kelsen's doctrine is often associated with the realisation of the hierarchical structure of the legal order. This includes various aspects. Firstly, it is about the *context of validity*. For a real event to be understood as a legal act, it must be interpreted as such by the standards of the legal system. This results in a context of conditional and conditional acts from an individual concrete order of an administrative body or a judicial judgement up to a general administrative act, on to a parliamentary law, and finally to the constitution. This can be traced back to a historical first constitution. However, to be able to interpret this act as a legal act, the assumption of its validity must be made—as mentioned above—and this is the function of the basic norm.

Kelsen's most important student, Adolf Julius Merkl, worked out that the legal system can be understood not only statically but also in its dynamic flow. The relativity of the creation and application of law shows, in Merkl's words, "double face." It is wrong to say that the content of a subordinate legal act results entirely from its previous legal basis, nor does it represent—as is sometimes claimed—a completely new judicial creation. Rather, both elements are linked in accordance with constitutional rules of creation. Thus, a constitution can provide for a strict binding of the administration to the law or also assume its greater freedom, i.e., discretion.

A further insight is that the hierarchical structure of the legal order also has a derogatory function. The legal system itself can provide mechanisms for the destruction ("derogation") of law, such as authorising a constitutional court to annul unconstitutional laws. In the doctrine of constitutional jurisdiction so prominently advocated by Kelsen, the structural element of the hierarchical structure finds an answer in the construction of the positive constitutional order.

V. Concluding Remarks

The Pure theory of law is a *positivist legal theory*. It is based on the interest in describing the orders issued by a social authority as precisely as possible. In comparison to other legal positivist theories, the Pure theory does have a high degree of self-analysis. As a theory of law, it is not a self-contained whole, but is to be critically further developed; Kelsen did not leave behind a dogmatic structure.

In relation to *legal technique,* the Pure theory offers a very well-suited basis for differentiating and refining legal forms. The importance of this is evident, for example, in the case of (EU) Community law. In relation to legal science, which, as legal dogma, occupies itself with the interpretation of positive law, the Pure theory leads to an insight into the relativity of the respective standpoint and, thus, to a restraint that is well-suited to legal science.

It is not overlooked that the full explanatory value of the Pure theory becomes particularly apparent with regard to *modern legal orders based on explicit codification.* The Pure theory would, and indeed does, have less use value in connection with a simplification of the legal order. This does not mean, however, that according to its scientific theoretical concept it would not be suited to describing *any* form of legal order. If one understands the "positivising" of the law in a legal-sociological sense as the visualisation of the changeability of law, then the Pure theory offers the key to seeing law as a tool available to man.

Even though the "technocratic" character of the Pure theory corresponds to a particular type of law formation, positive law, in particular a constitutional order, can take other routes in its understanding of itself, in its self-interpretation. Legal-theory differentiations do not have to be reflected in positive law. Thus, referring to natural law, particular basic values can be accorded eternal validity, or the literature can be given the character of a source of law. This is also true, however, for the legal technique dimension: the *validity concept* itself is open to a *positive law formation.* Precisely legal orders that are very differentiated with regard to legal technique may contain statements concerning what is to be regarded as the valid legal norm. As a result—and this is not without irony for a legal positivist—the legal concept of positive law can be different from the legal-positivist concept of law.

9 Social Norms and the Internal Point of View

An Elaboration of Hart's Genealogy of Law*

Philip N. Pettit

1. Introduction

A. Hart's Methodology

One of the most remarkable things about Herbert Hart's classic study *The Concept of Law*, first published in 1961, is that without advertising the fact, perhaps even without recognising it explicitly, he introduces a way of doing philosophy that was quite at variance with the spirit of that time in Oxford.[1] It was a time that had been dominated in philosophy by J. L. Austin, who died in his late forties, just the year before Hart's book appeared. In the style of the period, Hart presented his work as an analysis of the concept of law. But he offered very little of the analysis of linguistic usage, common or professional, that we might have expected; in that regard, he broke from the ranks of his colleagues in Oxford and in the philosophical world in which Oxford then stood supreme.

What Hart offered instead might be described as a philosophical genealogy of the concept of law: an account of how it would plausibly, even inevitably, have gained currency in a society that previously lacked the concept—or, indeed, the practice—that it might have been used to articulate.[2] He begins with an imagined society that we might describe as Normitania, where informal norms of conduct have emerged among its residents: these he calls primary rules. He then shows how various difficulties would have prompted a set

* This paper was originally published in the *Oxford Journal of Legal Studies*, 2019, Volume 39, Issue 2, Pages 229–258. We bear responsibility for any errors that may have occurred in reprinting or editing.

1 H. L. A. Hart, *The Concept of Law* (3rd edn, OUP 2012) vi. For an argument that his project does not belong with ordinary sociology or the analytical philosophy of his time, see L. Green, 'Introduction' in H. L. A. Hart, *The Concept of Law* (3rd edn, OUP 2012) xlv–xlvii. For an account of his relationships with his philosophical contemporaries, see N. Lacey, *A Life of HLA Hart: The Nightmare and the Noble Dream* (OUP 2004). For signs of Austin's influence on Hart's work on responsibility, see Ibid.

2 J. Gardner, 'Why Law Might Emerge: Hart's Problematic Fable' in D. d'Almeida, J. Edwards, and A. Dolcetti (eds), *Reading HLA Hart's the Concept of Law* (Hart Publishing 2013).

DOI: 10.4324/9781003728603-11

of adjustments among the people involved and how these, without any central contract or planning, would have given rise to secondary rules governing the interpretation, amendment and application of primary rules. He invites us at that point to agree that, by almost any standards of interpretative practice, it would be natural to cast this regime of primary and secondary rules as a system of law: that it deserves the name, to coin a term, of Lexitania.

The idea, as I read him, is that if the Lexitanians had a phrase for that combination of rules, as they surely would have done, it would correspond in our language, by natural criteria of interpretation, to the notion of a system of law. If we go along with that idea, then there are a number of benefits in prospect. We may take the story about how Normitania leads to Lexitania to direct us to the sort of thing that deserves to be conceptualised as a system of law and to how it can get to be conceptualised as such among its officials and subjects. We may take it to illuminate the role or function of the system, explaining why it is a more or less inevitable feature of a certain sort of society. And we may take it to demystify law in the positivist fashion that attracted Hart; the story does not have to appeal at any point to natural law or moral value.[3]

Hart's methodology harks back to the 18th-century idea of a conjectural history; it has parallels, for example, with the story that David Hume tells about the emergence and utility of the concept and custom of ownership.[4] It has come back into vogue in recent times, as when Edward Craig offers us a conjectural genealogy of the concept of knowledge,[5] and Bernard Williams a similar genealogy for the ideas of truth and truthfulness.[6] I have relied on it myself to provide a genealogy of ethical practices and concepts.[7] In this usage, the word refers to a counterfactual exercise, and should be distinguished from genealogy in a historical sense. Equally, it should be distinguished from the debunking sort of genealogy offered, for example, in Nietzsche's *Genealogy of Morals*; a debunking genealogy of any norms, legal or moral, would deprive them of the motivating and related power they may have seemed to possess.[8]

As I construe the genealogical method, it breaks with conceptual analysis in its standard form, but serves a similar purpose.[9] By contrast with standard analysis, it does not itemise the connotations of the target term or concept—in this case, that of law; filter out those connotations that we would want to see preserved across any cases where we applied the term; and then, relying on this

3 Note, however, that to allow for versions of positivism developed in the wake of Hart's work, it is not blocked from appealing to people's subjective judgments or valuations.
4 D. Hume, *A Treatise of Human Nature* (OUP 1978) s 3.2.2.
5 E. Craig, *Knowledge and the State of Nature* (OUP 1990).
6 B. Williams, *Truth and Truthfulness* (Princeton UP 2002).
7 P. Pettit, *The Birth of Ethics: Reconstructing the Role and Nature of Morality* (Oxford University Press 2018).
8 F. Nietzsche, *On the Genealogy of Morals* (CUP 1997).
9 Pettit (n 7); P. Pettit, 'Analyzing Concepts and Allocating Referents' in A. Burgess, H. Cappelen, and D. Plunkett (eds), *Conceptual Engineering and Conceptual Ethics* (OUP 2019).

method of cases, seek to identify the property identified by the stripped-down set of connotations. Rather, it describes how an interpretatively equivalent concept might have emerged in tandem with a corresponding practice—how concept and practice might have co-evolved—and invites the conjecture that our own concept of law serves a similar role and identifies a similar referent: a system of primary and secondary rules.

B. *The Aim and Plan*

My aim in this article is not to defend Hart's genealogical method or narrative, only to extend it into the past, spelling out a story that his narrative presupposes. This is the story, cast in the same genealogical mould, of how a society might give rise to the primary rules that he postulates. In other words, it is a story about how Normitania might have emerged in a world without norms: in Prenormitania, as we may describe it.[10]

The developed story extends the temporal reach of Hart's genealogy, taking it back to the earlier stage where primary rules are supposed to emerge spontaneously. In doing so, it evades a familiar problem raised for the spontaneous emergence of norms of a kind with the emergence that Hart presupposes. In order to see the problem, assume, as all sides do, that norms require enforcement. Why should people who are not altruistic enough to conform to norms of their own accord be altruistic enough to practice enforcement, bearing the associated costs of effort or embarrassment, for example? The problem can be resolved if enforcement does not require performing a costly intentional action, but only observing how someone behaves, and being seen by that person to observe them. The story told here, which is broadly faithful to Hart, shows how enforcement can take that non intentional form and vindicates Hart's assumption about the emergence of primary rules in Prenormitania.

But a good part of the interest of providing a prequel to Hart's genealogy is that doing so supports a rich psychological model of what it means for people to take an internal point of view, as he calls it, on the rules that they follow. According to Hart, the internal point of view is that which is held by people who are insiders to the society, not outside observers, and in particular insiders who willingly abide by the rules: they do not submit only in the manner of detached outliers.[11] The genealogy of primary rules developed here identifies different dimensions in an internal point of view: different ways in which it may contrast with the view that outside or detached observers will take of rules. It extends the psychological depth of the genealogy, as it extends its temporal reach.

10 The account of norms given in this chapter, and their connection with laws, appears in a more streamlined version in Chapter 1 of Philip Pettit, *The State* (Princeton University Press 2023).

11 Hart (n 1) 89–92.

While the story focuses only on primary rules, the account it offers of the internal viewpoint that people in Prenormitania will adopt on those rules naturally extends, with suitable amendments, to the secondary rules on which Hart concentrates.[12] According to the story, primary rules will not only get to be established as universal regularities of behaviour in Prenormitania; in terms to be explained later, they will also come to be matters of perception, internalisation and ratification, and will be registered in the process as matters of personal commitment. Norms that achieve that status will count in an intuitively rich sense as enjoying an internal status in the perception and psychology of agents.

While the discussion that follows is meant to be faithful to the spirit of Hart's treatment of law, providing an extension that I hope he would find congenial, it is not designed as an exegesis or defence of his views. Thus, it ignores the vast literature that explores and often questions those views. It focuses only on the two aims cited: first, to tell a story about how the primary rules that he postulates might have emerged spontaneously in Prenormitania, as he thinks secondary rules would have emerged in Normitania; and, secondly, to show how essential to that process would have been the adoption of an intuitively internal point of view on the emergent rules.

In the conclusion at the end of the article, I look briefly at the main remarks that Hart makes about primary rules and argue that they apply to the sorts of social regularities or norms explored here. But the point in this exercise is to vindicate the claim that the role he ascribes to primary rules in grounding a legal system is precisely the sort of role played by the social norms introduced here. It is not to suggest that the genealogy provided for those norms is guided by reflection on Hart's comments.

Apart from that conclusion, the argument of the article is developed in three main sections. In the first, I draw on familiar stories about the emergence of social regularities to explain why we would expect universal, reputationally supported patterns of cooperative conduct—collectively beneficial norms—to appear in Prenormitania; other, objectionable norms are liable to have appeared there as well, of course, but they are not relevant to this project. In the second, I argue that, in all likelihood, those cooperative norms ought to achieve a distinctive social status among the population: as a matter of common awareness, they ought to be perceived as norms by members; to

12 Hart (n 1) 90. Hart assumes that in the case of secondary rules the internal point of view will involve a 'much extended and diversified' vocabulary, with new terms appearing like 'jurisdiction' and 'validity'. He suggests in that passage that primary rules will attract the internal point of view for most people in a 'simple regime of primary rules'. But he later allows that secondary rules may have to be seen from the internal point of view only by officials (115–117). Indeed, he seems to take this to be enough also for various first-order rules, on a par with primary rules, that are endorsed under secondary procedures; that may be because such rules need not be collectively beneficial in the manner of spontaneously supported primary rules: they may be introduced under minority pressure. None of these features undermines the relevance of the extension to his genealogy that is proposed here.

be internalised by them, not treated as making unnecessary and unwelcome demands; and to be ratified communally, as the members present them to youngsters and newcomers as norms that they will be expected to follow. The third and final section takes this line of thought further; it argues that there is a perfectly ordinary, pre-moral sense of commitment in which the members of the society will be personally committed to conforming to those cooperative norms, granting others a claim to censure any failure on their part to do so.

2. The Emergence of Universal Patterns of Cooperative Behaviour

A. *Some Assumptions*

There are a number of assumptions that we have to make about Prenormitania in order to explain the emergence of primary rules there. Many of these are so obvious that they may pass without remark, but five are particularly salient. They are all fairly plausible, and Hart himself endorses them, sometimes implicitly, sometimes explicitly, in his own story about the transition from Normitania to Lexitania.

A first assumption is that the members of this society are self-regarding to the extent that they are especially, if not exclusively, concerned about their own welfare and the welfare of those close to them. A second is that they are relatively rational in adopting measures for the promotion of that welfare: they are reliable in forming beliefs about available opportunities, for example, and in selecting appropriate means of action. And a third, more specific assumption is that they have the use of natural language. However rudimentary this language is, it allows them to communicate in the standard, distinctively human manner.[13]

While these first three assumptions are only implicit in Hart's discussion, he explicitly mentions another two. One is that the members of the society he explores enjoy 'approximate equality' with one another. None is 'so much more powerful than others, that he is able, without cooperation, to dominate or subdue them for more than a short period'.[14]

This is the most problematic of his assumptions, since most societies in history have been hierarchical, with one class or ethnicity or gender effectively

13 T. C. Scott-Phillips, *Speaking Our Minds: Why Human Communication Is Different, and How Language Evolved to Make it Special* (Palgrave Macmillan 2015). Speakers overtly convey their would-be attitudes to one another—how they take things to be, what they desire or intend to do—by advertising that that is indeed what they wish to convey. On this, see P. Grice, 'Meaning' (1957) 66 *Philosophical Review* 377; P. Grice, *Studies in the Ways of Words* (CUP 1989); S. Neale, 'Paul Grice and the Philosophy of Language' (1992) 15 *Linguistics and Philosophy* 509. They will do this truthfully if they actually have those attitudes, deceptively if they do not.

14 Hart (n 1) 195.

dominating others; they constitute the alphas in a world where there are also betas and gammas.[15] There are two possible defences for his approach, however, one quasi-philosophical, the other quasi-historical. The more obvious, quasi-philosophical defence is that, since Hart is looking at how the rules of a presumptively inclusive society might have emerged—and this necessarily in a counterfactual way—he can idealise the starting point without jeopardising the methodology described earlier.

The quasi-historical defence may be called upon if such idealisation is thought inappropriate. It consists in the claim that all that the genealogy needs strictly to suppose is, first, that there is one dominant class in the society, the alphas, among whom approximate equality obtains; second, that members of this class are likely to support cooperative rules, both primary and secondary, governing their interactions with one another; and, third, that there is nothing to stop those rules from extending to other classes in the society, if members of those classes manage to achieve more or less equal power with the alphas: this might come about spontaneously or, more likely, as a result of resistance and struggle. The cooperative rules that the genealogy would hold up as paradigm laws allowed to emerge on this model, as they undoubtedly emerged in the actual world, as rules governing primarily a privileged, relatively equal class: this, at any rate, provided there is no obstacle to their being extended to become rules governing everyone equally.[16]

Whether defended in the more philosophical or more historical manner, we will go along with Hart's assumption that Prenormitania is a society of equals in the attempt to elaborate his genealogy. Interpreted on the lines suggested, the assumption need not be as historically insensitive as it might otherwise seem.

15 This is certainly true of societies since the time of the agricultural revolution about 10,000 years ago; on the possibility of more equality in earlier groups, see C. Boehm, *Hierarchy in the Forest: The Evolution of Egalitarian Behavior* (Harvard UP 1999); C. Boix and F. Rosenbluth, 'Bones of Contention: The Political Economy of Height Inequality' (2014) 108 *American Political Science Review* 1. Hart (n 1) relaxes the assumption of equality in his discussion of international law.

16 In any hierarchical society of the kind envisaged in the genealogy, there would certainly be subjugating norms in place, expressing and enforcing the dominance of the alphas. But the idea is that such norms would be undone, and cooperative norms would be extended, if other people managed to gain equality with the alphas. To assume that there is a class of alphas among whom approximate equality holds is itself to idealise somewhat, holding out the possibility of a rule of cooperative norms before which all can aspire to be equal; it represents a more optimistic scenario than one where a single family dominates. The account later provided of how primary rules or social norms are likely to develop appeals to the economy of esteem, and this economy can explain the appearance of such subjugating norms: as honour among thieves may require hurting others, for example, so the same may be true of honour among alphas. See G. Brennan and P. Pettit, *The Economy of Esteem: An Essay on Civil and Political Society* (OUP 2004).

The fifth and final assumption that his and, indeed, our story needs is also more or less explicitly endorsed by Hart. This postulates that the members of the society are each dependent for their well-being on others reliably eschewing violence and deception and the like: on their practising what he casts as 'mutual forbearance and compromise'.[17] The assumption is that in Prenormitania it will be manifest to each member, as it will be manifest in any human society, that each needs to be able to rely on others for such basic forms of tolerance and cooperation.

B. Reliance, Reputation and Regularities

With these assumptions in place, it becomes intelligible why, for purely self interested reasons, each member of the society should display certain patterns of cooperative behaviour in dealing with others. Human beings may well be spontaneously cooperative, given the selectional advantage of such a disposition.[18] But while that disposition would increase the likelihood of cooperative behaviour in Prenormitania, we need not rely on its presence for postulating cooperation; the emergence of cooperative behaviour will be intelligible even if it is absent. Nor, for similar reasons, need we postulate that Prenormitanians are spontaneously disposed, for selectional reasons, to punish any defector by refusing to cooperate with them;[19] we need not rely on this possibility, even if it would help the case to be made for cooperation.

To start with a salient example, Prenormitanians may be expected to be truthful or sincere in making reports to one another and to be relatively careful about the reports they make. Each will depend on receiving reliable reports from others about features of the environment with which they are not immediately familiar: say, about whether the seasonal fish are returning to the river, whether the hunting prospects are better up north, whether the wild corn has begun to ripen, and so on. But if I am not reliable in the information I provide to you about such matters, I can hardly hope to find you reliable in providing information for me. And equally, I can hardly hope to get you to rely on me in any future scenario—to believe what I say—where it may be in my interest to secure your reliance.

Why should you bother to prove reliable when I seek information from you, since my proven lack of reliability will deprive you of a self-interested incentive to report reliably to me? Indeed, my lack of reliability may even provide you with a positive incentive to penalise me by not proving reliable; you may plausibly expect this to get me to rethink my attitude: to recognise that in

17 Hart (n 1) 195.

18 M. Tomasello, *Why We Cooperate* (MIT Press 2009); M. Tomasello, *A Natural History of Human Morality* (Harvard UP 2016).

19 E. Fehr and S. Gachter, 'Altruistic Punishment in Humans' (2002) 415 *Nature* 137.

exchanges with you, honesty is the best policy. And why, even more tellingly, can I expect to be able to get you to rely on me in the future, accepting what I say, if I have proved unreliable in the past? Once bitten, as the proverb goes, twice shy.

What holds in these regards for me, of course, will hold by the same token for you. And by that same token, it will hold for anyone who is likely to relate to another in a similar way: to relate, now as someone in need of information, now as someone in a position to provide it; now as someone anxious to get another to rely on them, now as someone whose reliance the other desires. In effect, it will hold for everyone insofar as everyone is bound to operate within relationships of mutual dependence with others.

Summing up this lesson, then, we Prenormitanians are each bound to be concerned to have a reputation among those with whom we interact for reliability as reporters. And this concern is bound to prompt us, at least in the general run of cases, to report truthfully and carefully to one another. In that run of cases, there will be little or no difficulty in telling the truth; there will not be particularly huge benefits, personal or even collective, to be won by deception; it will not be easy to hide our deception from those we mislead; and we will not be subject to impulses or passions that would overwhelm our recognition of the case for proving reliable.

Reliable truth telling has two salient characteristics: it is a collectively beneficial pattern or regularity in the sense that everyone is better off in any society to the extent that everyone reliably tells the truth to others; and yet it is an individually burdensome pattern in the sense that each may be better off still if they can rely on others to tell them the truth, while doing so themselves only when it suits their interests. The observations about truth telling highlight the likelihood that, despite its being individually burdensome in some cases, Prenormitanians will be generally disposed to support such a collectively beneficial pattern.

The points made in support of this conclusion apply also with other collectively beneficial, individually burdensome patterns or regularities. They argue that as you and I, and other members of the society, will generally tell the truth, so will we be generally non-violent in our behaviour towards one another, non-coercive in seeking to elicit one another's responses, faithful to the promises we make and, if there is a sense of ownership in place, respectful of property. Despite being collectively beneficial, any such pattern will be individually burdensome: we are each likely to wish that we could get away with breaching it opportunistically, while others reliably conform. Still, the reputational points made in support of the claim that Prenormitania is a truth telling society argue equally that it will be a society where non-violence, non coercion, promise-keeping, and so on are common patterns of behaviour. That they are behavioural patterns of this kind does not yet mean, of course, that they count as norms, let alone social norms: more on this in a moment.

C. *Multilateral, Reputational Support*

The reputational mechanism on which this story of cooperation relies generates a pattern of bilateral interaction and cooperation that resembles the pattern described in game-theory as tit-for-tat reciprocation.[20] This pattern applies whether the members in a pair of interactants act simultaneously in each encounter, take turns in acting or sometimes act simultaneously, sometimes take turns. A person follows the tit-for-tat strategy just in case they cooperate in the first interaction—they tell the truth, avoid violence, coercion and theft or keep their promises—and in every later episode they do whatever the other party did in the previous encounter with them: they cooperate if the other cooperated, they defect if the other defected.

Strictly speaking, tit-for-tat patterns might emerge in suitable forms of behaviour—say, in avoiding violence or even in providing assistance—in the absence of language; the reputational mechanism required does not require communication. It is not surprising, then, that there is some evidence that such patterns materialise among the members of many different species, not just amongst human beings.[21] But the presence of language means that the reputational mechanism can assume a particularly powerful, multilateral form. It can generate an encompassing economy of esteem.[22]

The desire to be thought cooperatively reliable by a partner gives you an incentive to cooperate, in the bilateral model considered up to now, insofar as such behaviour manifestly provides the other with evidence of your disposition to be cooperative with others—or at least to be cooperative with those who cooperate with you. But the presence of language—or, more generally, of a means of communication—has an effect that transforms the model, giving it a multilateral rather than just a bilateral character.

Language will enable you to give evidence of wanting to be reliably cooperative yourself by means other than actual cooperation. Giving favourable or unfavourable reports to third parties on the performance of others whom you can identify by name or description will provide evidence of that kind. If you gossip about the failure of others, then you manifestly stick your neck out, as we say: you invite the charge of hypocrisy, not just uncooperativeness, if you fail to prove reliable yourself. And by putting more at reputational stake in this way—by linking failure to a greater cost—you communicate all the more credibly your claim to be a cooperative, reliable agent yourself. By gossiping about the failures of others to third parties, you will invite them to think that,

20 It only resembles tit-for-tat, since it need not make requirements of the exacting kind imposed in game theory models. It need not require retaliation in response to any single defection, for example, and need not require a continued pattern of retaliatory defection until the other begins to cooperate. R. Axelrod, *The Evolution of Cooperation* (Basic Books 1984).

21 M. Nowak, 'Five Rules for the Evolution of Cooperation' (2006) 314 *Science* 1560.

22 Brennan and Pettit (n 16).

running the risk of being named a hypocrite if you fail to cooperate, you must definitely be a reliable cooperator.

In view of the impact of language, Prenormitania will be a gossipy society, in which you and I realise that if we let down someone in an interaction, that may have multilateral as well as bilateral costs. The betrayal may not only lead the person you let down not to cooperate with you in future; it may also deny you the possibility of securing the cooperation of others among whom word of your defection has spread. Language will allow your victim's bad opinion of you to propagate and gain wider currency, giving you a bad name: a standing reputation for being unreliable.

This reputation may not only come to be shared widely in your local networks, or in the society at large, it may even come to be shared widely as a matter of common awareness. This will happen if the evidence leads each, not just to form a bad opinion of you, but to become aware that each holds such a bad opinion, to become aware that each is aware in turn of this, and so on.[23] At that point, you will not only be esteemed badly by each, suffering a consequent degree of shame; you will be badly esteemed in the public manner associated with stigma.

D. *Regularities and Norms*

The multilateral reinforcement of the reputational mechanism will give rise to an economy of esteem insofar as each of us in Prenormitania gains a particularly powerful motive for seeking to behave cooperatively in the general run of cases. These are cases, as we characterised them earlier, where there are no particular difficulties that block our cooperative behaviour, there are no enormous benefits to be won by defection, it is not easy to hide defection and we are not overwhelmed by countervailing impulses or passions. In any such case, each of us may be tempted to defect on the particular person we are dealing with: the bilateral reputational incentive may not be powerful enough to ensure cooperation. But that temptation will be much weaker in the presence of the multilateral reputational incentive that comes onstream with communication and language. The concern for how we are likely to be seen by others in general—the concern with our good name—should serve to keep most of us onside in most relevant cases.

These observations support a claim that various collectively beneficial, if individually burdensome, patterns of cooperation will emerge in Prenormitania. Each such pattern or regularity, R, will satisfy broadly the following conditions, whether R involves reliably telling the truth, reliably avoiding violence or coercion, promise-breaking or theft. Almost everyone in the community conforms to R, at least when dealing with those who have not breached R in

23 D. Lewis, *Convention* (Harvard UP 1969). A more detailed account of common awareness is offered in the next section.

a previous encounter. Almost everyone expects such conformity to attract a favourable reputation among others and/or nonconformity to attract an unfavourable reputation. Almost everyone is supported in their conformity to R by expecting such reputational benefits and costs. The sorts of regularity that R exemplifies contrast with mere conventions, such as the convention of driving on the right or driving on the left hand side of the road.[24] Conventions, unlike the regularity of truth telling, are grounded in the attraction for each of us, including each of us in Prenormitania, of doing the same thing as others—securing a desired form of coordination—and need not attract or depend in any way on the expectation of reputational benefits. Thus, conforming to a convention is not individually burdensome, and does not give rise to freeriding problems, in the manner in which the regularities we are envisaging may do. You will not be tempted, on approaching another car, to break convention, drive in the same lane and risk a head-on collision.[25]

The three conditions they satisfy mean that the sorts of regularity envisaged here are distinct not just from mere conventions, but also from a number of other social regularities that may arise in any society, including Prenormitania. Thus, the fact that they are generally maintained in people's behaviour, as the first condition stipulates, distinguishes them from standards honoured more in the breach than in the observance, such as a supererogatory ideal that we routinely applaud but rarely realise. The fact that they reflect the mutually expected attitudes of agents toward conformity, as the second condition holds, means that they are distinct from regularities to which others are manifestly indifferent, such as the regularity whereby most people sleep at night, not during the day. And the fact that they are supported by that expectation, as the third condition holds, means that they are distinct from regularities such as that involved in taking steps to guard against penury in old age; it is unlikely that people are motivated to display such prudence by expecting that others will think well of them for doing so.

How to characterise the universal patterns or regularities captured in our conditions? For want of a better term, we may describe them as norms that obtain among the members of the society. But as we shall see in the third section, there is good reason to regard them as pre-social rather than properly social norms. For all that has been said here, as we shall see, they may not be generally perceived as norms to which almost everyone conforms; the

24 Ibid.

25 E. Ullmann-Margalit, *The Emergence of Norms* (OUP 1977). Leslie Green (n 1) xxii–xxiii argues rightly that Hart is mistaken to suggest in a later comment that his theory applies mainly to rules that have a conventional, coordinating aspect. Individually burdensome rules, on which *The Concept of Law* focuses, are not mere devices of coordination, like the convention governing the side of the road on which to drive.

regularities involved may obtain without this being registered by the people who sustain them.[26]

E. *The Role of Excuses*

Before moving on to the discussion of perception, it may be useful to mention one feature of the pre-social norms that we might expect to emerge in Prenormitania. This is that it is bound to be possible within an economy of esteem for someone to breach a norm, be seen to breach the norm and yet avoid the reputational costs of doing so.

Suppose, for example, that I mislead you by a report that the blackberries on the other side of a local hill have ripened. It may be that you go in search of them and find they are still not fit for picking or find instead that they have all been picked already. And imagine that I convince you either that they really looked ripe to me—this, perhaps, because I had seen them in the setting sun—or that someone picked them between the time I observed them or made my report and the time of your search. Imagine, in short, that I can credibly explain my having misled you either by appeal to misleading evidence or a changed world.

In such a case, it would be self-defeating of you to treat me as if I had breached the norm of truth telling by not being careful or truthful in the report; it would lead you to expel me unnecessarily from the community of those you can generally rely on. And so, we may expect you to keep me within that circle if you accept a misleading-evidence or changed-world explanation. In virtue of having this effect, the explanation counts as an excuse; it enables me to get off the reputational hook.

The observation suggests that while the economy of esteem will motivate people in Prenormitania to act in a way that establishes a norm of truth

26 Anticipating discussion in the next section, social norms must plausibly satisfy the three clauses given, plus a fourth clause to the effect that the first clause, or even all three clauses, are fulfilled as a matter of common awareness. For an earlier version of this conception of social norms, see P. Pettit, 'Virtus Normativa: Rational Choice Perspectives' (1990) 100 *Ethics* 725, reprinted in P Pettit, *Rules, Reasons, and Norms* (OUP 2002) and Brennan and Pettit (n 16); the current version appears in P. Pettit, 'Value-Mistaken and Virtue-Mistaken Norms: Political Legitimization Without Morality?' in J. Kuehnelt (ed), *Political Legitimization Without Morality?* (Springer 2008). Also see P. Pettit, *The Robust Demands of the Good: Ethics with Attachment, Virtue and Respect* (OUP 2015); Pettit (n 7). The notion of a social norm picks up points made in a variety of approaches. See e.g. P. Winch, *The Idea of a Social Science and its Relation to Philosophy* (Routledge 1963); J. Coleman, *Foundations of Social Theory* (Harvard UP 1990); E. Sober and D. S. Wilson, *Unto Others: The Evolution and Psychology of Unselfish Behavior* (Harvard UP 1998); J. Elster, *Alchemies of the Mind: Rationality and the Emotions* (CUP 1999); S. Shapiro, *Legality* (Harvard UP 2011). For an insightful development of the idea of reputationally supported norms, see K. A. Appiah, *The Honor Code: How Moral Revolutions Happen* (Norton 2010). For an overarching theory that is reconcilable with that adopted here, although it uses terminology somewhat differently, see G. Brennan and others, *Explaining Norms* (OUP 2013).

telling—and, of course, norms of non-violence and the like as well—it will operate in a relatively nuanced way that leaves room for letting those who breach such norms occasionally off the hook. This observation about excuses will be important later, in our discussion of ratification. It applies straightforwardly to full excuses of the kind illustrated, but also extends to corresponding partial excuses, as we generally call them; to excuses of a distinct non-epistemic kind such as 'I was coerced to say what I did'; and, indeed, to the exemptions relevant in cases where someone is not functioning properly as a person.[27]

3. The Perception, Internalisation and Ratification of Cooperative Norms

For all that we have said about the norms that are likely to emerge and stabilise in Prenormitania, it should be clear that they are not likely to be seen by agents from within anything like Hart's internal point of view. That point of view presupposes that those who conform to the rules see them as general rules, and take an attitude towards them that contrasts with that of an outsider or outlier. But, for all that has been said up to now, Prenormitanians may not be able to see the norms to which they conform as general rules of this kind and may not be able to adopt any attitude whatsoever towards them.

A. *Perception*

The cooperative norms whose emergence is documented in the previous section may constitute universal patterns that escape the notice of those who sustain them. Adam Smith famously argued that various aggregate economic regularities may emerge behind people's backs 'by an invisible hand'; strictly, he should have said by a not necessarily visible hand.[28] The story told about the emergence of norms of truth telling, non-violence, non-coercion and the like has a similar character. For all it stipulates, the patterns that emerge as a result of people's each seeking to have the reputation for being reliable cooperators may be regularities of the same, unnoticed kind.

You and I, and everybody else in Prenormitania, may be led by reputational pressures to cooperate reliably in the domains illustrated without anyone noticing that this is what more or less everyone in the society does: that it constitutes a more or less universal pattern. Confronted now with one interlocutor or interactant, now with another, you may confidently expect that person

27 See J. Gardner, *Offences and Defences: Selected Essays in the Philosophy of Criminal Law* (OUP 2007). The observation connects with some of the comments made by Richard Holton on how legal rules may have exceptions, although he concentrates on cases where a failure to stick by a rule is not so much excusable as justifiable: this, in virtue of intuitively more important considerations trumping the case for abiding by the rule. See R. Holton, 'The Exception Proves the Rule' (2010) 18 *Journal of Political Philosophy* 369.

28 A. Smith, *The Theory of the Moral Sentiments* (Liberty Classics 1982) 184–185.

to be cooperative; in that sense, you may believe of everyone you confront, or are even liable to confront, that they are cooperative. But you may not register this as a general truth; you may not register the truth of the proposition that everyone, or almost everyone, is cooperatively disposed.

For all that has been said so far, then, it may be true that, for any rule or norm like that of truth telling or non-violence or whatever, you as an agent in the society will prefer in any instance to act in a way that happens to involve conforming to the rule; you will have a powerful reputational incentive to act in that manner. But it need not be true that you prefer to conform to the rule or norm under that description of what you do: you may not be aware that there is a general rule or norm to conform to.

It is highly likely, however, that as a regularity like truth telling or non violence or whatever gets established in a society, it will come to be perceived as an aggregate fact about how people behave in the society: the evidence of its obtaining will be there for all to see. Indeed, it is likely that it will come to be perceived in this way as a matter of common awareness among the members of the society. Not only will the evidence be there for all to see; it will be there for all to see that the evidence is there for all to see; it will be there for all to see that it is there for all to see that the evidence is there for all to see; and so on. In short, the evidence will not just be accessible, but accessibly accessible, accessibly accessibly accessible, and so on in a recurring pattern. The universal regularity of truth telling or non-violence or whatever will be established as a matter of common awareness: each will be aware that it holds, aware that each is aware that it holds, aware that each is aware that each is aware of this, and so on in the usual hierarchy.[29]

That a norm in the sense characterised earlier is perceived by all, as a matter of common awareness, means that it deserves to be cast as a properly social norm. It will be clear to you, as it will be clear to each, that conformity is the local norm, as we say. It is the norm in the statistical sense of being a routine, expected pattern in the society. And it is the norm in the regulative sense of constituting a *sine qua non* condition for anyone hoping to gain acceptance in the society: fail to live up to it, and you will count as an outsider or an offender.[30]

29 Lewis (n 23). This does not require that everyone is actively aware at each level in the hierarchy of the claim that common awareness supports there; that would be impossible for any finite mind. All that it need require is that each is disposed, should they confront and understand the relevant question at any level, to answer in the affirmative.

30 The argument for its being a matter of common awareness that a regularity exists suggests that it will also be a matter of common awareness that the other two clauses in our characterisation of a norm are satisfied. Similar observations about the evidence accessible to each party, accessibly accessible to each, and so on, apply with these clauses as well as with the first. Thus, in all likelihood, it will not only be the case that it is a matter of common awareness that almost everybody conforms to the regularity, R; it will also be a matter of common awareness that almost everybody will expect conformity to attract a positive reputation and/or non-conformity a negative, and that this expectation will support people's tendency to conform.

At this point in the genealogy, it may be thought that the internal point of view makes a first appearance. You will not just have a reputational incentive to act in a way that happens, perhaps unbeknownst to you, to involve conforming to a norm like that of truth telling; you will now have a reputational incentive to conform to the norm as such: to conform consciously or knowingly to the norm. Thus, it will at least be possible for you and others to have a general attitude towards the norm, and the question is whether acting on the reputational incentive means that that attitude will constitute an internal point of view.

The reputational incentive on which you act will be that if you do not conform with the universal pattern involved, then you will not be one of the gang; your social identity and allegiance will be in doubt. You will not be in tune with how things, as we others may say, are done around here. This suggests that, recognising the incentive on offer, you will not view the norm from an outsider or outlier perspective; you will display the sort of profile that Hart associates with the internal point of view.

But does the suggestion stand up to reflection? Why think that having a self interested, reputational incentive for conforming knowingly to the norm marks off your attitude from that of an outlier who conforms unwillingly to it? After all, the unwilling outlier in a community might also conform knowingly to a norm and might have a self-interested incentive for conforming.

Nothing much hangs on how we decide this question. But a possible reason for thinking that the internal point of view already enters at this point is that there is a salient difference between acting to avoid a reputational penalty for being out of line with others and acting to avoid, say, a physical penalty for being out of line. A concern with the reputational penalty involves a concern for how you stand in the opinion of others, whereas a concern with the physical penalty may not involve anything of that character.

Even if the self-interested, reputational concern that leads you to abide by a norm like that of truth telling or non-violence is distinct in this way from the fear of a physical penalty—and even if it is taken to mark the first appearance of an internal point of view—it has one feature in common with the fear of a penalty that is worth noting. This is that it has a causal-instrumental character. If you fail to conform in this or any instance, then the consequence you fear is a downstream, causal effect: viz., that you will get a name for being unreliable in relevant exchanges and, more generally, for not accommodating recognised expectations.

While the causal-instrumental consideration is more or less bound to support conformity in this way, however, it is important to notice that the consideration may be relevant without being the conscious, motivating reason why you or anyone else generally conforms. You and others may be actively moved, not by self-interested calculation, but by sheer habit or even by more idealistic considerations. And yet it may remain the case that the causal-instrumental consideration plays an important role in supporting your compliance.

This will happen in an obvious way if the self-interest is effectively motivating only with the motivational help of habit or idealism. But it may also happen, and may be more likely to happen, even when habit or idealism are the only motives driving the behaviour. In this case, the causal-instrumental consideration can play an important back-up role, being there to prompt you to conform in the event that the more regular motive fails: in the event, for example, that habit falters or idealism wanes. The consideration may be salient enough to alert you or any would-be defector to the self-interested costs of defection and to put you back on track. It may monitor your behaviour, coming into play if, and only if, it is needed; it may make it robust over scenarios where the usual generators of conformity fail.

B. Internalisation

We have seen that a norm may obtain in a society without being perceived as a norm and that it is only with perception that it deserves to be cast as a properly social norm. But the next, surprising point to notice is that a norm may be perceived as a norm, and be in that sense established, without being internalised among people: this, on a more or less intuitive understanding of what that involves.[31] Internalisation connects with Hart's notion of the internal point of view, but it is not exhaustive of the idea, as will be shown by the account presented later.

In order to see what internalisation means, and why it need not materialise with some norms, it may be useful to consider the phenomenon of pluralistic ignorance, as it has been described by two psychologists, D. A. Prentice and D. T. Miller.[32] In an experiment that they conducted on a university campus, they found that while the students they studied generally conformed to a regularity of drinking a certain amount of alcohol at parties and other events, while they generally expected that conforming to that regularity was essential for maintaining a suitable reputation in the eyes of others and while they were therefore generally motivated to drink the prescribed amount, the expectation that each of the others would disapprove of a failure to conform was mistaken. In fact, most of the students thought that the amount in question was excessive and would have preferred not to be constrained by the norm they combined to sustain.

The drinking norm in operation among the students in this example is a genuine norm, by our account. It is a regularity that meets all the conditions in our earlier characterisation, since almost everybody conforms, almost everybody expects conformity to be essential for reputation and almost everybody is motivated by that expectation to conform. Moreover, plausibly, it is a regularity that obtains as a matter of common awareness in the student body

31 R. D. Cooter, 'Structural Adjudication and the New Law Merchant: A Model of Decentralized Law' (1994) 14 *International Review of Law and Economics* 215.

32 D. A. Prentice and D. T. Miller, 'Pluralistic Ignorance and Alcohol Use on Campus' (1993) 64 *Journal of Personality and Social Psychology* 243.

involved: it is a perceived norm, established as a socially routine and socially regulative pattern.

But however far it qualifies as a norm, and however fully it is perceived as a norm on all sides, the drinking rule does not enjoy internalisation in the sense invoked here. It is true, as with any perceived norm, that each agent in the group has a causal-instrumental reason to conform, expecting to suffer a serious reputational cost in the event of not doing so; that expectation is supported by the perception that conformity is the socially routine, regulative pattern. But the striking thing is that while everyone recognises that conformity is the general pattern, and forms the corresponding expectation about the reputational stakes, no one apparently prefers that that pattern should obtain. Each would prefer, presumably, that the norm in place amongst them should require the consumption of a lesser amount of alcohol or perhaps allow the consumption of none at all.

This observation allows us to define internalisation. Any perceived norm that leads most or all members of a group to do X is going to be supported by the expectation among members that defection will have reputational costs, and compliance reputational benefits. But, as we can now see, members may not generally prefer that X-ing be the established pattern—they may each prefer a feasible, salient alternative, Y-ing—and, as a consequence, may not think ill of someone who fails to do X—or well of someone who does X—and thereby impose a reputational sanction. In that case, we can say, the norm will not be internalised. In order for the norm to be internalised, the members of the relevant group must generally prefer that X-ing be the established pattern—rather than any feasible, salient alternative, if indeed there is one—and must, in consequence, be disposed to think ill of someone who fails to abide by it and well of someone who lives up to it.

It may be that many norms obtain despite the fact of not being internalised in this sense by those who sustain them.[33] And it may be that some norms are internalised but only very reluctantly on the part of some: they may prefer that a norm obtains only because more appealing alternatives are infeasible. Norms of a kind that benefit some at a cost to others are unlikely to be internalised by those others, or at least unlikely to be internalised enthusiastically. But the cooperative sorts of norms at the focus of discussion here are not unbalanced in that manner, and are likely both to be internalised and internalised with enthusiasm.

Everyone in Prenormitania stands to benefit from people's generally conforming to norms like those of truthfulness, non-violence and non-coercion, keeping promises and, at a stretch, respecting property; this last case will be problematic to the extent that the local understanding of property is contested. People may each wish they could themselves breach those norms while others conform, but that alternative is not only infeasible; being a pattern

33 Pettit, 'Value-Mistaken and Virtue-Mistaken Norms' (n 26).

that no one else could be expected to support, it hardly counts as an alternative at all. Among the alternatives in any area, then, they are going to prefer that everyone should conform to the sort of norm mentioned: truth telling, non-violence, non-coercion, fidelity to promises or respect for property.

The upshot is that the pre-social norms characterised in the first section are not only likely to be perceived as social demands in Prenormitania, but also to be internalised spontaneously by those who live under them; henceforth I shall take the internalisation they attract to be of the enthusiastic variety. Indeed, those norms are likely to be internalised as a matter of common awareness. This is because similar points to those that were invoked in earlier cases apply here. The evidence of internalisation—the clear appeal of the norms—will itself be evidently available to all. The fact that it is evidently available to all will itself be evidently available to all. And so on in the usual pattern.

The perception of a norm as a norm may already introduce an internal point of view among those to whom it applies, as tentatively suggested earlier, with each having a causal-instrumental, reputational reason for complying with the norm. But the internalisation of the norm certainly marks the advent of an internal point of view. It puts into play a new respect in which the viewpoint of members contrasts with the detached perspective of outsiders or outliers.

Insofar as you internalise a norm like truth telling or non-violence, you will not only have a causal-instrumental reason for conforming; you will also be responsive to the consideration that by conforming you contribute a necessary element to the universal pattern of truth telling or non-violence, where that is a pattern that you prefer to obtain, given that you cannot feasibly hope to freeride. Your conformity is necessary to that pattern, because if you did not conform, the pattern would not obtain. As a matter of its nature as an act of conformity, then, the action will have a property that makes it attractive to you: the property of making universal conformity possible. By conforming, you help to realise that property, where realising it is an immediate, constitutive effect rather than an effect of a downstream, causal kind.[34]

Because the realisation of that property is an effect of what you do—it is something you bring about by conforming—it still counts as an instrumental reason for conforming. But it is a constitutive, not a causal, reason. And it is a reason that may not reflect any concern for your own interests; this is consistent with the genealogy, although not required by it. You may be inclined to act in the relatively disinterested way required spontaneously, rather than for any ulterior motive of self-interest. Or you may embrace that behaviour as a personal ideal: recognising that you would want to act on the disinterested

34 P. Pettit, 'Three Mistakes About Doing Good (and Bad)' (2018) 35 *Journal of Applied Philosophy* 1.

inclination even if you were impeded by laziness, lassitude or distraction, you may be moved by that very consideration to overcome any such impediment.[35]

C. *Ratification*

As they have been characterised so far in the genealogy, cooperative norms of truth telling, non-violence and the like are bound to attract the support of members on the basis of self-interest, although they may also happen to appeal to their spontaneous inclinations or ideals, or answer to their unthinking habits; in that case, the self-interest will provide back-up reinforcement: it will monitor the behaviour of any member, being ready to play an active part in motivating compliance if, but only if, the independent inclination or ideal fails.

For all that the genealogy requires, then, the norms established will recommend themselves to people in a purely personal perspective; they are rules of behaviour that people each have their own personal reasons—albeit reasons of a similar kind—for adopting. Social ratification, as envisaged here, would introduce yet a further dimension to their way of viewing the norms. It would lead them to see the norms as standards that they support as a community and are obliged, for that reason, to honour as members.

The ratification of a norm presupposes its internalisation, as its internalisation presupposes its perception. To ratify a norm, by the account adopted here, is to accept that you cannot object to anyone's avowing a favourable attitude towards it in your name as a member of the group. In order to understand what ratification involves, then, it is essential to move away a little from the main line of argument and introduce the notion of avowal.

Avowal is a way of communicating an attitude that contrasts saliently with giving a report on the presence of the attitude. If I report on an attitude of my own, and I turn out not to display the attitude, then, as noted at the end of section 1 I can seek to excuse myself on the grounds that I was misled about my mind or that I changed my mind since making the report. Asked about whether I trust Jones, for example, I may report that I think that I trust Jones but am not quite sure. In that case, if it turns out that I later behave as if Jones is not trustworthy, I may excuse my miscommunication by saying that I must have been wrong about myself—that it seemed to me that I felt a trust I turned out not to display—or that I ceased to trust him after I made the report. Avowing an attitude contrasts with reporting insofar as it sets aside the misleading-mind excuse (pledging an attitude, which sets aside the changed mind excuse as well, will be discussed shortly). Suppose that, in answer to the

35 M. Smith, *The Moral Problem* (Blackwell 1994). Instrumental reasons are often wrongly taken to be necessarily causal-instrumental and necessarily self-interested. The sort of reason envisaged in the text is instrumental in the sense that you act on an instrumental reason when you return a book in order to keep a promise, or help me out because that is what friendship requires.

query, I say: yes, Jones is trustworthy. In that case, by standard conventions, I cannot explain my later acting as if Jones is not trustworthy by saying that I must have got my attitude wrong. Under those conventions, as I understand avowal, I avow my belief that Jones is trustworthy rather than just reporting it. I take a greater risk in communicating my attitude than a report would involve, since I will not be able to invoke the misleading-evidence excuse for a miscommunication. And, of course, I thereby make my communication more credible. Why, you may think, would I opt for an avowal instead of a report unless I was very confident of my trust in Jones?[36]

As I can avow a belief or other attitude in my own name, so can I avow it in the name of others, too. I can assume the authority to speak for them, as in saying 'Jones enjoys the trust of all of us,' or something of the kind. If others allow me to avow such an attitude in their name as well as mine, then they will not be able later to say that I got them wrong. They might say this of a journalist reporting on their attitude, but they could not say it of someone they treated as a spokesperson with the right of avowal.

Others would give me the right to make that sort of avowal in their name in the unlikely event that they had made a pledge to act according to whatever attitudes I ascribe to them, at least in a certain domain. In pledging an intention to act in that way, they would each have had to communicate an intention to live up to my words in a way that denies them access both to the misleading-mind and to the changed-mind excuse. They could not later excuse a failure to live up to my words either by claiming that they had misread their own intention or by saying that they had changed their minds. In making a pledge, they would have set aside both the misleading-evidence excuse that avowing forecloses and the changed-mind excuse that it still allows.

By Hobbes's account of group agency,[37] individuals who wish to incorporate as an agent—a company, for example, or a commonwealth—must pledge in this way to follow the words of a spokesperson, authorising an individual or a majoritarian body to speak in their name as a group.[38] Outside that special context, however, it is vanishingly unlikely that others might pledge to let me speak for them, allowing me to ascribe the attitude to them on such a basis that they cannot excuse failing to display it by saying that I got them wrong. Why, independently of the pressures of group agency, would others pledge to act on any attitudes that I ascribe? Why would they authorise me *ex ante*

36 For a general, broadly congenial account of avowal, see D. Bar-on, *Speaking My Mind: Expression and Self-Knowledge* (OUP 2004). For my account of avowing and the pledging mentioned in the next chapter, see P. Pettit, 'Making Up Your Mind' (2016) 24 *European Journal of Philosophy* 3; Pettit (n 7).

37 T. Hobbes, *Leviathan* (E. Curley ed, Hackett 1994) Ch 16.

38 P. Pettit, *Made with Words: Hobbes on Language, Mind and Politics* (Princeton UP 2008); P. Pettit, 'Group Agents Are Not Expressive, Pragmatic or Theoretical Fictions' (2014) 79 *Erkenntnis* 1641.

as someone who can speak for their attitudes—even their attitudes in quite a restricted domain—with the status of an avower?

While others are unlikely to give me an *ex ante* authorisation to speak for them, however, there is another way in which I might manage to avow an attitude in their name: I might bet on their *ex post* authorisation and hazard something that counts by conventional or contextual criteria—these will make it clear that I am not merely playing the role of a reporter—as an avowal of a shared attitude. Saying that Jones enjoys all our trust, for example, I might bet on no one objecting to my claiming the role of their spokesperson. And if I get away with the presumption, facing no objection, I will count it as having avowed the attitude successfully in the name of all. Others may not have said 'Yea' *ex ante* to my communication of their attitude but, despite having the opportunity to do so, they will not have said 'Nay' *ex post*. In that sense, they will have virtually, if not actively, authorised my speaking for them.[39]

Given this account of how someone may avow an attitude on behalf of others, it should be clear that any member of Prenormitania will be positioned to avow a favourable attitude on the part of all towards any of the cooperative norms that are perceived and internalised in the community. Given the entrenchment of those norms as a result of their being manifestly perceived and internalised on all sides, it is going to be a safe bet that others will not object to anyone's presuming to avow such an attitude on the part of the society as a whole.

But why would someone be motivated to exercise this capacity for making an avowal in the name of all? Because doing so is bound to be reputationally attractive. The reputational concern, as noted earlier, will give people an incentive to gossip about others who fail to conform, since this will make it manifestly more costly for them to let others down themselves; it will expose them to the charge of hypocrisy. As that motive explains why people will have an incentive to gossip about how far others conform, so it will give them an incentive to avow on behalf of all a favourable attitude towards cooperative norms. By doing so, as by gossiping about others, they will stick their necks out, raise the cost of not conforming themselves and increase the confidence of others that they are reliable conformers.

The members of Prenormitania will not only have the general ability to avow a favourable attitude towards cooperative norms in the name of the society, and they will not only have a personal, reputationally based incentive for doing this: they will also have lots of opportunity for making such avowals.

39 By standard accounts of conversation, that is what we routinely do as we presume to contribute to a shared body of attitudes in speaking with others, where the absence of objection by any other means that our contribution gets to be registered by each participant as part of that corpus: part of the common ground between us; see R. Stalnaker, 'Assertion' in P. Cole (ed), *Syntax and Semantics: Pragmatics* (Academic Press 1978); D. Lewis, *Philosophical Papers* (Vol. 1, OUP 1983) Ch 13.

It will be clearly appropriate to do so in teaching the young about how they should behave, in introducing new arrivals to the society and, of course, in reminding offenders of how they have erred. In each case, it will make perfect sense to claim to speak for the society as a whole in claiming that this or that pattern is how we do things around here and how we expect people generally to behave.

Back now to ratification. If any member of Prenormitania has the capacity, the motive and the opportunity to avow in everyone's name a favourable attitude towards cooperative norms, then this is certain to be a matter of common awareness: the evidence that that is so will be accessible to all, accessibly accessible to all, accessibly accessibly accessible to all, and so on. But if it is a matter of common awareness that anyone can avow such an attitude in your name or mine, it will equally be a matter of common awareness that, because we internalise the norm—and not just, for example, because it would be embarrassing to do so—none of us can demur; the conditions that make any such avowal appropriate will make it inappropriate for us to object. As a matter of common awareness, then, we each not only favour cooperative norms individually, but also favour them collectively as members of the community who identify with how things are done there. We ratify the norms together, giving them our shared, social imprimatur.

Ratification in this sense takes the internal point of view further than perception and internalisation, setting up a new dimension of contrast with the perspective of the outsider or outlier. In Prenormitania, it turns out that we not only each see the norms as attractive from an individual perspective, internalising them readily, we also see them as attractive in our social identity, joining with others in supporting and celebrating them. Insofar as the norms have the authority of the community behind them in this way, they will present to us, ironically, as imposing requirements from without. We may favour them in our social identity, but that identity is only part of who we are. So, the very ratification of norms to which we are party in that identity may give them the aspect of obligations to which we are subjected, willy-nilly, in our capacity as individuals.[40]

40 If Hart's story about primary—and, by extension, secondary—rules explains ratification, then that may help to answer the criticism, roughly, that he cannot account for the fact that when a regime of law is in place, members of the society will take the law to rule on how each ought to behave, at least in important respects, providing a basis for exhorting themselves or others to conformity. Shapiro (n 26) formulates this sort of challenge in one way; for other formulations, see Joseph Raz, 'About Morality and the Nature of Law' (2003) 48 *American Journal of Jurisprudence* 1; D. Plunkett, 'Legal Positivism and the Moral Aim Thesis' (2013) 33 *Oxford Journal of Legal Studies* 563.

4. The Personal Commitment that Cooperative Norms Attract

A. *The Internal Point of View*

The appearance in Prenormitania of cooperative regularities that are generally perceived, internalised and ratified as norms means that the society now well and truly deserves the name of Normitania. Those regularities constitute social norms of broadly the kind that Hart casts as primary rules. And they establish the starting point for his genealogy of law: for his argument that Normitania is likely to give way to Lexitania.

The genealogy of Normitania highlights the fact that members of the society are likely to adopt a point of view on their shared norms that is saliently different from that of outside or detached observers; it fleshes out the idea of the internal point of view. Those on the outside will see the norms only as a basis for predicting how members will behave in various circumstances and, if they enter the society, how they will be expected to behave themselves. But the members of Normitania will generally perceive, internalise and ratify them as norms, adopting a stance that marks them off as insiders and, unlike outliers, as more or less willing adherents.

There is one further feature of how Normitanians will see those norms that this final section introduces; it consists in their viewing the norms as matters of personal commitment. This feature is bound to appear when conditions like those documented in the two previous sections have been realised; in that sense, it is a derived, not a novel, development. But it is worth highlighting because it reveals a further contrast between their point of view on the norms they sustain and the point of view of outsiders or outliers. It uncovers another dimension in the notion of an internal point of view.

B. *Responsibility Ascribed and Invited*

The norms considered so far are all socially constructed rules, as Hart emphasises that primary rules are socially constructed. But even though they are social constructs—better perhaps, social precipitates—there is a question as to how far we in Normitania invite others to hold us responsible to them.

The norms are patterns to which we each hold one another to account insofar as we react negatively to defection: we refuse to cooperate with offenders, we gossip about their offences and we indict them with failing to live up to socially ratified expectations. In reacting to defection in such ways, we may be said to hold one another responsible for conformity to the established norms: to hold them to account. And, that being manifest, we each expect to be held responsible for conformity ourselves.

But there is a difference between our each expecting to be held responsible in this sense by others—this may be something we accept but regret—and our each positively inviting others to hold us responsible. To invite others to hold us responsible is to grant them a claim against us—an entitlement to hold us to the norms—recognising that they have an important standing in our lives. And it turns out that we in Normitania cannot help but issue such an invitation to one another, and confer such an entitlement.[41]

C. Commitment

The paradigm case where I invite responsibility as well as expecting to be ascribed responsibility is marked by the notion of commitment, as it is used in ordinary exchange. When I have committed myself to act in a certain way, I clearly give you a claim over me that I should act in that way. And if I act contrary to my word, then I wrong you by denying you that claim. Suppose I commit myself not to tell a hurtful story about you in certain company and I do then tell that story. I will do you a disservice insofar as I hurt you by the story I tell. But I will do you a distinct disservice insofar as I deny you the claim that my commitment gave you. In virtue of having made the commitment, I owe you my silence on the matter in question, to invoke a familiar commercial metaphor, and I fail to discharge that debt.

The most salient way in which the residents of Normitania might invite others to hold them responsible for conforming to cooperative norms, giving others a distinctive claim against them, would be by committing themselves to live by those norms. In ordinary usage, however, the notion of commitment belongs with morality, being tied up with ideas of right and wrong, obligation and permission. And it would offend against the spirit of Hart's approach to introduce a moralised notion into a genealogical narrative. So is there a non moral counterpart that might serve the role of such commitment instead? As a matter of fact, there is.

As already noted, to report about one or another of your attitudes—a belief, a desire, an intention or whatever—is to leave open two sorts of explanations for not displaying such an attitude later that may get you off the reputational hook: first, that you were misled about your own mind in making the report; and second, that you changed your mind since making it. Those can each serve as excuses that you might well make if a report about a third person's mind turned out to be false. And if your communications about your own attitudes

41 For an analogue of the distinction between my expecting to be held responsible to certain norms and my inviting others to hold me responsible, consider the difference marked in recent moral theory between being held responsible from a third-person and a second-person standpoint: S. Darwall, *The Second-Person Standpoint: Morality, Respect, and Accountability* (Harvard UP 2006). I may be blamed from a third-person standpoint for doing something that hurts another or that breaches a duty I have, or that offends against a general precept of behaviour. In this sort of case, broadly described, I may be said to do wrong because I do bad. I may be said to do wrong in another more complex case, however, not so much because I do bad—although I may indeed do something that is independently bad—but rather because I act, as we say, in a way that wrongs someone: I act contrary to a claim that by common assent they have over me.

were of a similar kind—if you spoke about yourself as you might speak about another—then you might claim to explain and excuse a miscommunication on either basis.

But, as emphasised, two sorts of speech acts are distinct from attitudinal reports in manifestly setting aside such excuses. The avowal of an attitude sets aside the misleading-mind excuse, as in communicating a belief that Jones is trustworthy by saying simply 'Jones is trustworthy' or an intention to X by saying 'X-ing is the thing to do' or, in a suitable context, 'my intention is to X'. And the pledging of an attitude, which may be possible only with intentions, involves setting aside both excuses at once, as in saying 'Rely on me: I am going to X' or simply 'I promise to X'.[42]

Avowals and pledges involve commitment in a game-theory rather than a moral sense. They are acts of communication in which I as speaker choose to stake my reputation on the attitude I self-ascribe being as I characterise it. In the case of avowing an attitude, I foreclose the possibility of excusing a miscommunication by saying: 'I must have got myself wrong: I thought that is what I believed or intended.' In the case of pledging an intention to X—in effect, making a promise to X—I foreclose that possibility and also the possibility of saying 'I changed my mind since speaking with you.'

In each case, it is manifest that I am staking my reputation on being right about the attitude I self-ascribe and, seeing that I am doing this, you are in a position to be much more assured about the presence of the attitude than if I had merely reported it. I make a commitment in the purely descriptive sense of putting my money where my mouth is. I take on a risk that would manifestly lack sense unless I had special knowledge of the attitude: this, presumably, because of having a degree of agential control over whether I develop and display the attitude.[43]

The upshot of these observations is that there is a non-moral sense, perfectly consistent with Hart's genealogy, in which residents of Normitania may commit themselves to abiding by the social norms or primary rules that emerge in their society. They may make a pledge, in the sense introduced, to act as the norms require. And if they do commit themselves in that way, then they may be said to invite one another to hold them responsible to cooperative norms or primary rules.

So is there any ground for thinking that those agents must commit themselves to the emergent norms? Yes, it transpires, there is. But in order to see

42 Here and elsewhere, I set aside complications arising when the content of the avowal or pledge bears on a past time or is highly qualified, say in probabilistic terms. For a fuller treatment, see Pettit (n 7).

43 See V. McGeer, 'Is "Self-knowledge" an Empirical Problem? Renegotiating the Space of Philosophical Explanation' (1996) 93 *Journal of Philosophy* 483; R. Moran, 'Self-Knowledge: Discovery, Resolution, and Undoing' (1997) 5 *European Journal of Philosophy* 141; V. McGeer, 'The Moral Development of First-Person Authority' (2008) 16 *European Journal of Philosophy* 81.

why that is so, it is necessary to reintroduce an idea also canvassed earlier: that of doing something virtually rather than actively.

As discussed earlier, people may authorise you to avow their attitudes in either of two ways: actively or virtually. They will actively authorise you to do this if they say 'Yea' to the proposal that you should speak for them. They will virtually authorise you to do this if you carry on as if you were authorised and if they have the opportunity to object but choose not to do so. In each situation, they exercise control over your speaking for them: in the one case, by saying 'Yea' to your doing so; in the other, by refraining from saying 'Nay' in response to your presuming to do so.

As authorisation and control may be virtual, so too may commitment. Suppose that I am expected to behave in a certain way, as a matter of common awareness between me and those I interact with. And suppose that I do nothing to reject this expectation that is held about me when there is opportunity for me to do so. The fact that the expectation of others is manifest between us—is a matter of common awareness—will mean that I can hardly say, in seeking to excuse the fact that I disappointed them, that they got me wrong or that, while they got me right, I changed my mind after they formed the expectation. Given I knew they hold that expectation, they may reasonably ask why I didn't say anything to remove it. The fact that I said nothing, consciously allowing them to misconstrue my intention, means that I pledged in a virtual sense to behave as they expected me to behave. I didn't say 'Yea' to their expectation, but I could have said 'Nay' and I didn't.

It should be clear that when social norms are fully established in Normitania, being perceived, internalised and ratified as a matter of common awareness, each of us in the society is virtually committed or pledged to complying with them. We are each in a position where, as a matter of common awareness, others are going to expect us to conform unless we distance ourselves from the norms. And if we do not distance ourselves—if we do not say 'Nay' to the expectations—then we must be taken as acquiescing to those expectations and, in effect, committing to live up to the norms.

The upshot of this is that we in Normitania not only sustain the sorts of cooperative norms explored here, perceiving, internalising and ratifying them as norms; we also each virtually pledge ourselves to abide by those norms, making conformity a matter of personal commitment. In other words, we not only expect to be held responsible for conforming to the norms, but also each invite others to hold us responsible; we give others a claim against us, in the event of our failing to conform.

That cooperative norms like those envisaged here are matters of personal commitment in this sense is not an extra feature in the way in which perception, internalisation and ratification count as extra features. The fact that the norms are matters of perception, internalisation and ratification means that they have to display the committal property as well. But it is well worth emphasising that property, because it highlights yet another respect in which those norms attract an internal point of view on the part of those who sustain them. That you and I commit to the norms, inviting others to rely on our conformity, maximises the contrast between our attitude towards the norms and the attitude of an outsider or an outlier.

5. Conclusion

A. The Upshot

According to the account developed in this article, there is value in extending Herbert Hart's account of how, under suitable conditions, the secondary rules of a legal system would have more or less inevitably emerged from a society governed only by primary rules: how Normitania would have naturally given way to Lexitania. Specifically, there is value in seeking to tell a similar genealogical story as to how primary rules or norms would have emerged themselves: how Prenormitania would have given way to Normitania.

The value in this exploration, so I suggested, is twofold. It vindicates something that Hart presupposes: that there is every reason to think that primary rules or norms would naturally get established in more or less any society. And it helps to give us a sense of how the people among whom they emerge would relate to those rules in the manner of insiders and willing adherents; it substantiates and enriches Hart's claim that people would have an internal point of view on the rules. We saw that, emerging under the impetus of a reputational motor, primary rules would naturally come to be perceived, internalised and ratified by people and that this would mean that they get to be matters of personal commitment on the part of each.

B. Primary Rules and Social Norms

Do the social norms whose emergence we have described really correspond to primary rules, as Hart conceives of those rules? Or do they represent a somewhat different picture of the rules that, by his account, precede the appearance of a properly legal system? The account given of those norms does not aspire to be an exegesis of Hart, as I stressed, not being developed from an interpretation of the things he says about primary rules. But there is still a question as to how far it may call for a revision of Hart's own account of primary rules. The answer to that question, I submit, is that while the account may regiment primary rules in some measure, it is not revisionary in any substantive way.

If this is so, then there are two respects in which we should expect to find a fit between social norms, as we have cast them, and primary rules. First, there should be a high degree of convergence between the extension of social norms and that of primary rules. Secondly, there should be a high degree of convergence between our conception of those norms and Hart's conception of primary rules; his comments on those rules ought to apply in general to norms that are reputationally supported and, to cite their underived features, are perceived, internalised and ratified.

C. *The Extensional and Conceptual Fit*

The first requirement of fit is that our norms of truth telling, non-violence and non-coercion, keeping promises and respecting property should correspond broadly to what Hart has in mind when he speaks of primary rules. And it is clear that they do, since they impose more or less the same prohibitions or restrictions on people. 'Primary rules,' he says, 'must contain in some form restrictions on the free use of violence, theft, and deception to which human beings are tempted but which they must, in general, repress, if they are to coexist in close proximity to each other.'[44] And he adds immediately, in a phrase redolent of the time, that 'such rules are in fact always found in the primitive societies of which we have knowledge'.

The second requirement of fit is that there is something in Hart's conception of primary rules—indeed, rules in general—that answers to our stipulations that social norms should be reputationally supported and should be perceived, internalised and ratified as norms. He is not explicit on any of these specific issues, but the tenor of the discussion fits very well with the tenor of the presentation here.

Are primary rules reputationally supported for Hart? Well, they are certainly supported, as he argues in various contexts, by 'social criticism and pressure for conformity'.[45] And given that primary rules are 'wholly customary in origin', he says that 'the social pressure may take only the form of a general diffused hostile or critical reaction which may stop short of physical sanctions'. Specifically, the pressure 'may be limited to verbal manifestations of disapproval or of appeals to the individuals' respect for the rule violated; it may depend heavily on the operation of feelings of shame, remorse, and guilt'.[46] The comments come close to acknowledging that reputational motives are crucial in getting people to conform to primary rules.

Does Hart suggest that primary rules are going to be perceived as norms in Prenormitania? Absolutely. With those rules in mind, he implies that they will be taken on all sides as collectively beneficial and individually burdensome, something that could not be the case unless they were perceived as norms by all: registered by all—and, indeed, registered by all as a matter of common awareness. On the one side, he says that they are 'thought important because they are believed to be necessary to the maintenance of social life or some highly prized feature of it';[47] on the other side, he presumes that it will be 'generally recognized that the conduct required by those rules may, while benefiting others, conflict with what the person who owes the duty may wish to do'.[48]

44 Hart (n 1) 90.
45 Hart (n 1) 57.
46 Hart (n 1) 86.
47 Hart (n 1) 87.
48 Hart (n 1).

As he thinks that primary rules are bound to be perceived as norms, so Hart is clear that they are also going to be internalised. When people do not internalise a rule, they abide by it only in the manner of the students in our example of pluralistic ignorance. Hart recognises that where secondary rules have been established, people may differ in the basis on which they conform to any rule, primary or secondary, and that some may even resemble the students in conforming reluctantly, without a preference for general conformity playing any role in their psychology: they may conform to the rules without internalising them. However, he insists that this cannot happen much in a society where primary rules operate in the absence of secondary rules. In such a society, he thinks, 'those who reject the rules except where fear of social pressure induces them to conform' can only be 'a minority'; otherwise they would not be numerous enough to enforce the rules: 'those who reject the rules would have too little social pressure to fear'.[49]

This remark suggests that Hart would take a negative line on the question raised in section 2 concerning whether the internal point of view can enter before internalisation. He would apparently deny that the internal point of view has appeared at the stage where people conform to something they perceive as a norm but only for reputational reasons. Assuming that 'the fear of social pressure' he speaks of in this passage is not just a fear of physical penalty—assuming that it includes a concern with reputation—he would seem to hold that internalisation of a norm is required for the appearance of the internal point of view.

Finally, does Hart think of his primary rules as socially ratified? He does not use that language, of course, but the language that he does use strongly suggests that in our terms those who live under primary rules see them as expressions of a collectively shared attitude within the society. He thinks of the rules as being imposed on people, under the effect of 'social criticism and pressure',[50] 'as a common standard' sponsored from without, not just within.[51] Thus, he holds that people see their requirements as matters of obligation, not as matters of personal interest, inclination or ideal. 'Characteristically, rules so obviously essential as those which restrict the free use of violence are thought of in terms of obligation. So too rules which require honesty or truth or require the keeping of promises.'[52]

Given the fit between the social norms for which this article has provided a genealogy and the primary rules that Hart posits in his story about law, it is reasonable to claim that what we have done is to extend or elaborate his

49 Hart (n 1) 91–92. The insistence that this cannot happen is undermined, of course, by the possibility of pluralistic ignorance, as the earlier discussion makes clear. Hart does not seem to have registered that possibility.

50 Hart (n 1) 57.

51 Hart (n 1) 86.

52 Hart (n 1) 8.

genealogy. That extension gives a greater temporal reach to the genealogy, as I put it at the beginning, explaining why even a pre-legal society ought to be characterised by something like his primary rules. It also gives a greater psychological depth to the story, providing us with an enriched sense in which it is bound to be true that the members of that society see those rules from within an internal point of view.

10 The Planning Theory of Law

Scott J. Shapiro

Hart famously characterized the "essence" of law as "the union of primary and secondary rules."[1] In doing so, Hart sought to draw our attention to the *systematicity* of legality. In a legal system, every primary rule is linked to every other rule by virtue of their common validation by the secondary rule of recognition. Compare the law to the rules of etiquette. Insofar as etiquette consists just in those norms of politeness that members of a group accept, there is no one rule which is responsible for the existence of all others. The rules of etiquette, therefore, are not systematically interconnected; they simply form a simple set of separate standards. By contrast, legal systems are *systems*: the existence of any primary rule can always be traced to the very same source.

While Hart thought that systematicity distinguishes law from related phenomena, he does not go so far as to claim that it is unique in this regard. For it is clear that other normative systems also contain secondary, as well as primary, rules. Condominium associations, for example, have rules about who can change the rules of the condominium and which rules residents are required to follow. Condo by-laws are thus systematically interconnected in the same way as legal rules are; yet, condominium associations are not legal systems. At best, the existence of secondary rules provides only a partial answer to the question "What is law?" It constitutes the "essence" of law in the ordinary meaning of the term (i.e., the main idea or gist) rather than the technical, philosophical sense (i.e., the complete set of properties the possession of which makes the object in question the thing that it is and not something else).

My aim in this chapter will be to develop an account of the essence of law in the strict philosophical sense. In doing so, I will try to isolate the distinctive nature of legal institutions by contrasting them with closely related phenomena, such as parenting, clubs, organized crime, condominium associations and so on. I hope to show through this comparative process that legal systems are institutions of a very special kind: they are compulsory planning organizations that have a moral aim and bear a privileged relation to other planning

1 This phrase is the title of chapter 5 of *The Concept of Law*.

DOI: 10.4324/9781003728603-12

organizations. I will claim that these properties constitute the essence of law insofar as their instantiation makes the law *the law* and not something else.

I. The Planning Thesis

The main idea behind what I call the "planning theory of law" is that legal activity (i.e., the exercise of legal power) is the activity of social planning. Legal institutions plan for the communities over whom they claim authority, both in the sense of telling their members what they may or may not do, as well as authorizing some of these members to plan for others. Call this idea the "planning thesis."

Planning thesis: Legal activity is an activity of social planning.

"Planning" here refers to the activity of formulating, adopting, affecting, applying, enforcing and repudiating plans. The planning is "social" in that its function is to guide, organize and monitor the behavior of members of the community. Legal rules of a particular system, then, are just the general plans, or plan-like norms, that are formulated, adopted, affected, applied and enforced by legal officials of that system for members of a certain community.

Planning, on this view, is not just activity that we do just for ourselves, but one we can do for others as well. For example, I plan my children's lives, the law school administration plans the faculty's lives and the Ann Arbor City Council plans the lives of the residents of Ann Arbor. To be sure, authorities don't completely plan out our lives—we plan it too, but their plans override our plans when we they conflict.

Central to the planning theory is the claim that legal activity is more than just the activity of formulating, adopting, affecting, applying and enforcing norms. It is the activity of *planning*. One reason that the planning theory emphasizes the planning nature of the law is to highlight the often-overlooked incremental feature of legal regulation. In the law, as in ordinary life, agents don't usually settle on an entire course of action all at once. Rather, they typically fill in our plans over time, at first setting the basic ends to be achieved, and preliminary steps to be taken, and then settling on means to achieve those ends as the time for carrying out the plan approaches. Because the nature of planning is crucial to our understanding of the nature of law, I would like to dwell on the incremental nature of planning for a moment.

The Partiality of Plans

I am sitting at my desk in my office and thinking about what to do for dinner tonight. Should I eat out or cook dinner at home? Since I feel a bit guilty about having frequented restaurants so often lately, I decide on the latter option. I now have a plan, namely, to cook dinner at home tonight. Admittedly, it is not much of a plan, because I have no food at home to cook. So, the question with which I started (where to eat?) has been replaced with a new query (where should I get food to cook?).

I respond to this new query by forming an intention to buy the food from a supermarket. And so, I now have two plans: one to cook dinner tonight and one to buy food at the supermarket. These plans are clearly related to one another. Buying food at the supermarket is a means to cooking dinner at home tonight. When one plan specifies a means for accomplishing, or a way of realizing, the end fixed by another plan, we will say that it is a "sub-plan" of the second. Thus, the plan to buy food at the supermarket is a sub-plan of the initial plan to cook dinner tonight.

Of course, by adopting these two plans, I have also created a third plan, namely, the plan to cook dinner by buying food at the supermarket. This larger plan, we might say, has two parts to it: the first is the plan to cook dinner tonight and the second is the plan to buy food for dinner at the supermarket. These parts are related as means to an end: the second part is a sub-plan of the first.

As Michael Bratman has shown, planning typically involves the creation of these larger plans.[2] When I initially form my intention to cook dinner tonight, my plan simply identifies my end goal. But if my plan is going to work—that is, if it is to organize my behavior so that I may attain the goal I set for myself—I have to specify the means as well. I must decide which meal to make, what kind of food to buy, where and when to buy it, whether to make enough for leftovers, which knife to use when preparing the food and so on.

Bratman notes that these larger plans are typically partial. They begin as empty shells and, as more details are added, they become more comprehensive and useful. Plans are almost never exhaustive because there is rarely a need for a full specification of every step necessary to achieve a goal. My plan to cook dinner tonight will not specify the correct way to hold the knife when I cut the food because I have the skills necessary to accomplish the task without deliberation or reflection.

As plans are filled in, they thus naturally assume a nested structure. My plan to make dinner tonight specifies the overall goal I wish to achieve. My plan to buy food from a supermarket, as we mentioned, is a sub-plan of the overall plan of making dinner. My intention to buy chicken at the supermarket after work is, in turn, a sub-plan of the plan to buy food at the supermarket and, thus, a sub-sub-plan of the overall plan to cook dinner tonight.

The nested structure of plans explains how past deliberation shapes present planning. When constructing my plan, I take my prior decisions about means and ends as given. These plans and sub-plans are settled and not up for reconsideration. Rather, my present deliberation is confined solely to those options that are not ruled out by past decisions. If I have decided to go to Stop & Shop to buy food, I figure out how to get there, not whether it might be better to go to Pathmark instead.

2 Michael Bratman, *Intention, Plans, and Practical Reason* (Harvard University Press 1987) 28–30.

As Bratman points out, plans not only organize our behavior, but they also organize our thinking about how to organize our behavior.[3] The planner sets ends to be achieved and determines which means are best suited to achieve those ends. Once selected, these means are treated as new ends and lead the planner to determine which new means ought to be adopted. By fleshing out plans in this manner, the planner ensures that, according to his beliefs, he will perform all the necessary actions in the right sequence and thus realize the overall ends of the plan.

Of course we need not settle all outstanding issues at once. While I should soon decide when to buy the food for dinner, I can probably wait until I arrive at the supermarket to decide what to make and how much to cook. And I certainly can wait until I get to the kitchen before settling on which knife to use. Indeed, there is a pragmatic argument for leaving certain aspects of plans open until the time for action nears. Settling on a course of conduct far ahead of time in the absence of complete information is a risky thing to do. By leaving our plans for future actions somewhat sketchy, we provide the measure of flexibility necessary to enable us to fill in the details as our visibility substantially improves.

The Path of the Law

As we have seen, plans do not normally leap like Athena from Zeus' head, fully mature at the time of birth. Planners usually begin with partial plans and fill in the details over time. Law follows the same route. Schemes of legal regulation are rarely created all at once. They are typically assembled piece by piece, starting off either as broad standards which are refined over time, detailed regulations which are unified by the development of general standards, or a hodgepodge of rules which are supplemented bit by bit as new problems arise.

Consider as an example of legal planning the law of business competition in the United States. The first major piece of federal regulation was enacted in 1890 in the form of the Sherman Antitrust Act. Section 1 of the Sherman Act, for example, provides: "Every contract, combination in the form of trust or otherwise, or conspiracy, in restraint of trade or commerce among the several States, or with foreign nations, is declared to be illegal." The Sherman Act, however, does not specify which activities are "restraints of trade." It simply sets out a very broad standard, prohibiting any activity of restraining trade that results from contract, combination or conspiracy.[4]

3 Ibid. 32–35.

4 Or at least this is the way that the federal courts have regarded section 1. According to Herbert Hovencamp, courts treat the Sherman Act "as 'enabling' legislation—an invitation to the federal courts to learn how businesses and markets work and formulate a set of rules that will make them work in socially efficient ways." Herbert Hovencamp, *Economics and Federal Antitrust Law* (West 1985) 52. See also Frank Easterbrook, "Vertical Arrangements and the Rule of Reason" (1984) 53 *Antitrust Law Journal* 135, 136 ("The Sherman Act of 1890 told the

Subsequent litigation under the Sherman Act forced federal courts to interpret and develop the limited guidance they had received. In 1911, for example, the Supreme Court held that only "unreasonable" acts that restrain trade violate the Sherman Act.[5] In subsequent cases, the Court clarified this ruling, maintaining that certain acts—price-fixing, bid rigging and market allocation schemes—are so anti-competitive that they are unreasonable per se and hence illegal.[6] It also held that other activities must be judged according to the so-called rule of reason, that is, on a case-by-case basis to ascertain whether, on balance, the anticompetitive effects of the business activity harm the consumer more than they benefit the firms in question.

As it turned out, many in Congress were unhappy with the doctrine emerging from the courts. In an effort to overturn certain precedent, as well as provide greater guidance, Congress enacted the Clayton Antitrust Act of 1914. According to section 2 of the Clayton Act, price discrimination that "substantially lessens competition or tends to create a monopoly in any line of commerce" counts as a "restraint of trade" under section 1 of the Sherman Act, while according to section 6, labor activities such as boycotts and strikes do not. Congress provided further direction in 1936 by enacting the Robinson-Patman Act, which specifies in greater detail which activities count as price discrimination under the Clayton Act and, hence, as illegal restraints of trade under the Sherman Act.

In the same year that Congress enacted the Clayton Act, it passed the Federal Trade Commission (FTC) Act, which prohibits all forms of "unfair competition in or affecting commerce." This standard is broader than section 1 of the Sherman Act, in that all unreasonable restraints of trade are unfair methods of competition but not vice versa. Subsequent legislation by Congress specified which acts are to be considered unfair methods of competition under the FTC Act, such as the misbranding of wool (as per the Wool Products Labeling Act), fur (the Fur Products Labeling Act) and textile fibers (the Textile Fiber Products Identification Act). The FTC Act also created a new administrative agency, the Federal Trade Commission, and directed it to promulgate rules prohibiting practices deemed to be unfair methods of competition under the Act. Since then, the FTC has promulgated numerous regulations, including extremely detailed rules regulating the branding of wool, fur and textile fiber products.

Federal antitrust law, therefore, did not come into being all at once. It resulted from multiple acts of planning, following a mostly top-down path:

---

courts to make up a law on the subject of restraint of trade"). Others have imputed to section 1 more determinate content. See, e.g., Robert H. Bork, *The Antitrust Paradox: A Policy at War with Itself* (Free Press 1978) 20.

5 *Standard Oil Co. of New Jersey v. United States*, 221 US 1 (1911).

6 *United States v. Trenton Potteries Co.*, 273 US 392 (1927); *Continental TV Inc. v. GTE Sylvania Inc.*, 433 US 36 (1977).

Congress began with broad standards, such as prohibitions on "restraints of trade" and "unfair methods of competition," which were then refined by more detailed standards. These narrower standards, such as those set out in the Clayton Act, "rule of reason" and the Wool Products Labeling Act, were then further fleshed out by the Robinson-Patman Act and FTC regulations. At times, the planning has gone in the opposite direction, as when Congress broadened the prohibition on unreasonable restraints of trade in the Sherman Act to include all unfair methods of competition as specified in the FTC Act.

The social planning that created antitrust law has also followed a decentralized process. In addition to Congress, the federal courts have played a very substantial role in the development of this body of law. And the grant of administrative authority to the FTC confers on them the primary responsibility for social planning in the area. They are empowered, in other words, to adopt those sub-plans they deem to best realize the legislative plans set out by Congress.

Because the development of the federal antitrust regime has taken place over many decades involving numerous actors and agencies, social planning in this area has experienced a considerable degree of repudiation and revision. Thus, Congress has overturned Supreme Court precedent, the Supreme Court has reversed the decisions of other federal courts, including the rulings of earlier Supreme Courts, federal courts have struck down administrative rulings through the exercise of judicial review, Congress has repealed and amended earlier legislation and so on. And, of course, the federal antitrust regime preempted and largely displaced state common law regulation of business competition which had reigned for several centuries. In this sense, legal regulation differs from ordinary, non-legal planning, where the shorter life span of plans renders repudiation and revision a less common, though not entirely unusual, phenomenon.

Common Law as Bottom-Up Planning

In contrast to the top-down planning characteristic of some forms of legislation, common law reasoning represents the paradigm of bottom-up legal planning. Consider for example the development of the tort of negligence. Until the early part of the 20th century, courts were mostly content to develop very case-specific rules regarding the civil duties of ordinary care. Duties were classified based on the capacities of the defendant (adult, child, blind, mentally challenged, etc.), relationship of the defendant to property (owner, renter, bailee, etc.) and the kind of relationship the defendant bore to the victim (defendant as common carrier, manufacturer, salesman, employer, landlord, etc.; victim as passenger, customer, employee, renter, stranger, etc.) Courts then began to broaden the standards of liability and eventually settled on the modern rule of negligence law, which holds that everyone owes everyone else a duty of reasonable care.[7] These courts, in other words, engaged in bottom-up social planning. By adopting a consolidating standard of liability, they moved up the legal planning tree, converting previous rulings into sub-plans of a much more general plan.

The bottom-up nature of common law reasoning is motivated by two different institutional considerations. The first is the political conviction that courts are not the appropriate venues for large-scale social planning: duly elected representatives ought to set broad policies in democratic societies, not the courts. This perceived deficit in legitimacy also explains why common law courts are not usually empowered to develop standards with arbitrary elements. Judges may not, for example, enact a rule which requires swimming pool owners to build a fence 40 inches or higher to protect neighboring children from drowning. They are merely authorized to promulgate non-arbitrary standards such as "swimming pool owners must take reasonable precautions in protecting children from hazards on their land." This restriction to principled standards greatly reduces the power of courts to engage in social planning. If no common law rule may contain arbitrary elements (e.g., whether a fence should be 40 or 41 inches high), there is an inherent limitation to how specific, and hence comprehensive, judge-made plans can be.

Aside from considerations of political legitimacy, the common law tradition has also been skeptical about the value of abstract moral reasoning. Concrete cases, it has often been thought, provide the rich detail judges need to make good decisions and provide the base off of which analogies can be made to other concrete cases. Courts are authorized to take a broader view only when there has been sufficient judicial experience with low-level decision-making. Vigorous and prolonged engagement with the concrete implications of various legal rules enables courts to figure out how various aspects of social policy hang together and thus licenses them to consolidate specific rules into more expansive legal standards.

The bottom-up nature of common law social planning is also evident in the power that courts have to "distinguish" precedents. Even when a past case announces a rule framed at a certain level of generality, a court may contract the scope of the rule by holding that it applies only to certain facts of the past decision which are not present in the current case.[8] In distinguishing precedent, courts in essence split general rules into narrower ones which are more closely tied to the facts of each case. The practice of distinguishing manifests yet again the common law's distrust of high-level theorizing and the comparative faith it places in decision-making based on concrete and detailed fact patterns.

7 *Donoghue v. Stevenson* [1932] AC 562 (HL); *MacPherson v. Buick Motor Co.*, 217 NY 382 (1916).

8 Joseph Raz, *The Authority of Law: Essays on Law and Morality* (Oxford University Press 1979) 183–189.

By claiming that legal planning is an incremental process, I do not mean to suggest, however, that schemes of legal regulation are never created all at once. On certain occasions, especially in civil law countries, legislatures have enacted entire codes, either encompassing the whole field of legal regulation (the Code of Justinian, the Napoleonic Code, the Prussian Civil Code) or subject-specific ones (penal, tax, bankruptcy codes). In most of these cases, however, these systematic collections of rules simply "codify" existing law, presenting the rules in an orderly manner and resolving contradictions between customary, decisional and statutory materials.

It is not hard to understand why one-shot comprehensive legislation is generally avoided. As we have seen in the case of personal planning, committing to a course of conduct far in advance of action is inherently risky. Because the future is often unclear and human beings do not have the ability to consider every single contingency, it often makes sense to wait until more information is available before deciding how to respond. Aside from the moral perils of premature planning, there are political risks as well. Enacting a comprehensive regulatory scheme usually requires legislators to make very hard choices. By contrast, setting broad policies enable them to take credit for solving a social problem without incurring the costs of imposing restrictions on specific individuals and groups. The delegation of planning to judicial or administrative bodies is not only efficient in a large range of cases, but expedient as well.

The Positivity of Planning

By characterizing legal activity as planning activity, my aim thus far has been to highlight the incremental nature of the law's regulatory behavior. But the parallel does not end there. As I would now like to show, legal activity also seeks to accomplish the same basic goals that ordinary garden-variety planning does, namely, to guide, organize and monitor the behavior of individuals and groups. It does this by helping agents lower their deliberation, negotiation and bargaining costs, increase predictability of behavior, compensate for ignorance and bad character and provide methods of accountability.

Consider laws regulating motorists. Rules that require drivers to be a certain age, pass a test, inspect their cars every year, wear seat belts, buy liability insurance, stop at red lights, ride on the right side and not over 55 mph and under the influence of alcohol are all part of a comprehensive regulatory regime. Their aim is to guide and organize the behavior of many different individuals so as to achieve a very complex and contentious goal, which is safe, fast and fair driving, in an arbitrary environment. They do so by serving as paternalistic measures that compensate for cognitive incapacities, weakness of the will and ignorance; coordination devices that render behavior more predictable; and ethically acceptable guidelines that ensure that motorists will not interfere with one another while simultaneously obviating the need to deliberate, negotiate and bargain about what behavior is reasonable under the circumstances.

Other examples of legal rules which guide and organize the behavior of community members include rules limiting the legal capacity of minors (paternalistic measures that compensate for cognitive incapacity), prohibitions on the use of certain recreational drugs (paternalistic measures that compensate for weakness of will), laws regulating pharmaceuticals (paternalistic measures that compensate for ignorance), rules designating legal tender (solves coordination problems by rendering behavior more predictable), voting laws (enables shared activities to take place by reducing deliberation and negotiation costs and rendering behavior more predictable), business competition law (forestalls shared activities by guiding behavior that is deemed injurious to others), nuisance rules (prevents individual behavior from interfering with others unfairly and, in the process, lowers negotiation and bargaining costs associated with ethical conflicts) and contract law (confers power on persons to plan for others).

Laws are able to perform these functions for exactly the same reason that plans can, namely, they are *positive* norms. By simply referring to norms designated as authoritative, the individuals in question need not deliberate, negotiate or bargain. They can simply rely on the norm in question to settle their practical doubts or disagreements. Compare such norms to moral rules and principles that have not been similarly marked off as binding by planning or custom. In order to resolve any practical doubt or disagreement, individuals would have to deliberate, negotiate or bargain precisely the activities that are circumvented by plans. Moreover, moral norms are not able to solve coordination problems because morality concerns itself with principled action and coordination problems arise because of their arbitrary nature. There are no moral rules telling motorists which side of the road to ride on, whether to use clamshells or silver coins as legal tender, whether the president should be at least 35 or 36 years old and so on. Norms which have been designated in advance can solve such problems precisely because human beings have the ability to make arbitrary choices.

Legal Activity as Settling, Dispositive and Purposive

Planning is not only a process that produces norms in an incremental fashion but (1) is supposed to settle questions about how to act; (2) disposes their addressees to obey; and (3) is purposive, i.e., it not only produces norms but has the function of producing norms. I would quickly like to show that legal activity meets these three conditions as well and, thus, the central idea of the planning theory, namely, the planning thesis, is valid.

1. *Settling*: There is an old joke that goes: "Gravity. It's Not Just a Good Idea. It's the Law!" The joke works not only because it is crazy to admonish people to obey the laws of physics, but equally because it isn't crazy to insist that they heed the laws of political institutions. It makes perfect sense to say, for example, that legislation requiring passengers to wear their seat

belts is not "just a good idea." Legal institutions are neither in the business of offering advice nor making requests. They do not present their rules as one more factor that subjects are supposed to consider when deciding what they should do. Rather, they claim the right to *settle* normative matters in its favor and to demand compliance. For this reason, deliberating or bargaining with officials about the propriety of obedience normally shows profound disrespect for them, and for the law's authority. Regardless of whether seats belts are a good idea, passengers are required to buckle up—after all, it's the law.

It is important not to overstate the law's claim to authority. That the law purports to settle normative questions should not be taken to mean that the law demands that its dictates be followed *come what may*. Laws, like all plans, are typically defeasible. When compelling reasons exist, the law will normally permit its subjects to reconsider its direction and engage in deliberation on the merits. The catch here is that the law claims the right to determine the conditions of its own defeasibility. It attempts to settle when the quandaries it has resolved become unsettled. Thus, in jurisdictions that accept a necessity defense, persons are allowed to break the law if doing so is the choice of the lesser evil. The availability of a lesser evil, therefore, is a reason that the law recognizes to be compelling enough to defeat its own mandates.

2. *Dispositive*: The dispositive nature of legal activity can be seen by attending to the "general efficacy" condition on legal systems. All legal philosophers agree that legal systems exist only if they are generally efficacious, i.e., they are normally obeyed. General efficacy does not require that community members actually accept the law's legitimacy; they may comply out of fear of punishment, habit or peer pressure. But if most fail to conform to the dictates of the regime claiming authority, then such a community cannot be said to have a legal system. If we accept the correctness of the general efficacy condition, which I think we should, we must conclude that legal activity is dispositive in nature. For according to the general efficacy condition, if an activity did not generate a general disposition to obey in a certain community, then it would not be legal activity.
3. *Purposive*: Finally, it is clear that legal activity is purposive in nature. The legislative process does not just happen to produce laws as a side effect of its pursuit of some other end. Its very point is to create norms that are supposed to settle questions about how to act. Similarly, the function of adjudication is to apply norms to others. Evaluations are not just happy accidents but what courts are supposed to churn out.

Legal Activity as Social Planning

As I have tried to argue, not every way of guiding conduct counts as "planning." Indeed, planning is a very distinctive way of guiding conduct. For this reason, the planning thesis makes a strong jurisprudential claim. According to it, legal activity is not simply the creation and application of rules. It is an incremental process whose function is to guide, organize and monitor behavior through the settling of normative questions and which disposes its addressees to comply under normal conditions. In this section I hope to have established the plausibility of this position.

To argue that the exercise of legal authority is describable as the activity of social planning is not to say that it can only be characterized in this way, or that this model is the most useful for all purposes. Many legal scholars have argued, for example, that the law is often expressive in nature. Thus, when the law permits people to protect themselves when confronted with deadly force in public even if they could safely retreat, it is plausible to suppose that the law aims to express a judgment about socially proper behavior, namely, that "real men" don't back down from fights.[9] The planning thesis, of course, does not preclude this interpretation. It simply points out that when the law serves an expressive function, it does so through *planning*. Thus, the law expresses its attitudes about gender not by relating proverbs about how real men behave or giving sermons, issuing advice, performing ritual dances, and so on, but rather by permitting them to kill even when they could retreat in total safety.

The planning thesis does not simply state that legal activity is an activity of planning; it claims that it is an activity of *social* planning. The planning is "social" in three different senses. First, the activity creates and administers norms which represent *communal standards of behavior*. Members of the community are required to conform to these standards and are held accountable by legal officials if they do not. Second, the planning regulates most communal activity via *general policies*. The law's primary mode of address is not naming particular individuals; actors are regulated only insofar as they instantiate the general description set out in the rules. Third, the planning regulates most communal activity via *publicly accessible standards*. Secret plans that satisfy the formal requirements of the system are possible, but if most legal regulation is inaccessible to those to whom they apply, then these plans are not the result of social planning and hence not law.[10]

If legal activity is social planning activity, then it follows that legal authorities are social planners. In other words, they exercise their power by formulating, adopting, repudiating, affecting and applying plans. Of course, legal authorities often do things other than engage in social planning. Most notably, they support the social planning effort through law enforcement. When the

9 Dan Kahan, "The Secret Ambition of Deterrence" (1999) 113 *Harvard Law Review* 413, 429–430.

10 To say that legal planning regulates most communal activity via general and publicly accessible standards is not to claim that most laws are general and publicly accessible. Most laws in a legal system might be private bills addressed to individuals or secret, but as long as the bulk of the activity regulated is governed by open policies, then the regulation counts as social planning.

plans do not succeed in guiding conduct, the master plan of the system normally authorizes certain officials to impose costs on the violators.

II. The Shared Agency Thesis

Virtually everyone would agree that certain aspects of legal activity are shared activities. When Congress legislates, its members are acting together in creating law. Similarly, judges on an appellate panel are engaged in the shared activity of adjudication. The planning theory, however, makes a stronger claim. Not only are some aspects of legal activity shared, but so is the whole process. Legal activity is a shared activity in that the various legal actors involved play certain roles in the same activity of social planning: some participate by making and affecting plans and some participate by applying them. Each has a part to play in planning for the community. Call this the "shared agency thesis."

Shared agency thesis: Legal activity is shared activity.

In order to engage in the shared activity of social planning, it is not necessary for legal authorities to intend to act in a collective manner or be committed to its success. He, she or they may be completely alienated from the legal process. A legal authority is simply required to accept the shared master plan of the system. This plan specifies the part that each is supposed to play in the shared activity of social planning: who has authority to plan with respect to what subject matter and over whom, and who has the duty to apply and enforce these plans made by these authorities.

The shared agency thesis may be justified by two different considerations. First, it accounts for the core intuition that some legal officials are related to one another in a special way: they are each members of particular legal systems. We recognize, for example, that French judges, ministers, legislators and law enforcement personnel are part of the French legal system, as opposed to the British legal system. Likewise, British officials belong to the same system, but not to the French system. The shared agency thesis explains these common-sense distinctions. We distinguish between different groups of legal officials because we recognize that different groups are engaged in different collective activities. Furthermore, we sort officials based on the shared activity in which they are supposed to participate: officials of a particular legal system are members of the same system just in case they are supposed to work together in planning for a community. Thus, French legal officials are *French* legal officials because they are supposed to work with each other, and not with British legal officials, in governing their country.

The idea that legal activity is shared activity is also meant to explain how it is that legal systems are able to do what they typically do. For the functions we normally attribute to legal systems—maintaining order, redistributing wealth, protecting the rights of at least some parties, providing facilities for private ordering, settling disputes—are goals that are usually unachievable solely by individual agency. In communities that have legal systems, it is normally not possible for any one person, or a cohort of uncoordinated persons, to establish and maintain control over the entire population, redistribute their wealth, protect their rights and resolve their disputes. In order to achieve these political ends, collective and concerted action is essential. Members of the group must work together and do so in an organized fashion.

The Design of the Master Plan

It goes without saying that designers of legal systems do not merely intend *that* legal participants plan—they very much care how they plan. The framers of the US Constitution were not, for example, indifferent between democratic, communist, socialist, theocratic and monarchic forms of government. They were committed to a form of democratic self-rule, and this commitment explains why the US Constitution has the content that it does.

The design of a legal system will, therefore, be a function of the substantive goals that designers intend to advance. The relation between planning hierarchies and substantive goals may either be intrinsic or instrumental. It is intrinsic when the goals themselves demand that certain individuals be empowered to act in certain ways. The promotion of democratic self-rule, for example, requires that the citizenry have some say in determining the rules of the system. A system designed to further such a goal, therefore, will make provisions such as elections, representation, voting and protection of free speech so that individuals are empowered to determine the terms and direction of social interaction.

The relation between structure and goal may also be highly instrumental. Federalism, for example, is often justified by the effect that partial decentralization has on the protection of individual liberty. In theory at least, depriving the centralized authority of certain power diminishes its ability to oppress the citizenry. Moreover, by removing barriers to internal migration, the units that make up the federal system are forced to compete for residents, thereby giving them an incentive not to enact abusive regulations. Finally, dividing authority between sets of rivalrous political actors enables the participants in each set to serve as checks to the encroachment of the others.

When legal systems are designed to achieve certain moral or political goals, it is often possible to recover the goals of a system by a close examination of its master plan. For example, a system that made provisions for voting, representation, elections and some protection for public deliberation would be one in which democratic self-rule was prized. By contrast, an institutional structure that empowered clerics to decide matters of principle and policy and minimized the degree to which secular forces can affect the direction of the law would be a system in which religious values were being promoted.

Reverse engineering, however, is not the only method available for ascertaining the goals of a system. Usually, legal systems are proud of their objectives and proudly proclaim them to the world. Consider for example the preamble to the US Constitution:

> We the People of the United States, in order to form a more perfect union, establish justice, insure domestic tranquility, provide for the common defense, promote the general welfare, and secure the blessings of liberty to ourselves and our posterity, do ordain and establish this Constitution for the United States of America.

The preamble sets out, either explicitly or implicitly, the following goals of the federal system: (1) democratic self-rule; (2) political and economic integration; (3) personal security against domestic and foreign threats; (4) promotion of the general welfare; and (5) protection of the individual from governmental tyranny. These goals are served by the institutional arrangements set out in the Constitution. For example, the goal of democratic self-rule is furthered by the creation of a dual system of political representation, one based on population (for the House of Representatives), the other based on statehood (for the Senate), the mandate of periodic elections for congressional representatives and for the president, the institution of majority voting to enact legislation, supermajority voting to ratify and amend the Constitution, the protection of freedom of speech and the press, etc. Political and economic integration is furthered by the creation of a national Congress comprising representatives from every state, the grant to Congress of the power to regulate foreign and interstate commerce, the denial of power to the states to close their borders to other states or impose on them import duties, the grant of power to the Senate and the president to enter into treaties with other countries and the denial of such power to the states, etc.

The diversity of goals that legal systems are designed to achieve is actually quite striking. Some legal regimes aim to build "a classless communist society," others intend to advance "the cultural, social, political, and economic institutions of . . . society based on Islamic principles and norms," while still others seek to "secure the right to work, housing and education, and to promote social care and social security and a good living environment."[11]

It is important to note that legal officials can be committed to the substantive political or moral goals of a regime without agreeing on comprehensive worldviews. This, as we have seen, is typical of shared activity: participants may converge on a set of common goals despite differing on more fundamental beliefs and values. One can be a Kantian, utilitarian, Aristotelian, libertarian, Rawlsian, Christian, Muslim or Jew and still believe in the moral necessity of promoting democratic self-rule and protecting individual rights. But these officials may not even be committed to the aims of the legal system in which they participate. This, we have also seen, is a typical feature of *massively* shared

11 USSR Constitution preamble; Iran Constitution preamble; Sweden Constitution arts I and II.

agency: participants may share a plan even though some are not committed to the success of the joint activity.[12]

The Unity of Law

As I argued at the beginning of this section, one reason to accept the shared agency thesis is that it provides an intuitive account of group membership within a legal system. Group membership, on this view, is constituted by the shared activity in which its members are supposed to participate. Just as my friends and I are members of the Cooking Club because we are supposed to cook together, officials are members of the same legal system because they are supposed to participate in the same collective activity of social planning.

The shared agency thesis also provides a natural way to define norm membership in a legal system. We might say that two laws are part of the same legal system just in case they are created and applied by officials of the same legal organization. The *unity* of a set of legal norms is thus derived from the *sociality* of legal participants. What makes it the case that the laws of a particular system are laws of that system is that they are the products of the activity of *one group* sharing a plan and working together in planning for a community.

Put more precisely, the law of a certain system consists in (1) the master plan shared by a group of planners; (2) those plans created in accordance with, and whose application is required by, such a master plan; and (3) those plan-like norms (such as customary norms) whose application is required by such a master plan. New York statutory law is New York law, for example, because it was created in accordance with, and its application regulated by, the master plan shared by a certain group working together in governing New York State. Executive orders of the New York State governor are also laws of New York State because the governor shares a plan with the legislature and they both

12 I do not mean to suggest, of course, that all legal systems have been designed in advance. Historically, certain fundamental aspects of legal systems have arisen purely through custom. The model of shared agency I developed in *Legality* accounts for these cases by requiring only that the shared plan be designed "at least in part" with the group in mind. Groups may share plans, in other words, even though parts of their plans have not been planned for the group. A plan is shared if at least *some* part of the plan was designed for the group and group members see the non-planned parts as means to carry out the ends of the shared activity. Thus, the master plan of a legal system may contain many customary parts, so long as it also contains non-customary parts and the officials see the customary parts as *sub-plans* of these non-customary parts. To be sure, when large portions of a legal system arise purely through custom, it may turn out that there is no ideology that underlies the system's institutional structure, no coherent set of political objectives at which the shared activity aims. I say that there *may* be no ideology for two reasons. First, convergence in practice is often the product of common beliefs and values. Second, legal officials may theorize previously untheorized customary aspects of a certain system and develop the system in the direction of this new ideology. These officials are then properly seen as designers of the legal system, reworking the crooked timber of custom in the hopes of making it straight.

work together in governing New York. On the other hand, New Jersey law is distinct from New York law because New Jersey officials do not share a plan, and hence do not work together, with New York officials.[13]

III. Offices, Institutionality, and Compulsion

Thus far, I have argued that legal activity is the shared activity of social planning. Unfortunately, this description cannot be considered a complete answer to the identity question for law. Consider parenting. My wife and I plan for our family together. We consult with each other about how our children should treat other people, who should set the table, what we will eat for dinner, where we will go on vacation, and so on. We also apply each other's rules and enforce them when necessary.

Official Activity

One reason why my wife and I are not the law is that we are not "officials," that is, we do not occupy offices. Offices are non–ad hoc positions of authority. They are designed to deal with recurring sets of issues and, as such, have long life spans and admit of different occupants. The presidency of the United States, for example, is an office because it persists from term to term and its normative character does not change merely because one president vacates and a new one assumes power. Presidents come and go but the presidency remains.[14]

It is an essential feature of an office, therefore, that holders of power are "fungible," namely, that the rights and responsibilities that attend to the office do not depend on the identity of those who inhabit the office. If X and Y are both eligible to occupy office O, then X and Y will have the same rights and responsibilities when they occupy O.

Because offices are meant to serve a recurring set of issues, they normally possess two other properties, none of which is necessary but are typically

13 Although the account of shared agency I sketched requires that there be one shared plan, it is possible to relax this requirement without changing the essentials of the approach. Thus, we could say that a law is a member of a legal system if it was created in accordance with, and its application is regulated by, a set of plans that the relevant official group shares. We can further stipulate that a group shares a *set of plans* if and only if (1) each plan of the set was designed, at least in part, for that group so that they may engage in a joint activity; (2) the members of the group accept the parts of the plans that apply to them; and (3) the members of the group commit to not interfering with the parts that apply to others. On the planning theory, therefore, the content of a legal system does not depend on the unitary nature of its shared plan. Rather, it ultimately depends on the fact that someone conceived of officials *as a group* and developed a set of instructions for them so that they may govern a community. Whether we treat the instructions addressed to this group as forming one plan or many is, in the end, immaterial.

14 Indeed, it is a noteworthy feature of offices that they can exist even while empty, e.g., papal interregna, where the papacy remains while the College of Cardinals decides the new pontiff.

present. First, offices are typically stable. Rights and responsibilities should not fluctuate over time but remain constant throughout. Second, turnover in occupancy is not only possible, but an expected occurrence.

By these measures, parents do not occupy offices. Although parenthood is fungible, its normative character is not typically stable. The rights of parents decrease over time and, in many cultures, are taken to cease, or nearly so, upon the maturity of their children. Even in societies where parental rights remain constant throughout life, parental responsibilities typically change and diminish as children grow. Nor is parental turnover expected. Although a parent may die or have their rights legally terminated and another person takes their place through adoption, such changes are unusual. Parents normally stay the parents of their children—for better or worse.

Because legal activity must be an activity conducted by officials, parental planning cannot be legal in nature. By contrast, legislators, judges, police officers, regulators, and clerks are officials, if any are, and as a result they may properly be thought to engage in legal activity.

Institutional Activity

When my wife or I want to make a rule for our family, we have to do it the old-fashioned way, namely, by issuing a command or granting permission. If I wish to order my daughter to pick up her toys before she goes out to play, I must intend that she pick up her toys at that time and express that intention to her.

Legislatures, on the other hand, can bypass that drudgery. They can get some staff attorney (or lobbyist) to draft legislation and then simply follow some formal procedure, such as raising their hands at a certain time, in order to enact it. They need not intend that those obligated by the rule follow it. Indeed, they do not even have to know which rule they are enacting. As long as they follow the procedures set out in their rules, their acts are legally valid and a new plan will have been created.

As we have seen, the normativity of law is "institutional" in nature, which is to say that the legal relations may obtain between people independent of the particular intentions of those people. This institutionality is made possible by the structure of master legal plans. Master plans not only contain authorizations, but instructions as well, namely, plans which specify how the authorized power should be exercised. These instructions will typically set out formal procedures which allow people to exercise power even without the intention to do so. Thus, if part of the master plan of a legal system validates a rule if a majority of legislators simply say "Yea" after the rule is read, then the rule is legally valid if a majority of legislators do say "Yea" after the rule is read. The rule will be valid even if those enacting it had no intention of enacting it or even knew that their actions would lead to enactment. By contrast, my wife and I have no formal rules for how to make rules in our family. If we want to exercise our power, we have no choice but to intend that something happen and express that intention directly to those whom we wish to bind.

The introduction of institutional normativity is a revolutionary advance in social planning. Plans can be adopted without the planners actually intending that the community act accordingly. As a result, the community need not worry about whether the planners had these intentions. They can know that they are legally obligated simply because the planners followed the right procedures. Of course, the institutionality of law is ultimately grounded in intentions. Rules are legally valid because they were created pursuant to a rule that most officials accept. If officials stopped accepting the plan, then the plans created in accordance with it would cease to be legally valid as well.

Compulsory Governance

Let us say that any group that engages in a shared, official and institutional activity is an "organization." It follows then that legal systems are *planning organizations*. Legal officials constitute such organizations because they are engaged in a shared activity of social planning, occupy offices and are capable of instituting normative relations irrespective of particular intentions. By the same token, parents are not legal systems because, even though they are shared planners, they do not constitute a planning organization.

There is a sense, however, in which parental authority is closer to legal authority than the powers exercised by other planning organizations. Let us return to the Cooking Club, Inc. The hierarchical relationship that exists between the supervisors and any particular staff member is entirely contingent on the will of the staff member. If the staff member no longer wants to work for the company, he or she may quit and, as a result, will no longer be subject to the planning power of the designated supervisor.

By contrast, the parent-child relationship is not terminable at will. At least until maturity, children cannot "quit" their parents and are subject to parental norms even against their will. Parental authority, we can say, is "compulsory" because consent is not a necessary condition for the applicability of its requirements. Legal authority is similar in this regard. For it is *never* a valid legal defense to claim that one has not consented, or no longer consents, to the authority of the law. Acceptance is always irrelevant to the legal validity of official action and to its applicability.

The compulsory nature of the law's authority is clearly central to its efficacy as an institution of social planning. Compliance with the law is often onerous, sometimes extremely so. If one could be relieved from paying one's taxes, complying with military conscription, serving on a jury, driving under the speed limit and so on, simply by repudiating the law's authority, then one would expect many people to avail themselves of this option, or at least have legitimate concerns that their law-abidingness will be exploited by others availing themselves of this option. Conditioning authority on consent is a luxury that the law normally cannot afford.

The compulsory nature of the law, however, might appear puzzling. Unlike parents, who are more informed and mature than their young children and as a result can bind them even against their wills, how can a plan legally obligate competent adults in so involuntary a fashion? The mystery dissolves once we recall our analysis of legal obligation claims. On the planning theory, to say that laws legally obligate is to say (at least on the perspectival interpretation) that they morally obligate *from the legal point of view*. From the perspective of legal institutions, in other words, their plans morally bind regardless of whether those who are bound consent to their authority. Thus, just as I claim the power to morally bind my six-year-old son to clear the table after dinner even if he objects, the law claims the moral power to obligate irrespective of the will of its subjects.

As I have emphasized before, although the legal point of view purports to represent the moral point of view, it may fail to do so. In some cases, it will be unable to morally obligate without the consent of the governed; indeed, if the system is sufficiently unjust, the law may be incapable of morally binding even *with* their consent. Yet, from the law's own point of view, the compulsory nature of its demands is morally legitimate. And this conviction in its own rectitude is expressed by legal officials when they describe themselves as having the *right* to be obeyed and those who fail to comply as *wrong* and as deserving punishment for their *guilty* actions.

IV. The Moral Aim Thesis

According to the planning theory, the law is not simply a compulsory planning organization—it is a compulsory planning organization with a distinctive aim. The fundamental aim of the law is to rectify the moral deficiencies associated with what I will call the "circumstances of legality." When a community faces moral problems which are numerous and serious, and whose solutions are complex, contentious or arbitrary, certain modes of planning such as improvisation, spontaneous ordering, private bargaining, communal consensus or personalized hierarchies will be costly to engage in, sometimes prohibitively so. Unless the community has a way of reducing the costs and risks of planning, resolving these moral problems will, at best, be expensive and, at worst, impossible. On the planning theory, the fundamental aim of the law is to meet this moral demand in an efficient manner. By providing a highly nimble and durable method of social planning, the law enables communities to solve the numerous and serious problems that would otherwise be too costly or risky to resolve.[15] Call this the "moral aim thesis."

15 The primary method by which legal systems should resolve moral problems depends on the nature of political morality. On one view, political morality is largely determinate, namely, it provides answers to most political questions. Given this conception of political morality, the law should solve moral problems primarily by revealing these answers to those who need

Moral aim thesis: The fundamental aim of legal activity is to remedy the moral deficiencies of the circumstances of legality.

To say that the fundamental aim of the law is to compensate for the infirmities of custom, tradition, persuasion, consensus and promise is not to suggest that the law *never* relies on these other mechanisms. When simpler methods of organizing behavior work, it would be irrational to abandon or overturn them in favor of accomplishing the very same ends through more sophisticated methods. Thus, when customs or contracts solve moral problems, the law will typically let them stand. Indeed, legal systems often rely on custom and contract when they judge these methods to be superior methods of solving moral problems than legal planning.

Moreover, to say that the law's mission is to address the moral defects of alternative forms of social ordering is not to claim that legal systems *always* succeed in their mission. The law may end up pursuing immoral objectives or simply replace private moral mistakes with public ones. Indeed, the sheer diversity of political objectives that actual legal systems have attempted to secure throughout human history suggests that the law often fails in its primary mission. What makes the law *the law* is that it has a moral aim, not that it satisfies that aim.

By asserting that legal systems have a characteristic aim, the planning theory bucks the trend among legal positivists who have been skeptical of such claims.[16] These positivists, of course, do not deny that legal systems pursue particular ends. Rather, they worry that there is no aim that is both universal *and* non-trivial.[17] For consider any particular aim: the defense of human rights, promotion of democracy, protection of private property, redistribution of wealth inequality, etc. It always seems possible to find or imagine some legal regime which is not dedicated to such an end. These particular aims are too parochial to play the necessary universalizing role. On the other hand, if we impute an end which is plausibly universal, such as coordinating social activity

---

them and secondarily by selecting arbitrary solutions to coordination problems. Others regard political morality as largely indeterminate: it provides very little by way of specific guidance about what the law should be. Political morality, in other words, does not tell us what kind of property, contract, criminal, constitutional and tax laws we must have. On this conception, the law resolves moral problems primarily through a process that Aquinas called "determinatio," namely, the determination and filling out of the details that are left indeterminate by morality. The law is needed not so much to reveal the answers to moral questions, but rather to *create* them. On this conception of political morality and the role that law plays within it, see Arthur Ripstein, *Force and Freedom: Kant's Political and Legal Philosophy* (Harvard University Press 2009).

16 H. L. A. Hart claimed that the law has a function, which is the guidance of conduct, but clearly did not think that this function was unique to law. See H. L. A. Hart, *The Concept of Law* (Joseph Raz and Penelope Bullock eds, 2nd edn, Clarendon Press 1994) 249 (hereinafter *CL*).

17 For a clear expression of this skepticism, see Leslie Green, "Law as a Means" in Peter Cane (ed), *The Hart-Fuller Debate in the Twenty-First Century* (Hart 2010).

or guiding conduct, we end up with an empty truism. Of course, the law does those things, but so do games, religion, etiquette and so on.

The moral aim thesis, however, posits an end that is neither parochial nor empty. It is not parochial because it does not claim that the law is supposed to pursue any substantive end. It is agnostic, in other words, about which particular moral problems and opportunities the law should address. The law, we said, is a universal means, adapted to solve any kind of moral problem. But the aim the planning theory attributes to the law is not empty either, for it specifies one that only legal systems pursue, namely, the rectification of the moral defects associated with the circumstances of legality. Any normative system coordinates social activity and guides action. But only a legal system is supposed to address those problems that less sophisticated methods of coordinating social activity and guiding action are unable to resolve.

Happy Accidents

The moral aim thesis is bolstered by several considerations. First, it explains why we think that law is invaluable in the modern world but not, say, among simple hunter-gatherers. The former is the paradigm of the circumstances of legality, whereas the latter is its antithesis. Second, the moral aim thesis explains why legal systems which are unable to solve serious moral problems are criticizable. No one blames baseball for failing to alleviate poverty or protect populations from natural disasters, but a legal system which ignores such problems, or addresses them incompetently, is subject to rebuke.

There is a third consideration which supports the moral aim thesis and which shows why the end it attributes is central to the law's identity. Consider sophisticated crime syndicates like the Japanese yakuza or the Sicilian mafia. These firms are compulsory planning organizations: their members engage in collective planning designed to further shared criminal ends, they occupy offices (e.g., the don, consigliores, capos, lieutenants, bodyguards, hitmen), their normativity is institutional in nature (e.g., the Yamaguchi-gumi of Japan has 18,000 members and as a result has an extremely complex hierarchical structure) and they do not require consent before imposing their demands on their victims. Yet, these criminal organizations are not legal systems.

We can see, therefore, that though all legal systems are compulsory planning organizations, not all compulsory planning organizations are legal systems. What, then, distinguishes the non-legal compulsory planning organizations, such as the firms just mentioned, from the legal ones? I think it is plausible to say that the difference is one of aim. If we want to explain what makes the law *the law*, we must see it as necessarily having a moral aim, an end that criminal organizations do not necessarily possess.

I am not suggesting that organized crime never produces morally good benefits. Indeed, some studies have shown that organized crime arises and flourishes in societies where established legal systems fail to provide adequate levels of dispute resolution, property rights enforcement and protective services. Criminal enterprises act as black-market entrepreneurs who supply much-needed social services and thereby fill important niches left by weak state institutions.[18] According to the moral aim thesis, the difference between legal systems and these criminal syndicates is not that the former are *in fact* morally better than the latter; rather, the distinguishing factor is that it is in the nature of the former that they are *supposed to be* so. In other words, it is part of the identity of law to have a moral mission, whereas it is not in the nature of non-legal criminal syndicates to have such a mandate.

There is a sense, of course, in which both legal systems and these criminal organizations are supposed to solve moral problems, namely, as a matter of substantive morality. Morally speaking, everyone should act morally, which clearly includes criminals as well. The claim I am advancing here, however, is a metaphysical, not a moral, one. A legal system cannot help but have a moral aim if it is to be a legal system; whereas a criminal organization that did not have a moral aim would still be a criminal organization, though it would likely be a morally bad one.

Additional support for the moral aim thesis can be gleaned from the diverse reactions we have to situations in which morally good consequences are produced. When organized crime happens to solve moral problems, these occurrences are treated by us as *serendipitous*, as happy accidents. By contrast, the moral benefits generated by a just legal system are not accidental or side effects of legal activity; rather, producing them is the very point of its activity. Legal systems are by their very nature supposed to be morally good, and when they are so, they fulfill their aim.[19]

Conversely, when a mafia don terrorizes a neighborhood, we don't think that he has *abused* his power or has acted in a *corrupt* fashion. It doesn't even make sense to accuse the mafia of being *unjust*, since the mafia does not fail at a task that by its nature it is supposed to perform. By contrast, legal systems can be unjust, and when they are, they fall short of their defining mission: unlike the yakuza or mafia, they fail not only morally but on their own terms as well.

Representing Moral Aims

According to the planning theory, the law has the aim that it does irrespective of the aim of legal participants. Imagine a legal system staffed by legal officials who merely pretend to pursue noble aims but are solely after their own

18 See, e.g., Curtis Milhaupt and Mark West, "The Dark Side of Private Ordering: An Institutional and Empirical Study of Organized Crime" (2000) 67 *University of Chicago Law Review* 41–98.

19 Morally good laws, we might say, are like true beliefs: laws should be moral just as beliefs should be true. Morally beneficial crimes, however, are akin to psychologically comforting beliefs. Beliefs need not make us feel good, although when they do, and they are true, we should count ourselves lucky.

material gain. It would nevertheless be true that the aim of legal activity in that system is moral in nature (much as the aim of assertion is to convey true information even though the asserter is lying). It is simply an essential truth about the law that it is supposed to solve moral problems.

This last point, though, raises a substantial concern. If we grant that the law does not derive its aim from any intention of legal participants, what makes it the case that the law has the aim that it does? On what basis do we impute a moral end to legal systems?

It might be thought that the law's aim is taken from the fact that legal officials at the very least pretend to pursue noble ends.[20] Unfortunately, this cannot be the full story either because it is possible to imagine a legal system staffed mostly by alienated bureaucrats who merely follow the rules because it is their job.

Here, I think it is crucial to distinguish legal elites from lower-level functionaries. The law possesses the aim that it does because high-ranking officials represent the practice as having a moral aim or aims. Their avowals need not be sincere, but they must be made. These representations may take many forms, either explicitly in speeches, ceremonial steles, preambles to constitutions, prologues to legal codes and judicial dicta, or implicitly through the atmospherics of ritual dress and speech, the construction of monumental buildings housing legal activity and the use of religious or moral iconography in legal settings. Perhaps most importantly, the moral aims of the law are represented through legal discourse. By describing legal demands as *obligating*, not merely obliging, and power as based on *right*, not merely might, elites present their practice as something other than a criminal enterprise or self-interested pursuit of pleasure, profit or glory. They depict it, in other words, as an activity that is supposed to solve moral problems and should be obeyed for that reason.

The foot soldiers have a role to play here as well. In their official capacities, they must speak their lines, namely, use moral language to describe the law. But the fact that they use moral terminology and concepts does not mean that they personally endorse, or are trying to make others think that they personally endorse, such moral evaluations. They may just be doing their job, one which requires them to evaluate conduct from the legal point of view.

Augustine famously asked: "Absent justice, what are kingdoms but vast robberies?"[21] Morally speaking, the answer may be nothing. But from a conceptual point of view, there is all the difference in the world. The kingdom is a kingdom because the king and his court represent it as having a moral mission. Members of the criminal syndicates we have been considering, by contrast,

20 Joseph Raz, *The Authority of Law: Essays on Law and Morality* (Oxford University Press 1979) 155 n 13. For Hart's criticism of this position, see H. L. A. Hart, *Essays on Bentham* (Oxford University Press 1982) 155–161.

21 Augustine, *City of God Against the Pagans* (R. W. Dyson ed, Cambridge University Press 1998) 147.

do not portray their threats as creating obligations and right for their victims. They drop the conceit that they are trying to solve the problems associated with the circumstances of legality—in fact, they realize that they *are* the problems of the circumstances of legality. It is that recognition, and their lack of shame about it, which make them mere criminals and not legal officials.[22]

V. Self-Certifying Organizations

At first, life at Del Boca Vista, a growing retirement community in South Florida, was paradise. Residents filled their days at this beautiful location by the ocean with swimming, sailing, bingo, shuffleboard and socializing. When disputes arose, over such things as parking spaces or proper attire at the pool, residents were able to resolve them privately or, on occasion, publicly at community forums through consensual deliberation and bargaining.

As more retirees bought condos in the sprawling complex, disputes between the residents increased, both in quantity and intensity. Life no longer seemed so pleasant. In an effort to reduce the bickering and tension, the residents agreed to form a condominium board consisting of a president, vice-president, treasurer and secretary. They set the task of the board as the enactment of regulations governing the common areas and the resolution of disagreements that might arise under the rules created.

The condo board of Del Boca Vista engages in a shared activity of social planning. It creates rules for the residents of Del Boca Vista and applies them in case of disputes. It is constituted by officials and their actions are governed by a complex set of rules that renders the intentions of the board members irrelevant for decision-making. Its rules are binding irrespective of consent. And its aim is to solve those moral problems that cannot be solved, or solved as well, through alternative forms of social ordering. But the condo board is not the law. Why not?

What Law Is Not

Distinguishing between private entities such as the condo board and legal institutions turns out to be trickier than it might first appear. For example, one might think that the condo board is not the law because it is not supreme within its territory.[23] In cases of conflict, Florida law trumps the condo rules. Since the law must enjoy supreme authority within a territory or over a group of people, the condo board cannot be a legal institution.

22 It follows from the moral aim thesis that if a criminal organization presents itself as dedicated to solving serious moral problems (think of Robin Hood and his Merry Men) it too might be eligible to be a legal system. The fact that others consider it to be mere organized crime does not change the reality of the situation.

23 See, e.g., Joseph Raz, *Practical Reason and Norms* (Oxford University Press 1999) 151–152 (hereinafter *PRN*).

This proposal is not sound, however, because supremacy is not a necessary condition for the legality of an institution. For if this were so, Florida would not have a legal system either. According to the supremacy clause of the US Constitution, federal law is supreme over state law. A supremacy requirement would rule out American-style federalism as a potential legal configuration, as well as the very possibility that international law could impose obligations on nation-states.[24]

Another tack would be to claim that legal systems are necessarily comprehensive, i.e., they claim the authority to regulate any kind of behavior, whereas the condo board's regulatory authority is highly circumscribed.[25] The condo board, for example, cannot tell people which foods they may eat in their apartments, which doctors they may see, how to make a valid will and so on. Florida law, by contrast, is capable of regulating any behavior it deems fit to regulate.

This response, however, is doubly wrong. First, the limited scope of the condo board's governance is a contingent matter. We can easily imagine residents granting the condo board a comprehensive police power and authorizing them to enact any regulation they see fit to make. Even so, the condo board would not be a legal system. Second, although modern legal systems are comprehensive planning organizations, premodern legal systems did not enjoy universal scope. In 13th-century England, for example, many legal systems coexisted alongside one another, each having limited subject matter jurisdiction. Manorial law governed feudal estates; mercantile law regulated commercial interactions among merchants; ecclesiastical law concerned church matters, which at the time included marriages and legitimation of offspring; and the common law and equity regulated everything else. Subject specificity and legality are not mutually exclusive.

Finally, it might be argued that the condo board is not a legal system because it does not enjoy a monopoly on the legitimate use of force within its territory.[26] The Florida state police, for example, may use force on the condo grounds in order to enforce Florida state law. Since all legal systems must possess such coercive control, the condo board cannot be a legal system.

24 Raz argues that the law's claim to supreme authority can be discharged simply by the authority claiming to *permit* other normative institutions to operate within its jurisdiction. He might then respond to the objection in the text by noting that states claim legitimate authority over the federal government by permitting the feds to regulate their affairs. Unfortunately, this response leads to paradoxes. For the states permit the feds to regulate in a very strong sense, namely, by accepting federal supremacy. But it follows that states claim supreme authority over the feds by denying their supreme authority over the feds. Relatedly, we might question whether for Raz supreme authority is too easy to claim. Many groups claim such a right. My wife and I permit the law to regulate our lives—does that mean that we claim supremacy over it?

25 See Raz, *PRN* 150–151.

26 Max Weber uses this criterion to define the State, not the law. See Max Weber, "Politics as a Vocation" in H. H. Gerth and C. Wright Mills (eds and trans), *From Max Weber: Essays in Sociology* (Oxford University Press 1946) 77.

The problem with this suggestion is obvious: if the condo board does not enjoy a monopoly on the legitimate use of force within its territory, neither does the Florida legal system. After all, Floridians are permitted to use force in certain circumstances. Suppose that the president of the board sees a resident attempting to burn down an apartment building. Florida law would permit the president to use non-deadly force, and in some instance deadly force, to restrain the resident. Hence, even the State of Florida does not have or claim a monopoly on the legitimate use of force within Florida. Indeed, a legal system that truly cornered the market on legitimate coercion would be a monstrous thing. To completely preclude others from using force would entail denying them, for example, the right of self-defense. While it is possible to imagine such a legal system, I doubt that any such regime has existed on the face of the Earth.

The Presumption of Validity

As we have seen, one cannot disqualify the condo board from being a legal system simply by showing that Florida is a superior planning organization. If supremacy were necessary for legality, then Florida would not have a legal system either, insofar as Florida law is subordinate to federal law. US law preempts state law just as state law preempts the rules of the condo board.

Nevertheless, there is a crucial difference between these hierarchical relationships that we have thus far overlooked. Although state law must comply with federal law, *federal law automatically presumes that state law complies with federal law*. Federal law, in other words, gives states the benefit of the doubt and thus permits state officials to enforce their law without first demonstrating the validity of their actions. By contrast, the states afford no comparable presumption to private entities such as condo boards. It is not enough for the private actors to be in compliance with state law: in many instances, private actors may not enforce their rules unless they first demonstrate the validity of their actions to some state actor.

To take a concrete example, suppose that the state legislature enacts legislation forbidding skinny-dipping in any pool, public or private. We will assume for the sake of the example that this rule is constitutional and does not conflict with any pre-existing federal law. Now imagine that some resident skinny-dips in the Del Boca Vista pool and the state police are notified. In order to enforce this rule, the Florida state police need not file suit in federal court to receive permission to pull the naked offender out of the pool. Nor must the state police contact the FBI. They can simply yank the skinny-dipper out of the pool and charge him with the crime of skinny-dipping.

Now suppose that the condo board enacts a similar policy forbidding skinny-dipping in the condo pool. How will the condo board enforce their rule against the offending resident? Not by physically apprehending the swimmer and ejecting him from the condo premises. For Florida, like many other legal systems, does not permit owners to enforce their property rights (as opposed to their right not to be physically harmed) through this form of self-help. Rather, they must call the police and hope that the police agree that the skinny-dipper is trespassing on their property. Furthermore, they are not permitted to change the locks on the resident's condominium. The condo board must leave criminal punishment to the prosecutor, court, jury and sheriff and await a civil judgment before they are permitted to change the locks.

The condo board, we can say, does not enjoy the same presumption of validity that state governments do. Even though both the condo board and Florida are required to comply with the rules of superior planning institutions, only Florida is presumed to be in compliance with those rules and, hence, only it is allowed to enforce its own rules without federal permission. But since the condo board is not so presumed, it often has the burden of demonstrating to the state that the rules it wishes to enforce are valid under Florida property and contract law. Without making such a showing, the condo board violates Florida law, even though it is enforcing legally valid claims.

It might be helpful here to introduce the notion of a "general presumption of validity." X enjoys a general presumption of validity from a superior planning organization Y whenever Y does not require X to demonstrate the validity of its rules before they are enforced. In other words, when X enjoys a general presumption of validity from Y, Y places no "prior restraints" on X's enforcement powers. X may enforce its rules without making a case to Y that its rules are valid.

By contrast, a planning organization X does not enjoy a general presumption of validity when, under some circumstance, the superior organization Y requires X to demonstrate that its rules are valid before they are enforced. In situations where their rules are not presumed valid, these organizations are forbidden from enforcing them. They are subject to a rule of prior restraint. If they wish to enforce, or have another enforce, a rule, they must make a case to their superiors demonstrating the validity of their claim and hope that their superiors agree.

Call a planning organization "self-certifying" whenever it is free to enforce its rules without first demonstrating to a superior (if one exists) that its rules are valid. A planning organization, therefore, will be self-certifying whenever it is supreme or enjoys a general presumption of validity from all superior planning organizations. By contrast, a planning organization is not self-certifying whenever it is required to demonstrate that its rules are valid before it may enforce or have another enforce them. A planning organization, therefore, is not self-certifying whenever it has a superior, and this superior does not accord it a general presumption of validity.

According to the planning theory, the law is a self-certifying planning organization. Even when legal institutions lack supreme authority, they enjoy a general presumption of validity from all of their superiors. For this reason, the condo board is not a legal institution. In many cases, Florida does not presume that the condo board acts validly. The condo board cannot, for example, physically remove trespassers from the condo grounds, break into apartments to collect unpaid maintenance fees or change the locks. To do any of these things, the condo board must appeal to some legal official or body, hope that they agree that the condo board's legal rights are being violated and either direct law enforcement personnel to exercise coercion or permit the condo board to do so themselves.

It is easy to see why self-certification would be valuable to a planning organization. For when an organization cannot certify the validity of its valid rules, its ability to govern is greatly diminished. It cannot enforce its rules whenever it deems fit: in many cases, it must first submit its proposal to another organization and hope that their superior agrees with their judgment and certifies their claims. This burden of prior restraint not only results in delays, perhaps serious ones, but puts subordinates at the mercy of their superiors. Like being official and institutional, self-certification contributes significantly to the law's nimbleness as a planning organization.

By the same token, it is usually in the interest of the law to deny self-certification to powerful groups within its territory. In not extending the benefit of the doubt to others, the law plays a gatekeeping function: by requiring them to convince a competent legal tribunal that their rules are valid, it ensures that groups that can abuse their power do not do so. Furthermore, denying groups the presumption of validity also reduces the risk that feuding will break out. As Locke emphasized, long-running battles and cycles of revenge often result from the absence of neutral arbiters. If a group cannot take "the law" into its own hands, but must submit its claims to an impartial tribunal, the dangers associated with the state of nature are greatly diminished.

Because self-certification plays an important role in characterizing legal institutions, and since this property has not been previously identified or discussed in the literature, a few clarifications of it are in order. First, a self-certifying organization does not necessarily enforce its own rules. An organization is self-certifying when it is *free* to enforce its own valid rules without first having to establish their validity before some superior official or tribunal (if one should exist). Thus, the medieval Icelandic legal system was self-certifying even though its officials did not enforce the law because they *could have* enforced it if they so chose.[27] Whether a legal system avails itself of the freedom to enforce is immaterial to its status as self-certifying.

Second, self-certification does not imply that the organizations which enjoy it are completely free to use any enforcement method they wish. US states, for example, are prohibited by the Eighth Amendment from using cruel and unusual punishment in order to enforce its criminal laws. To claim that an organization is self-certifying is to say that the permissibility of using a certain method of enforcement is never conditioned on the certification of its rules by a superior. Some methods may be forbidden, but those that are permitted

27 On the medieval Icelandic legal system, see William I. Miller, *Bloodtaking and Peacemaking: Feud, Law and Society in Saga Iceland* (University of Chicago Press 1997).

are permitted without prior certification. The Eighth Amendment, therefore, does not destroy the states' presumption of validity because this constitutional provision does not impose a prior restraint on the use of cruel and unusual punishment. Rather, it imposes a blanket prohibition on this enforcement method. In other words, the prohibition on cruel and unusual punishment *would have* destroyed the presumption of validity if states had to convince the federal government that their laws are constitutional in order to use cruel and usual punishment or to get the federal government to use such methods. But since no one is permitted to use such methods, the fact that states are so prohibited does not affect their status as self-certifying.

Third, while non-supreme but self-certifying organizations enjoy a general presumption of validity, this presumption is rebuttable. Plaintiffs, for example, may sue a state in federal court and make the case that the state's behavior violates federal or constitutional law. In such circumstances, the presumption of validity evaporates, thereby shifting to the state the burden of demonstrating the validity of their actions.

Degrees of Legality

Although I have described self-certification as a binary property—either an organization has it or it does not—it is probably best to see it as something that comes in degrees. Some organizations that are not completely self-certifying may be virtually so if they are *almost* always free to enforce their rules without certification by a superior. State legal systems in the United States are virtually, but not completely, self-certifying because under rare circumstances they are required to shoulder the burden of establishing the validity of their rules to a federal tribunal before they may enforce their own rules. Section 5 of the Voting Rights Act, for example, requires certain states (so-called covered jurisdictions) to submit proposed changes in voting procedures to the Justice Department or a federal district court for pre-clearance before it may enforce these new procedures.[28]

Other properties that are constitutive of legality also come in degrees. Thus, some organizations may be virtually, but not completely, compulsory. Many legal systems, for example, allow certain groups the right to refuse obedience to certain laws out of reasons of conscience. While they are not allowed to "quit" the law entirely, they may quit some part of it under limited circumstances.

28 42 U.S.C. §1973c. It is interesting that parenting is more self-certifying than state legal activity because parents never face preclearance requirements. If I want to enforce the rules of the house, I never have to call the police or file suit against my child in family court; I can simply punish my child.

Indeed, it is plausible to suppose that legality itself is not a binary property but also comes in degrees.[29] The more self-certifying or compulsory an organization is, the more legal it should be considered. Ordinarily, we call something "law" when it lies towards, but not necessarily on, the end of various spectrums. We think that states have legal systems because they are virtually self-certifying. Preclearance requirements such as imposed by the Voting Rights Act are actually quite extraordinary, and may even be unique to the voting rights context.

In other cases, the property of legality will be even less fully instantiated, thus creating borderline instances of law. The United States Golf Association, for example, straddles the line between law and non-law. On the one hand, it is an organization which regulates the game of golf in the United States and Mexico and its activities are self-certifying (the USGA does not have to go to court in order to award or revoke titles). Thus, it styles itself the "national governing body of golf." On the other hand, it is not fully compulsory. One can, of course, not pay one's dues to the organization and not follow the rules which they impose on members. But it is compulsory in the sense that the USGA determines the official rules of golf in the United States and Mexico, and hence one cannot play golf (or at least the official version of golf) unless one follows the regulations they have enacted. One might also question whether the USGA has the moral aim characteristic of law. While the USGA does solve problems that would be difficult to solve otherwise, and thus improves human welfare, these problems are not of the same moral seriousness as those legal systems typically address. The best we can say about the USGA, therefore, is that it is like a legal system in some senses, but not in others, and leave it at that.

29 See, e.g., Raz, *PRN* 150.

Part III

Islamic Tradition

11 Law and Morality

Key Perspectives in Islamic Theology and Legal Thought

Muhammad Ammar Khan Nasir

Scholarly discourse among Muslim theologians and jurists regarding the ultimate source of morality largely converges on the notion that human beings possess an inherent ability to distinguish between good and bad from a moral perspective—a sentiment reflected across all cultures and societies. Nevertheless, Islamic tradition maintains that human reason alone is insufficient without divine revelation; thus, it emphasizes prophecy as a cornerstone of the divine plan for guiding humanity. To fully appreciate the depth and complexity of these discussions, it's essential to survey key perspectives and nuanced debates within the Islamic intellectual tradition, spanning various disciplines such as theology, jurisprudence, and political thought. This survey will also shed light on how classical debates inform contemporary Islamic discourses, particularly regarding issues at the intersection of modernity and Islamic law and morality.

Theological Perspectives

Debates in Islamic theology (*kalam*) encompass questions such as the extent of human reason's capability to discern the ultimate moral nature of things, the precise relationship between human moral knowledge and divine revelation, and the accountability of individuals before God based solely on their moral consciousness in the absence of divine revelation. In this context, the *Mu'tazilite* and *Ash'arite* schools represent two diametrically opposed conceptions, stemming from differing views about God's attributes, particularly whether God's actions are constrained by any moral principles or solely determined by His absolute free will.

I. Mu'tazilite *Perspective*

The *Mu'tazilite* school of thought anchors its debates in the context of the attributes of God, particularly the affirmation of God's justice (*'adl*). According to them, God, being an all-knowing and wise entity, does not act arbitrarily; instead, all His actions align with wisdom and justice. God's wisdom dictates that He abstains from purposeless actions, lies, and injustices. From creation to the responsibilities imposed on humans and the dispensation of

DOI: 10.4324/9781003728603-14

reward and punishment, every divine act operates on principles of justice and wisdom that are rationally explainable.

Mu'tazilites argue that while God is a voluntary agent and is not initially bound to perform any particular act, His inherent justice and wisdom necessitate that all His actions are good and not evil. In creating beings, God must act with the intention to benefit them since harming others is deemed evil and unbefitting for Him. They extend their understanding of good and evil to the divine commands and laws given to humans, arguing that God's commands must correspond to actions that are inherently good or beneficial to humans, and prohibition relates to inherently harmful actions.[1]

The *Mu'tazilites* believe that understanding good and evil is grounded in human interests. They assert that God's commands do not create moral properties but reflect the inherent goodness or evil of actions. For instance, God's permitting or forbidding an action does not establish its moral status but instead reveals its pre-existing nature. Thus, in their view, neither divine law nor human reason generates moral attributes; both simply recognize them.[2]

However, while human reason can grasp basic moral principles, such as the obligation to avoid purposeless harm, it cannot independently discern the specifics of what is beneficial or harmful without divine guidance. The knowledge of which particular actions hold goodness or evil belongs to the domain of the unseen. Consequently, the *Mu'tazilites* assert that there are two categories of actions that reason deems wrong. First, there are actions whose wrongness cannot be separated from them in any circumstance—reason inherently perceives them as wrong in any situation. Such actions are beyond the scope of alteration by divine law. The second category includes actions that can be seen as either good or wrong depending on specific conditions. Divine law can modify reason's judgment in such cases by revealing the harm in an action, based on knowledge beyond the reach of human reason but accessible through divine omniscience.

Given that the divine knowledge about the properties and attributes of actions is perfect and unerring, while human reason is limited and flawed, it follows that the divine pronouncements on actions may differ from reason's initial perceptions based on surface observations. Qadi Abdul-Jabbar elaborates that certain actions might appear wrong to reason but are deemed obligatory or recommended in divine law, such as obligatory and supererogatory prayers where humans face hardships, but these are made obligatory due to their underlying benefits. Conversely, some actions might seem beneficial to reason and be declared obligatory in divine law, like helping the needy

1 'Abd al-Jabbar ibn Ahmad al-Hamadhani, *Al-Mughni fi Abwab al-Tawhid wal-'Adl, Al-Ta'dil wal-Tajwir* (Mahmoud Muhammad Qasim ed, Al-Dar al-Masriyyah lil-Ta'lif wal-Tarjamah, Egypt, no date) 64, 65.

2 'Abd al-Jabbar ibn Ahmad al-Hamadhani, *Sharh al-Usul al-Khamsah* (3rd edn, 'Abd al-Karim 'Uthman ed, Maktabah Wahbah, Cairo 1996) 318.

through charity and expiations. Additionally, it is possible for certain actions, though permissible according to reason, to be prohibited by divine law due to associated evils, like prohibited acts of fraud, adultery, and eating during fasting in Ramadan.

The *Mu'tazilites* maintain that reason alone is not always capable of discerning the intricate details of what is beneficial or harmful in specific actions; divine guidance is essential to fully grasp these aspects. According to the *Mu'tazilites*, it is not necessary for humans to comprehend the detailed benefits embedded within divine commands and prohibitions, nor is such comprehension a condition for them to be considered morally binding. It is sufficient for reason to broadly understand that all divine commands are inherently beneficial because God is wise and cannot prescribe something that would harm humans.[3]

II. Ash'arite *View*

The *Ash'arites*, in contrast to the *Mu'tazilites*, explain God's attributes of justice and wisdom differently. They argue that the criterion for deeming an act just or unjust depends on the nature and status of the actor. If the actor is a dependent creature like a human, they are bound by the commands of their Creator and sovereign. However, if the actor is God, He is not subject to any moral principles since He is sovereign and the ultimate owner, beyond any binding laws. From this perspective, human actions are judged by what God has commanded and prohibited, while God's actions are determined by another rational concept—that an owner has the right to act as they wish with their property. Consequently, all of God's actions are inherently good, even if they might be considered wrong on the level of human morality.

Al-Ghazali illustrates this by referring to the allowance of injustice, sinfulness, and chaos among humans, and the suffering inflicted on animals by other animals or humans. He argues that if a master allows their subjects to fight, oppress, or kill each other, it is rationally considered wrong. Similarly, allowing harm to innocent animals is also rationally wrong. However, these occurrences are observed in the world, and while they may not be deemed good by human moral standards, they are considered good by the principle that God, as the master of the universe, has the right to act as He pleases, and thus, all His actions are inherently good.[4]

3 Al-Mughni fi Abwab al-Tawhid wal-'Adl, *Al-Tanabbu'at wal-Mu'jizat* (Mahmoud Muhammad Qasim ed, Al-Dar al-Masriyyah lil-Ta'lif wal-Tarjamah, Egypt, no date) 27, 28.

4 Abu Hamid al-Ghazali, *Al-Mustasfa min 'Ilm al-Usul* (Hamzah bin Zuhayr Hafiz ed, Dar al-Hady al-Nabawi, Mansurah/Dar al-Fadilah, Riyadh 2013) Vol. 1, 184.

The *Ash'arites* extend this principle to the domain of divine commands and laws. For instance, Al-Jurjani states:

> What is considered wrong according to us is what is prohibited by Shariah, whether it is prohibited for its inherent harm or for its undesirability, and what is deemed as good is what is not prohibited by Shariah, including the obligatory, recommended, and permissible actions. Reason has no judgment on the goodness or badness of things. This is not due to an inherent quality in the action before Shariah, as the *Mu'tazilites* claim. Rather, Shariah itself establishes and clarifies this. There is neither inherent goodness nor badness in actions before Shariah. If Shariah were to reverse the assessment, declaring what was inherently wrong as good and vice versa, it would not be impossible, as seen in the abrogation of commands from prohibition to obligation and from obligation to prohibition.[5]

Ibn Hazm further clarifies this point by stating that actions such as avoiding lying, *shirk* (associating partners with God), and injustice are necessary for humans solely because God has commanded them to do so. If God were to command the opposite—engaging in *shirk*, injustice, and lying—these actions would then become good, as there is no basis for deeming an action good or bad other than God's command.[6]

This underscores the Ash'arites' view that moral values are fundamentally rooted in divine command rather than any intrinsic quality of the actions themselves. Under this perspective, God's sovereignty encompasses the authority to define moral standards, and human moral reasoning must align with divine guidance.

Despite this, Ash'ari theologians, such as Al-Ghazali and Fakhr al-Din al-Razi, acknowledge that the concepts of goodness and badness can be considered rational (*aqli*) in the sense that the pursuit of benefit (*manfa'at*) and the avoidance of harm (*zarar*) are intrinsic to human nature. Human beings possess the inherent capacity to discern what is beneficial or harmful to them and to formulate strategies to achieve these objectives. Additionally, compassion is a fundamental aspect of human nature, psychologically compelling individuals to perform acts of kindness and to refrain from causing harm to others.[7]

5 Al-Sayyid al-Sharif 'Ali ibn Muhammad al-Jurjani, *Sharh al-Mawaqif* (Dar al-Kutub al-'Ilmiyyah, Beirut 1998) Vol. 8, 201–202.

6 Abu Muhammad ibn Hazm, *Al-Ahkam fi Usul al-Ahkam* (Ahmad Muhammad Shakir ed, Dar al-Afaq al-Jadidah, Beirut 1403 AH) Vol. 5, 73–74.

7 Al-Ghazali (n 4) Vol. 1, 184; Fakhr al-Din al-Razi, *Al-Mahsul fi 'Ilm Usul al-Fiqh* (3rd edn, Taha Jabir Fayyad al-'Alwani ed, Mu'assasat al-Risalah, Beirut 1997) Vol. 1, 130–131. In this regard, both Al-Ghazali and Al-Razi appear to align with Jean-Jacques Rousseau's theory, which

Nevertheless, for Ash'ari theologians, the rationality or naturalness of an action is insufficient for it to be regarded as a divine command. According to them, a moral injunction must be explicitly ordained by God to attain the status of a divine command. Only then can it be considered binding upon human beings, who are accountable to God for their actions. This divine command is a prerequisite for moral accountability and serves as a condition for the dispensation of rewards or punishments in the Hereafter.

Thus, while Ash'ari theologians recognize the rational and natural dimensions of moral actions, they maintain that divine sanction is essential for these actions to acquire religious and moral significance within the framework of Islamic theology. This nuanced position underscores the distinctiveness of Ash'ari thought in the broader discourse on the relationship between rationality, natural law, and divine command.

Two Illustrating Debates

To illustrate the general viewpoint of Islamic theological and legal thought regarding the capabilities and limitations of human reason in comparison to divinely revealed guidance, we can recount here two particularly interesting debates.

Al-Jahiz (d. 868), in his essay "Virtues of the Turks" (*Manaqib al-Turk*), narrates an interesting conversation between Emir of Khorasan Junayd ibn Abd al-Rahman and Khaqan, the Turkish king, which occurred during the conflicts between Muslims and Turks. The conversation revolves around the punishments for various crimes. Khaqan asks Junayd about the Islamic punishments for adultery, slander, and theft and responds to each explanation by praising the laws as excellent measures for preventing crime.

Then Khaqan enquires about the punishments for lying, slandering, and public flatulence in Islam. Junayd replies that such people are not accepted as witnesses, are kept away from positions of honor and respect, and are humiliated. Khaqan asks if that is all, and Junayd confirms that it is. Khaqan then explains that in his kingdom, he punishes these crimes by imprisoning slanderers, branding the anus of those who commit public flatulence with hot iron, cutting off the tongue of liars (just as Muslims cut off the hand of a thief), and banishing those who make others laugh by acting like clowns to ensure his people's minds are not corrupted.

In response, Junayd says that Khaqan relies on rational decisions in his laws, adopting what seems rationally good, while Muslims follow the prophets, believing that Allah knows the best outcomes of human actions and wisdom better than humans themselves. He notes that humans often see outcomes contrary to their plans. Upon hearing this, Khaqan acknowledges that this is

posits that the two basic human instincts of self-preservation and compassion serve as the foundation for natural law.

the most valuable insight Junayd has provided and that it has given him much to ponder.[8]

The exchange between Junayd and Khaqan on the differences between Islamic Sharia and Turkish law highlights their wisdom and understanding. Neither does Junayd attempt to convince Khaqan that his laws are irrational and that Islamic law is more rational (despite ample opportunity), nor does Khaqan dismiss Junayd's explanation as irrational. Their mutual understanding lies in comprehending the nature and limits of rationality itself.

Another debate that highlights the complexity of these discussions involved two medieval jurists, one from the Shafi'i tradition and the other from the Hanafi tradition. The debate centered on the permissibility of adultery, considering its social boundaries and restrictions: Is it rationally detestable and prohibitable aside from the Sharia's prohibition? The Hanafi jurist al-Jassas (d. 917) argued that adultery is rationally detestable because it inevitably affects matters related to lineage and guardianship of children. Therefore, considering mutual sexual enjoyment of men and women as permissible, disregarding these issues, is not rationally justified for the welfare of human society.[9]

The Shafi'i jurist, Alkiya al-Harasi (d. 1110), challenges this view, asserting that the necessity of establishing lineage stems from specific Sharia rulings. In their absence, he argues, lineage recognition would not be a rational obligation. Regarding the question of who would be responsible for the upbringing and guardianship of the child, al-Harasi argues that even if the father is known rationally, it does not necessarily follow that he must be responsible for the child's upbringing. This responsibility is also imposed by Sharia, and in the absence of such a ruling, people would be compelled to devise other rational ways to ensure the survival of the human race. From this reasoning, al-Harasi concludes that if there were no Sharia ruling, adultery would not be rationally detestable but rather completely permissible, as mutual sexual enjoyment with the woman's consent neither harms nor constitutes oppression for either party. In support of this, al-Harasi references the customs of the Arabs, among whom various forms of adultery and procreation through it were prevalent during the pre-Islamic period.[10]

The difference between al-Jassas and Alkiya al-Harasi underscores the importance of differentiating between two types of rationality: one grounded in Sharia preferences and the other operating purely on empirical grounds independent of Sharia injunctions. Al-Jassas seeks to elucidate the rational detestability of adultery based on a rationality defined by Sharia, where the responsibilities of preserving lineage, sanctity of relationships, and maintaining

8 Abu 'Uthman al-Jahiz, *Rasa'il al-Jahiz* ('Abd al-Salam Muhammad Harun ed and annot, Maktabat al-Khanji, Cairo 1964) Vol. 1, 178–181.

9 Abu Bakr al-Razi al-Jassas, *Ahkam al-Qur'an* ('Abd al-Salam Muhammad 'Ali Shahin ed, Dar al-Kutub al-'Ilmiyyah, Beirut 1415 AH/1994) Vol. 3, 260.

10 Al-Kiya al-Harasi, *Ahkam al-Qur'an* (2nd edn, Musa Muhammad 'Ali and 'Izzah 'Abd Atiyyah ed, Dar al-Kutub al-'Ilmiyyah, Beirut 1405 AH) Vol. 4, 287.

familial ties are already acknowledged. Within this framework, the rational impermissibility of adultery is established. Conversely, al-Harasi elevates the discourse from Sharia-based rationality to an autonomous and unbound reason, questioning what purely rational principle—without the decisive authority of Sharia—dictates that preserving lineage and forming family structures are necessary for human survival.

Ibn Khaldun's Analysis of Governance

The discourse around the relationship between reason and revelation is also vividly reflected in the works of Muslim theoreticians of governance and political power. A significant glimpse into this debate can be found in Ibn Khaldun's *Muqaddima* (Introduction), where he discusses three different kinds of empires and how they conduct public affairs.

Ibn Khaldun begins by emphasizing the natural necessity of human society and governance, seeing it as a product of human nature and the need for cooperation.[11] He discusses three types of governance: natural monarchy, political governance, and caliphate:

1. *Primitive authority*: Governed by power and domination, often leading to injustice as rulers impose their will on their subjects to satisfy their own desires and ambitions. This kind of rule tends to falter due to difficulty in sustaining obedience, often resulting in violence and social unrest.
2. *Rational governance*: This type of governance is based on societal laws and regulations established by wise and prominent figures of the state. It aims to ensure public order and worldly benefits. Such policies, although rational and aimed at managing worldly affairs effectively, are considered deficient because they lack divine guidance.
3. *Caliphate*: Described as the ideal form of governance, it integrates both worldly and religious duties. This system is based on divine law (Sharia), aiming at both worldly stability and eternal salvation. The Caliphate is viewed as governance that ensures the well-being of both this life and the hereafter, aligning with divine wisdom.

Ibn Khaldun concludes that while political governance based on reason can achieve some level of public order and prosperity, it remains inferior to governance rooted in divine revelation. The latter ensures that all aspects of life, including governance, are oriented towards ultimate spiritual and temporal well-being, grounded in principles revealed by God.[12]

11 'Abd al-Rahman ibn Khaldun, *Al-'Ibar wa Diwan al-Mubtada' wal-Khabar fi Tarikh al-'Arab wal-Barbar* (Khalil Shahadah ed, Dar al-Fikr, Beirut 1981) Vol. 1, 234.
12 Ibid. Vol. 1, 238–239.

This threefold categorization highlights the nuanced understanding of governance in Islamic thought, reflecting the continuous interplay between reason and revelation, and underscores the holistic nature of Islamic political theory that seeks to harmonize the material and the spiritual realms of human existence.

Discerning 'Objectives' in Divine Law

Another significant aspect of the Ash'arite conception of the relationship between Sharia and morality must be considered. Ash'ari theologians acknowledge that even though God's actions are not bound by any prior moral principles, He seeks to actualize certain benefits for human beings through His commandments and laws by His will and intention. This forms the foundation for the theory of the Objectives of Sharia, as propounded by Ash'ari jurists like al-Juwayni (d. 1085) and al-Ghazali (d. 1111), and fully developed by the illustrious 14th-century Andalusian scholar, al-Shatibi (d. 1388). The theory states that the guidance provided to humans through prophets is intended for the welfare and benefit of humanity. Human beings are required to follow certain principles and regulations in their individual and social lives to protect specific interests intended by the divine lawgiver.

A thorough examination of divine commands reveals that the entire process of legislation aims to safeguard five essential human interests upon which the worldly and spiritual well-being of humanity depends:

1. Religion
2. Human life
3. Lineage
4. Property
5. Intellect.

To protect religion, the lawgiver has prescribed acts of worship (such as faith, prayer, almsgiving, fasting, and pilgrimage); for the preservation of life and intellect, the law includes guidelines on customs (such as food, drink, clothing, and shelter); and to protect lineage, property, and in some aspects, life and intellect, the law encompasses transactions (such as buying and selling, marriage, retribution, and criminal law). The instructions provided by the divine lawgiver work at three different levels to protect these interests, which al-Shatibi refers to as necessities (ضروريات), needs (حاجيات), and embellishments (تحسينيات).

He explains that in the domains of worship, customs, and transactions, the protection of these three levels is the Objective of Sharia. Necessities ensure the minimum level of preservation, without which human life cannot continue correctly, leading to chaos, disorder, and total destruction. This protection must be on both ends—ensuring these interests are upheld positively and preventing anything that might harm them. Examples include the basic obligations and prohibitions stated in divine law, such as prayer and almsgiving in acts of worship, the permissibility of buying and selling in transactions, and the prohibition of murder, adultery, and theft.

Needs aim to provide ease and facilitate compliance with Sharia's laws, preventing undue hardship. This level includes all exemptions mentioned in Sharia to remove hardship caused by the original rules, such as the concession to skip fasting during illness and travel, the permission to hunt when slaughtering is not possible, and the permissibility of certain financial transactions like *Mudharabah* (a profit-sharing agreement between an investor and a manager), *Musaqah* (a partnership where one party tends to orchards or crops in exchange for a share of the produce), and *Salam* (a contract where payment is made in advance for goods to be delivered later), as well as holding the collective responsibility for paying blood money.

Embellishments refer to adopting praiseworthy habits and moral virtues and avoiding things that reason considers repulsive. Embellishments go beyond basic and needed interests, as their absence does not disrupt essential or needed interests but serves mainly for enhancement and beautification. Examples listed by al-Shatibi include maintaining cleanliness, covering oneself adequately, ensuring elegance in worship, observing dietary etiquettes, declaring slaves and women unfit for rulership, and prohibiting the killing of women, children, and monks during war.[13]

This profound understanding shows how the Ash'arite school bridges divine sovereignty with practical human welfare through a structured framework of Sharia's objectives.

Shah Waliullah's Framework

Comparing the perspectives of Shah Waliullah, the 18th-century Indian scholar, with those of al-Shatibi provides valuable insights into understanding the inner spirit of Sharia. Shah Waliullah offers a historical perspective on the relationship between reason, revelation, and God's purposes in his seminal work, *Hujjatullah al-Baligha*. He rejects the simplistic comparison of Sharia with commands given by a master solely to test a slave's obedience, emphasizing that Sharia laws aim at human welfare rather than mere obedience.[14]

While Shatibi employs an inductive method to derive the Objectives of Shariah by studying its injunctions and their interlocking principles, Shah Waliullah argues that this examination must also consider the social and historical milieu in which divine commands were revealed. He underscores that understanding divine laws requires supplementing the inductive method with

13 Abu Ishaq al-Shatibi, *Al-Muwafaqat* (Abu 'Ubaydah Mashhur bin Hasan Al Salman ed, Dar Ibn 'Affan 1997) Vol. 2, 17–23.

14 Ahmad ibn 'Abd al-Rahim al-Dihlawi, *Hujjat Allah al-Balighah* (Sayyid Sabiq ed, Dar al-Jil, Beirut 2005) Vol. 1, 27.

a thorough comprehension of their social and cultural environment. This approach helps derive and grasp the inner logic and rationality of Sharia laws through their relationship with evolving human cultures, providing a comprehensive historical and sociological context.

Shah Waliullah contributed significantly to the debate on the interplay between reason and revelation in determining the moral foundations for human actions. He proposed that human beings possess an intrinsic nature (*fitrah*) and an inherent capacity to reason (*'aql*), which collectively lead to the formation of consensual practical wisdom (*ra'y kulli*) in societies. This form of wisdom is instrumental in safeguarding the collective benefits and interests of communities, thereby guiding ethical and moral decisions to ensure justice and equity.[15]

Shah Waliullah elaborated on the evolution of human societies through four stages, referred to as "*Irtifaqat*." Each stage marks a progression towards a more sophisticated and organized collective life. Throughout these stages, *ra'y kulli* evolves alongside societal advancements, reflecting the continuous development of consensual wisdom that underpins social norms and practices. Despite different cultures adopting specific norms, rules, and customs according to their unique needs, *ra'y kulli* remains a consistent feature across all cultural manifestations, ensuring a common moral foundation.[16]

Furthermore, Shah Waliullah emphasized that divine guidance, through prophets and revelations, does not negate *ra'y kulli*. Instead, it builds upon this collective wisdom, using existing societal norms and values as foundational materials. Divine revelation aims not to completely replace these norms but to reform and refine them, eliminating any excesses or deviations.[17] The final Sharia, revealed through the Prophet of Islam, exemplifies this approach by incorporating two previously revealed sets of divine laws: the teachings of Abraham and the Mosaic law given to the descendants of Jacob. These laws serve as the basis for a universal and final Sharia intended for all of humanity.[18]

In essence, Shah Waliullah's theoretical framework offers profound insights into the relationship among human reason, the historical evolution of human societies, and divinely revealed injunctions and values. His perspective underscores the complementary nature of reason and revelation, illustrating how divine guidance enhances and perfects human wisdom to achieve a harmonious and just society. Despite giving utmost importance to pre-existing societal experiences and institutions, Shah Waliullah accords the final authority to reform them to Sharia, which is the ultimate arbiter for human actions, man-made customs, norms, and laws.

15 Ibid. Vol. 1, 99–101.
16 Ibid. Vol. 1, 82–99.
17 Ibid. Vol. 1, 162–167.
18 Ibid. Vol. 1, 213–223.

A Comparison With Western Natural Law Traditions

Pre-modern Western conceptions of law were largely iterations of natural law theory. These conceptions uniformly posited that law was grounded in a universal moral order, often tied to divine or eternal law, and that human laws derived their legitimacy from their alignment with this moral framework. Medieval conceptions of natural law were particularly deeply rooted in theology, viewing natural law as an extension of divine law, with its legitimacy derived from its reflection of God's eternal order. Theologians like Thomas Aquinas recognized that humans possess the capacity for moral reasoning and can discern right from wrong through rational reflection on natural law. However, they also emphasized the limitations of human reason, asserting that it is inadequate for fully comprehending divine law or the ultimate purpose of human existence, thereby necessitating the guidance of divine revelation. This principle subjected rulers and their actions to moral scrutiny, asserting that their authority was valid only to the extent that it conformed to higher moral law.

The emergence of a purely secular conception of natural law, detached from its theological foundations, was a distinctly modern development. This shift unfolded alongside the Enlightenment, as human reason began to be seen as autonomous and capable of determining moral and legal principles independently. This transition marked a turning point, decoupling natural law from its theistic roots and positioning it as a universal framework for governance within the secular, modern state. The rise of the modern state, in fact, facilitated this shift by seeking a foundation for legal and moral order that operated independently of religious institutions. This shift allowed natural law to be used as a foundation for secular governance, paving the way for modern legal positivism and the idea of state sovereignty independent of religious authority.

Against this backdrop, Islamic legal thought presents a framework that, in its essentials, aligns with the pre-modern theologically inspired natural law traditions of the West. Both traditions emphasize the harmony between human reason and divine guidance, insisting that political authority must remain subordinate to moral and divine law. These shared principles underscore a rich philosophical tradition that contrasts sharply with the secular, positivist turn of modern legal theories, offering a vision of law that is both morally grounded and divinely inspired.

Sharia and Modernity

The preceding discussion provides essential context for understanding and evaluating the Muslim theological perspective on various ethical issues, often viewed as key points of tension between Islam and modernity.

As established, the Islamic theological tradition recognizes Sharia, or divine command, as the ultimate arbiter of the moral status of human actions. At the same time, Sharia has evolved through successive revelations by engaging with and refining the laws and customs that human societies had deemed to serve their best interests. Human reason plays a pivotal role in uncovering divine purposes, both by examining the improvements Sharia has made to pre-existing customs and by hermeneutically interpreting Sharia injunctions. Through this process, underlying moral and legal principles, along with the human interests they aim to protect, are discerned.

This understanding underscores the well-known fact that Islamic law is derived from multiple sources. These include explicit divine injunctions found in the Quran and Hadith, rulings deduced through analogical reasoning (*qiyas*), laws developed to meet human needs and benefits (*maslahah*), and practices rooted in custom (*urf*). Despite this diversity, the legitimacy of these sources is fundamentally tied to Sharia, which is ultimately sanctioned by divine revelation. As such, Sharia holds supreme authority, and no source can override its explicit rulings.

It is also important to recognize that the interplay between these different sources can sometimes yield contradictory results. However, Islamic jurisprudence (*fiqh*) is equipped with internal mechanisms for resolving such conflicts. These mechanisms include principles of jurisprudence (*usul al-fiqh*) that guide the process of making preferences (*tarjih*) among conflicting evidences. Additionally, Sharia scholars (*ulama*) are afforded a significant degree of interpretative flexibility, allowing for a wide scope of legitimate scholarly disagreement (*ikhtilaf*) on particular issues.

This robust framework ensures that while Sharia remains the ultimate authority, the process of deriving and applying the law is dynamic and adaptable to changing contexts and circumstances. By appreciating the nuanced nature of Islamic legal theory, one can better understand the coherence and resilience of the Muslim theological position in navigating ethical questions that arise at the intersection of tradition and modernity.

For instance, there is a consensus within Islamic theology that practices such as charging interest on loans, adultery, incest, homosexuality, consuming pork, or drinking alcohol cannot be deemed morally acceptable, irrespective of their prevalence or acceptance in modern society. Despite their widespread acceptance in contemporary contexts, these actions remain unequivocally impermissible under Sharia.

However, changes introduced by modernity, particularly regarding women's rights—such as limitations on polygamy, the right to divorce, interaction with men in public spaces, and participation in social and political activities—can be approached with greater flexibility. This flexibility is permissible due to the lack of unequivocal textual evidence and the consideration of individual and societal benefits, which Sharia itself endorses. Therefore, these issues can be navigated through a nuanced understanding that aligns with both traditional Islamic principles and contemporary exigencies.

Traditional social hierarchies and class segmentation, although endorsed by early or medieval Islamic authorities, can be reevaluated in light of modern socio-economic realities and the ethical values emerging from these changes.

The evolution of societal structures necessitates a reexamination of historical endorsements, allowing for the abandonment of outdated practices in favor of more equitable and just frameworks.

Regarding Islamic punishments, it is crucial to recognize that they cannot be abrogated or evaluated solely against secular modern humanistic standards. Nonetheless, Sharia does not inherently favor the widespread implementation of such punishments. Instead, there is a significant emphasis on alternative methods of reforming offenders and preventing crimes. The restrictive application of these punishments aligns with the overarching goals of Sharia, which prioritize justice, compassion, and the welfare of the community.

Similarly, the pre-modern political framework within Islamic thought is adaptable to historical developments, allowing modern political concepts like democracy, equal citizenship rights for non-Muslims, the nation-state, self-determination, and international law to find legitimacy within the Sharia framework. Islamic jurisprudence showcases a remarkable capacity for integration, aligning democracy with *shura* (consultation) and *ijma* (consensus) and justifying equal citizenship through the Quranic principles of justice and equitable treatment of all individuals. The concept of the nation-state can be harmonized with *maslahah* (community welfare), while self-determination is supported by Sharia's emphasis on preventing oppression and ensuring autonomy. International law aligns with Islamic principles governing international relations and treaties (*siyar*), demonstrating Sharia's dynamic and integrative nature in engaging with modern political structures.

In conclusion, while Islamic theology maintains a firm stance on certain moral imperatives, it also allows for adaptability and reformation in response to evolving socio-economic conditions and ethical considerations. This balance between steadfast principles and contextual flexibility underscores the dynamic nature of Sharia in addressing contemporary challenges.

Index

Note: Page numbers followed by n indicate notes.

Made in the USA
Monee, IL
12 November 2026

ac584bf5-c2f8-4ae9-a4d8-0fdd239feec0R01